Training in Practice

Steve Truelove is a management trainer and human resource consultant. He specialises in the design and delivery of bespoke training programmes and assists in the design and operation of assessment and development centres for a variety of clients in both the private and public sectors.

The CIPD would like to thank the following members of the CIPD Publishing editorial board for their help and advice:

- Pauline Dibben, Sheffield University
- Edwina Hollings, Staffordshire University Business School
- Caroline Hook, Huddersfield University Business School
- Vincenza Priola, Keele University
- John Sinclair, Napier University Business School

The Chartered Institute of Personnel and Development is the leading publisher of books and reports for personnel and training professionals, students, and all those concerned with the effective management and development of people at work. For details of all our titles, please contact the publishing department:

tel: 020–8612 6204

e-mail publish@cipd.co.uk

The catalogue of all CIPD titles can be viewed on the CIPD website:

www.cipd.co.uk/bookstore

Training in Practice

Steve Truelove

Chartered Institute of Personnel and Development

Published by the Chartered Institute of Personnel and Development,
151 The Broadway, London, SW19 1JQ

First published 2006
Reprinted 2007 (twice)

© Chartered Institute of Personnel and Development 2006

Typeset by Kerry Press Ltd, Luton, Bedfordshire

Printed in Great Britain by the Cromwell Press, Trowbridge, Wiltshire

British Library Cataloguing in Publication Data

A catalogue of this publication is available from the British Library

ISBN 1 84398 150 5
ISBN-13 978 1 84398 150 3

Chartered Institute of Personnel and Development,
151 The Broadway, London, SW19 1JQ
Tel: 020 8612 6200
email: cipd@cipd.co.uk   Website: www.cipd.co.uk
incorporated by royal charter. Registered Charity No. 1079797

Contents

Part 5: Evaluate

Chapter 10 – Assessment   173

Chapter 11 – Evaluation   189

Figures and tables

Acknowledgements

My thanks are due to

Blackwell Business, publishers of the first edition who generously gave permission for this text.

Ruth Lake, commissioning editor at the CIPD for her patience and perseverance in bringing this book to fruition.

Andy Roberts, Managing Director of Knight Chapman Psychological for his help with psychometric material.

Anonymous reviewers who read through the proposal and first draft of this text and made many helpful suggestions.

Introduction

The first edition of this book was published by Blackwell Business in 1997 in response to the introduction of the Certificate in Training Practice as an attempt to produce a text which was suitable to accompany the new course. This edition has been considerably revised and enlarged to more fully reflect the current content of the programme, and to reflect some of the developments in training over the past nine years.

I have continued to try to adopt a policy of giving practical guidance from the point of view of the hands-on trainer who is new, or relatively new, to the role. I have also tried to give my personal opinion from time to time, and have given examples from my own experience. I know that some people may prefer a more formal and less personalised approach, but hope that they will still find valuable information in this text.

I have not included a lot of material about general management theory, wider human resources issues, or the kind of high-level strategic concerns which very senior people have to deal with. This is meant to keep the text focused on the needs of the training practitioner, and I hope that it is found to be accessible.

I have included a chapter on psychometrics. This is mainly because I think psychometric instruments can be of use, in some situations, to trainers, and because simple material outlining their characteristics is quite hard to find. If it is not relevant to you, I apologise.

A number of theories and academic models are described in the text. My policy has been to be selective about this – to include those that I believe all trainers should have a knowledge of, plus a few that I have found to be particularly useful. I believe that some textbooks written for trainers contain such a large amount of theoretical material, followed by in-depth discussion about it, that those new to the profession are daunted or alienated. In many instances, further reading will be required to gain a thorough understanding of the theories and models outlined here.

Structure

The book has been written to follow the training cycle – or rather, one of many training cycles! The 'standard' training cycle used in the United Kingdom has four stages:

- identification of training needs
- design of the training or development programme
- delivery of training
- evaluation.

However, I have structured the text to follow Goad's five-stage model (see Figure 1) – which essentially adds a development stage.

Stage 1
Analyse to determine training requirements

Stage 2
Design the training approach

Stage 3
Develop the training materials

Stage 4
Conduct the training

Stage 5
Evaluate and update the training

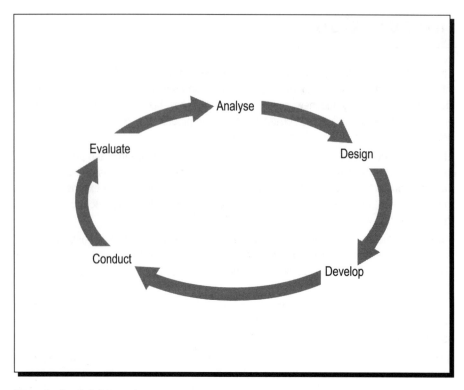

Figure 1 *Goad's training cycle*

Part 1 – Analyse
    Chapter 1: Introduction to the identification of training needs
    Chapter 2: Techniques for the identification of training needs
    Chapter 3: Agreeing learning needs within the organisational context

Part 2 – Design
    Chapter 4: The learning process
    Chapter 5: Designing learning events and strategies

Part 3 – Develop
    Chapter 6: Preparing presentation material
    Chapter 7: Preparing participative material

Part 4 – Conduct
    Chapter 8: Presentation techniques
    Chapter 9: Participative delivery techniques

Part 5 – Evaluate
    Chapter 10: Assessment
    Chapter 11: Evaluation
    Chapter 12: Psychometric testing

HOW TO USE THIS BOOK

Although I have attempted to arrange the book in a logical sequence, I hope that, for the most part, the text can be accessed as, and when, needed. I have tried not to assume any prior knowledge of training theories or techniques in the people who might buy this book. Inevitably, though, most readers will already have some existing knowledge and experience and will be able to skip the material that they already know. While I have given my thoughts about 'how it should be done', I hope it is clear that there is no single right way to go about the business of training. Read this, and all other training textbooks, with a sceptical and questioning attitude. If you are on a course and the tutors have views which are different from mine, you will have to make up your own mind about who (if anyone) is right. If you can, come up with your own ways of doing things that work for you.

I have given a 'Further reading' list at the end of each chapter. This has been kept fairly short, and there may be other texts which are equally good or better that are not listed. I have not read every textbook on training, and new material is being produced all the time. In addition, there are a number of training journals in publication which you could find useful.

I have given a number of website addresses at the end of each chapter – plus some useful contacts in Appendix 1. Inevitably, some of these will change or disappear – but I hope that most of them remain active and that some of these prove to be useful to you. New websites are appearing all the time – many of which provide a wealth of useful tools for the trainer.

The Activities

In order to facilitate its use as a set book for programmes leading to the Certificate in Training Practice, or similar programmes, I have included a number of Activities after each chapter. These aim to assist the understanding of concepts introduced in the text, or the application of techniques and development of skills. These are 'optional extras', primarily intended as group activities, but some of them could be adapted for individual use. I have included these because I have, myself, sometimes found such suggested activities in books extremely useful when running training events.

I have deliberately not included lengthy, detailed, instructions. The course tutors will be quite capable of adapting the activities to their own situations and conducting the necessary discussion, reflection and recording of learning points. If, as an inexperienced person, you lead any of these activities, you may wish to discuss with a more seasoned trainer the way in which the reviews and feedback might be best handled.

Similarly, I have not provided any model answers nor indicated how the activities usually progress. Again, I believe that the people leading the programme and the learners themselves will be able to deal with these relatively simple activities effectively.

FURTHER READING

Goad, T. W. (1982) *Delivering Effective Training*, San Diego, CA, University Associates

Useful website

www.arl.org/training/ilcso/goadmodel.html More detail about Tom Goad's training cycle, plus some other useful material

www

Analyse

Introduction to the identification of training needs

CHAPTER 1

Everybody is ignorant, only on different subjects.

Will Rogers

CHAPTER OBJECTIVES

When you have read this chapter you should be able to:

- **define what a training need is, with reference to the model devised by Tom Boydell**

- **describe factors which affect individual performance**

- **describe the key features of the motivation theories of Maslow, Herzberg and Vroom**

- **perform PESTLE and SWOT analyses**

- **discuss some of the major government influences on training practice.**

OVERVIEW

Before considering what techniques for identifying training needs are available to us, it may be useful to clarify one or two concepts. Firstly, let us look at a definition of the term 'training need':

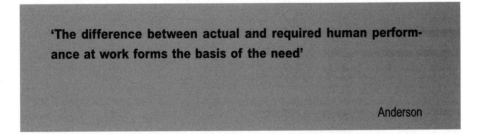

'The difference between actual and required human performance at work forms the basis of the need'

Anderson

This neatly sums up the concept. Other writers use terms such as 'performance gap' to convey the same concept. And it is in the sensitivity of this concept that our first difficulty lies. Remember that you are dealing with people, and that these 'gaps' may be sources of embarrassment, the beginnings of disciplinary proceedings, or the causes of deep-seated resentments for some people. It is all too easy to go blundering about – enthusiastically determining training needs with insufficient regard to the feelings of the individuals involved.

Attempts to soften this by using language such as 'not yet competent' can never be wholly successful. Many members of the training profession prefer to use the term 'learning need' rather than 'training need' because it is more learner-centred and covers a wider range of possible solutions than 'training need' does. However, the difference is rather subtle – especially for line managers to appreciate – and both terms are appropriate in many circumstances.

A further difficulty is that a training need is only one of several possible causes of the performance gap. The others are:

- poor resources
- lack of ability
- lack of motivation.

It is not always easy to determine the reason, or reasons, underlying poor performance. Many people find it easiest to blame others, or to blame poor resources. Of course, sometimes they are right to do so. Investigation is needed to determine where the root of the performance gap lies. There may be more than one of these factors involved.

Lack of ability

This refers to the individual's innate abilities, over which he or she has no influence. Intelligence, aptitude for learning, manual dexterity, and a range of other abilities can inhibit job performance. If this is the case, it may indicate poor selection procedures. Often, though, it is indicative of changes that have occurred in the job such that the job-holder is now struggling, whereas he or she could once cope. For example, many manual workers now have to deal with new technology requiring a set of abilities different from those previously needed, and many people who were recruited for technical jobs now have to deal directly with customers.

We are not all equally capable of learning new things. Mathematical ability, problem-solving, visual acuity, and so forth, vary widely between individuals. Training may not always produce any improvement.

Lack of motivation

Motivation is a complex subject. Poor motivation may be due to many things – boredom, lack of challenge, a feeling of being unappreciated, and resentment for some past wrong. Some people are much easier to motivate than others. The key question is whether or not the individual's motivation appears to have varied. Someone who was once highly motivated, and who is now indifferent, may be sending out strong signals: 'Something is wrong. I am not happy.'

It may not be easy to get to the bottom of the problem, nor is a solution always possible, but attempting to cure a motivational problem by inappropriate means may make matters worse. However, some training solutions may be highly motivational. Training gives people attention, which in itself can be motivating. It should stimulate them with new ideas – which can provide a fresh look at an old job. It can also put them in contact with other people whose enthusiasm may prove to be infectious.

Training need

The final reason for poor performance is lack of competence – that is to say, lack of knowledge or skills in someone who has the ability to acquire that knowledge or those skills. In other words, a training need. This may, in turn, be linked to poor motivation, or it may be due to lack of opportunity. Competence comes through learning. Learning comes either through experience or training, or through a combination of the two. However, trying to address a performance problem through training when it is really due to a lack of innate ability will not work.

At this point, I think it is helpful to introduce a simple framework for understanding training needs. That produced by Tom Boydell in 1976 distinguishes between three types of need:

- organisational training needs
- occupational training needs
- individual training needs.

Organisational training needs

An organisational training need is one that applies to the whole organisation. There are two main sub-categories:

Training needs which are generated by change
Changes such as:

- new products are being made or sold
- new technology has been introduced
- new legislation is affecting the organisation
- new managerial systems (eg Total Quality Management) are being introduced
- the ownership of the organisation has changed
- there have been acquisitions, mergers, disposals, or other structural changes.

Training needs which must be met to produce change
Changes to situations such as:

- productivity is too low
- morale is very low
- the corporate culture is inhibiting development
- people are not customer-focused.

Occupational training needs

An occupational training need is one that applies to a particular category of employee. It may be a consequence of a wider organisational change, or it may have arisen for one group of workers in isolation. Again, we can distinguish two main sub-categories:

Training needs which are generated by change
Changes such as:

- there is a new software package for Accounts
- there is a tighter system for access to the building to be operated by the security officers

- Personnel Officers and Training Officers are to be merged into new roles as Human Resources Consultants.

Training needs which must be met to produce change
Changes to situations such as:

- security officers are rather grumpy with visitors

- senior managers are still using gender-specific terms when referring to jobs

- middle managers are poor at solving problems

- higher output is required from production

- the fitters take a long time when repairing these machines.

Individual training needs

An individual training need may be thought of as an occupational need that applies only to a specific individual as opposed to the whole category of employees.

Training needs which are generated by change
Changes such as:

- one of the production crew is now responsible for completing production records

- Mark is going to be visiting the Madrid office quite frequently and will need to learn Spanish

- Jill has been asked to prepare a detailed training budget for the first time.

Training needs which must be met to produce change
Situations such as:

- if Kate could operate the switchboard, Mary could spend longer on the graphic design and we wouldn't need to use an agency

- if Martin could do some interviewing, Sue could become more involved in training

- if Paula could learn to speak Italian, we wouldn't need an agent over there

- Richard must start selling more.

Maintenance and development needs

Another way of thinking about training needs is to divide them into 'maintenance' and 'development' needs.

Maintenance needs are those training needs that must be met in order for the organisation, occupational grouping, or individual to maintain current performance. This can include training to 'keep the numbers up'. For example, an insurance intermediary may employ 100 telesales staff. If 15 per cent of them leave or transfer each year, then 15 replacements will have to be trained. Maintenance training also refers to the process of ensuring that performance does not deteriorate through sloppy practice or lack of feedback. Just as professional soldiers and top sportspeople train regularly to maintain skills, some workplace skills must be refreshed from time to time.

Development needs are those concerned with the promotion of new learning, taking an individual, an occupation, or even the whole organisation into new learning arenas.

Both types of need are equally important.

Yet another way of distinguishing types of need is to consider proactive and reactive training. Proactive identification of needs is concerned with anticipating needs before they arise; reactive identification is responding to problems after they have arisen. The way in which the concepts of maintenance/development and reactive/proactive interact can be illustrated by reference to Table 1.

Table 1 *Interaction of concepts of training needs*

	Maintenance	**Development**
Reactive	Correcting job performance failures	Helping people cope with new work
Proactive	Avoiding job performance failures	Helping people to prepare for future roles

It is tempting to regard being 'proactive' as good and being 'reactive' as bad. In fact, a balance must be struck. Organisations change so rapidly that not all needs may be anticipated, and the trainer must have a willingness and capacity to respond to line managers' urgent requests as they arise. If, however, no proactive identification takes place, the trainer will be constantly 'fire-fighting' and will have little opportunity to plan sensibly for the future.

LEVELS OF PERFORMANCE AND NEED

Tom Boydell has, in conjunction with Malcolm Leary, developed and expanded his analytical model with regard to learning needs. They believe that it is helpful to consider performance at three different levels. These are:

> **Level 1** Implementing (I_1)
>
> **Level 2** Improving (I_2)
>
> **Level 3** Innovating (I_3)

Implementing (I_1) is about doing things well. It is essentially about the performance gap between actual and desired performance – as defined by current standards. In many instances this will be basic training and maintenance training.

Improving (I_2) is about raising the performance of everybody – of the organisation as a whole – by raising current standards. This is where *continuous improvement* comes in.

Innovating (I_3) – unlike improving, which is about doing things better – is about reviewing what is being done and making changes to systems. For example, introducing new teamworking systems or devolving decision-making.

It will be noted that improving and innovating are both developmental. But Boydell and Leary make the point that all three levels interact and are of an additive nature. Thus, when improving (level 2) results in new standards being set, there will have to be implementation (level 1) of these standards. Innovation (level 3) will also require implementation of the new methods or systems, which will in turn lead to continuous improvement.

They have also analysed each of the three levels and identified different modes of learning at each level of performance. This is fairly involved, and the interested reader should refer to the original text. Of more immediate relevance is the way in which they see the three levels of performance interacting with the areas of need. In many ways, Table 2 below is an elaboration on the simpler table given in Table 1 above.

Table 2 *Organisational, group and individual needs at the three levels of performance*

	Organisational	Group	Individual
I_1: Implementing – doing things well	Meeting current organisational objectives	Working together to meet existing targets and standards	Being competent at the level of existing requirements
I_2: Improving – doing things better	Setting higher objectives and reaching them	Continuous improvement teams	Having and using systematic continuous improvement skills and processes
I_3: Innovating – doing new and better things	Changing objectives and strategies	Working across boundaries to create relationships and new products and services	Being able to work differently and more creatively with a shared sense of purpose

The idea of a framework like this is to help us to identify where needs might exist and their nature – and to help us to think of the questions we will have to ask in order to make sense of situations that are very often complex. Thus we might ask ourselves or others: 'Are we considering the whole organisation, or just one group within it?' Or 'Is the focus on meeting existing targets? Or are we looking at revising targets and making sure that these are reached?' Very often we get confusing answers to these questions: 'Well, we're not meeting existing targets – but we need to be doing better than those targets anyway.' This kind of framework can help in that we can point out to line managers, for example, that these are two different issues which may need to be separated and dealt with over different time-spans.

MOTIVATION THEORIES

There are many theories and models dealing with motivation. There are three that every trainer should be aware of.

Abraham Maslow's Hierarchy of Needs

One of the things Maslow noticed while working with monkeys early in his career was that some needs take precedence over others. For example, if you are hungry and thirsty, you will tend to try to take care of the thirst first. As we all know, we would die of thirst before we died of hunger. Thirst is a stronger need than hunger.

Maslow took this idea further and in the 1940s created his famous 'hierarchy of needs' – often represented as a pyramid. He laid out five broad layers: the physiological needs, the needs for safety and security, the needs for love and belonging, the need for esteem, and the need to actualise the self, in that order.

The physiological needs

These include the needs we have for oxygen, water, food, and various minerals and vitamins. They also include the need to maintain a normal temperature. Also, there's the need to be active, to rest, to sleep, to get rid of wastes and to avoid pain.

The safety and security needs

When the physiological needs are largely taken care of, this second layer of needs comes into play. We become increasingly interested in finding an environment free from threat. In many people, this set of needs results in a desire to have a home in a safe area, a secure income, and so on. Note that individual differences come into play more at this level – some of us have a higher need for security than others do.

The love and belonging needs

When physiological needs and safety needs are largely taken care of, a third layer starts to emerge. We begin to feel the need for friends, affectionate relationships and a sense of community. These needs, if unfulfilled, manifest themselves through feelings of loneliness and social anxieties. Typically, we will seek a long-term relationship with someone, perhaps through marriage, and will become a member of various social groupings. It is also a part of what most of us look for in a job or career. Individual differences are even stronger now.

The esteem need

Next, we begin to look for esteem. Maslow noted two versions of esteem needs. The lower one is the need to be respected by others – to have some status and recognition. The higher form involves the need for self-respect, including such feelings as confidence, competence, mastery, and independence. This is the 'higher' form because, unlike the respect of others, once you have self-respect, it's a lot harder to lose!

All of these four levels are termed 'deficit needs'. If you don't have enough of something, you feel the need. But if you get all you need, they cease to be motivating.

Self-actualisation

The last level is different. These are needs that do not involve satiation. Rather, they are likely to become stronger as we 'feed' them. They involve the continuous desire to fulfil potentials, to 'be all that you can be'. They are a matter of becoming the most complete, the fullest, 'you' – hence the term 'self-actualisation'. If you want to be self-actualising, you must have had your lower needs taken care of, at least to a considerable extent. Someone in a learning environment who is cold and hungry and afraid that he will lose his job will therefore have difficulty in concentrating on advanced management concepts. If someone else has a low sense of self-esteem, he or she may be defensive and unreceptive to feedback. When lower needs are unmet, we can't fully devote ourselves to fulfilling our potentials. This is important for trainers to remember when selecting venues, deciding on the length of the training session, allowing for social interaction, and so on.

Frederick Herzberg's motivator-hygiene approach

Research carried out by Frederick Herzberg and his colleagues produced a model (published in 1966) which is very useful in the work environment. Basically, he asked many people in different jobs at different levels two questions:

- What factors had led them to experience extreme dissatisfaction with their job?
- What factors had led them to experience extreme satisfaction with their job?

He collated the answers and concluded that two distinct sets of factors existed. One set of factors Herzberg called 'hygiene' factors. Their presence, he contends, does not motivate people in an organisation – yet they must be present or dissatisfaction will arise. By providing more of them 'you just remove unhappiness, you don't make people happy'. These match the lower three levels of Maslow's hierarchy.

Hygiene factors:

- policy and administration
- technical supervision
- salary
- interpersonal relations with supervisor
- working conditions.

The other set of factors – a group of 'satisfiers' – all related to job content. He called them the 'motivators'. These are concerned with achievement and responsibility, and match the top two levels of Maslow's hierarchy. Their existence yields feelings of satisfaction or, if absent, no satisfaction. To understand this model it is vital to appreciate that a state of feeling 'no satisfaction' is not the same as feeling 'dissatisfaction'. Herzberg likened trying to motivate people with pay incentives to offering carrots to a donkey to move. Incentives, he said, produce movement – not motivation.

Motivators:

- Achievement
- Recognition
- Work itself
- Responsibility
- Advancement

Although the factors are largely independent, remember that individual differences can apply and that, for example, a low salary might impact on the sense of recognition someone feels. The key points are that people must be treated fairly so that they don't feel dissatisfied *and* they must be allowed to realise their potential doing work which is interesting, meaningful, and challenging. Both sets of factors are important for optimum performance. Training and learning is vital for motivation – 'The more someone can do, the more you can motivate them.'

Victor Vroom's expectancy-valence theory

Vroom's theory of 1964 examines motivation. From the perspective of why people choose to follow a particular course of action he utilises three variables which he calls 'valence', 'expectancy' and 'instrumentality'.

Valence is the importance (or value) that the individual places upon the expected outcome of a situation. It can be positive (I want the promotion or attention), neutral (I don't care), or negative (I really don't want that job; I don't like being the centre of attention). A key point here is that our varying personalities and circumstances will affect the perception of the outcome (which may be a reward or punishment). In a training situation, the outcome (eg a certificate) may be highly valued by one person but of no value to another.

Expectancy is the belief that the individual has that he or she can attain the outcome. You will probably not feel motivated to attempt something that you think is beyond you – such as running a mile in less than four minutes – even if the outcome (a million pounds, for example) is highly valuable to you. A lot of sales training is based on trying to raise the expectancy level of being able to achieve targets, and a lot of other training aims to raise people's expectations of being able to perform new roles or employ new skills.

Instrumentality is the belief that the success of the situation is linked to the expected outcome of the situation. In a work situation, the perception of employees that they will actually get what they have been promised by management. In a training situation, whether passing the course really will lead to the 'dream job'.

Thus this theory of motivation is not about self-interest in rewards but about the associations people make towards expected outcomes and the contribution they feel they can make towards those outcomes.

TRAINING AND THE ORGANISATIONAL ENVIRONMENT

To state the obvious, training does not take place in isolation, but in the context of the organisation (or several organisations). To be effective, the training function must understand and analyse the organisational environment within which it operates. There are many ways of looking at organisations – a multitude of models and theories – which lie outside the scope of this book. Sometimes trainers regard these ideas as not directly relevant to their roles. Yet it is crucial that the training function operates in harmony with the rest of the organisation – and is seen to be a function which contributes to organisational success. We shall therefore consider a few fundamental terms.

Organisational objectives

The effectiveness of any organisation is measured in terms of the extent to which it achieves its objectives. This applies to not-for-profit organisations just as much as to commercial organisations. Everybody in the organisation should be focused on these objectives. And the role of training is to assist in the achievement of these objectives in a number of ways.

At a basic level, training is about ensuring that individuals are competent to perform their jobs. Indeed, many trainers operate in a very specific role in which they are required to teach people to perform a precise range of tasks in a particular manner and at a defined speed. But training can also play a more long-term strategic role. When training is involved with leadership, team and organisational issues, it is impacting on the achievement of these longer-term strategic objectives. When training includes activities which examine current methods, values and standards, it is contributing to the development of the organisation. In many ways, the 'Implementing, Improving, Innovating' model of Boydell and Leary is one of progression from the immediate to the strategic.

So to contribute effectively, we must, first of all, be aware of the organisation's objectives. In some organisations this is very easy: the objectives are plastered on the walls and constantly repeated. In other organisations, the objectives are closely guarded secrets known only to the top few in the hierarchy. In many cases, the objectives are stated in an incomplete manner. For example:

'To generate sufficient profit to finance continual improvement and growth of the business while providing our shareholders with an excellent return on their investment.'

This is an honest enough statement, but not very meaningful because it does not quantify anything. The company does not want to disclose its actual financial targets for its competitors to read, or for the stock market to judge it by. But we can look at the profit it made over the last few years to make our own estimate of what is likely to be sufficient. We can also look at the actual growth that has been achieved to make an estimate of what the directors are likely to be looking for over the next few years. Yet even as vague as it is, the objective statement makes it clear that this company wants to continue to grow and develop. The directors and major shareholders have approved this statement, and the trainers in that organisation must always be mindful of it.

Another example:

'The funding for the hospital is provided in the ultimate by the country's taxpayers. The Board of Directors is deeply conscious of the responsibility which this imposes on it and on the hospital. The financial policy of the Board is that every effort should be made to operate within this funding budget, to maximise productivity and to deliver optimum health care services.'

So in this case 'working within budgets' is going to be something that the line managers will be very conscious of at all times. When training needs and solutions are discussed, this must therefore be borne in mind. Note that the objectives may be found under a variety of headings including 'mission', 'values', 'goals', 'aims' and 'targets'.

Whereas overall corporate objectives apply to everyone, in practice they must be broken down into smaller objectives which apply to individual divisions, departments, teams and eventually individuals. This can cause conflicts. The classic example is that of the sales/production dilemma. Sales meets its objectives by promising to meet the customer's requirements for delivery and special needs; production meets its objectives by organising long runs of standard products. Good communication and relationships are therefore essential for both functions to operate effectively.

Even with the example objective from a hospital given above, the sub-objectives of delivering optimum health care and keeping within budget conflict. The objectives of the training function can often conflict with those of other functions. Training may require short-term expense, the release of key personnel and subsequent overtime costs, or the expenditure of management time and effort filling in forms about training needs or evaluation. There are many occasions when the training function is involved in change programmes that much of the organisation does not (yet) believe in – such as the introduction of a performance management system or multiskilling. In these cases, there may be concealed objectives elsewhere in the organisation such as making sure the new system does not work so that the status quo is maintained.

Other concealed objectives centre around organisational politics. A particular manager may be more interested in his or her own career than in the success of the organisation. Or he or she may be attempting to gain more status, control and influence for his or her own team. Some individuals bear deep-seated grudges against others in the organisation, or against the organisation as a whole. Yet others are marking time until retirement or until a better job comes along and are only interested in a quiet life. The training function may also be seen as a threat – particularly if it is introducing new ideas and procedures which may expose hidden weaknesses or poor performers. Or it may be seen as a tool of a 'slave-driving' management. All this must be considered when discussions are taking place.

Line and staff

The term 'line managers' has already been used several times in this text. It is a phrase that is much used, but not always fully understood – or is understood differently by different people. Many people use the term 'line manager' simply to mean their own immediate boss, or to mean the manager of any work group in any function – but these are not the original meanings. Alvin Toffler explains the origin of the terms 'line' and 'staff' in his book *The Third Wave*. The early American railroad companies were the giants of their day. They were massive in terms of numbers of employees, capital employed and geographical spread. They created new forms of organisation based on the centralisation of information and command. Employees were divided into two categories – line and staff. Line was concerned with the day-to-day operations of the railroad *line*. Staff was concerned with all the support work that was required to make this happen – accounting, marketing, legal, and so forth.

So 'line managers' are concerned with the core activities of the organisation. In a retail organisation they are the salespeople, in manufacturing the production people, in hospitals the medical people, and in a training consultancy they are the trainers.

Staff managers are in charge of the specialist support functions which make sure, for example, that proper procedures are followed in relation to purchasing or recruitment. There is often conflict between the line managers and staff managers because their objectives – although all contributing to the overall organisational objectives – are different. Staff functions, such as the training function in most organisations, may be perceived as peripheral. The line management, subject to constant day-to-day pressures, may resent the 'ivory tower' trainers who seem to have time to chat and reflect and talk about abstract models and theories. If that is the case, then the task of the training function is to change that perception. The line functions should see the training function as a valuable partner which enables them to better achieve their objectives.

The learning organisation

With his book *The Fifth Discipline: The art and practice of the learning organisation* (1990), Peter Senge popularised the idea of 'systems thinking' and focused the spotlight on *learning in the workplace* as no one had before. The reason for the impact of this idea was that Senge made the case for how learning can help managers to build successful enterprises.

According to Senge, learning organisations are

> 'organisations where people continually expand their capacity to create the results they truly desire, where new and expansive patterns of thinking are nurtured, where collective aspiration is set free, and where people are continually learning to see the whole together.'

Senge thinks that learning organisations require a new concept of leadership. Leaders must be designers, stewards and teachers. They are responsible for building organisations in which people continually expand their capabilities to understand complexity, clarify vision, and improve shared mental models – that is, they are responsible for promoting learning.

Many other writers have contributed towards the concept of the learning organisation, including Boydell and Leary who see the learning company as the ultimate stage in an organisation's development. What is important to remember is that the drive and vision necessary for the organisation to embrace these ideas must come from the most senior management. The training function can champion the ideas and can make a major contribution to their fulfilment, but can never succeed without the full commitment of the people at the top of the organisation.

Legislation and government influence

Some aspects of training are directly governed by legislation. In the United Kingdom the Health and Safety at Work Act (1974) requires every employer to provide instruction to ensure the heath and safety at work of all its employees. Other key pieces of legislation which have a direct impact on the work of the training function include the Race Relations Act (1976), the Sex Discrimination Act (1995), the Data Protection Act (1984), the Disability Discrimination Act (1995) and the Working Time Regulations (1998). In addition to these 'broad-brush' pieces of legislation, there are myriad regulations which apply to specific industries and occupations – for example, regulations concerning food hygiene, working in financial services, working in licensed premises and working with children. Whatever field you are training in, it is up to you to make sure that you are aware of the relevant legislation and comply with it. There is further consideration given to issues around discrimination later in the book.

Other than by means of legislation, the government seeks to influence skill development through providing a co-ordinating function. The United Kingdom has a history of periodically installing and later removing systems and infrastructure which affect training. At the present time, co-ordination takes place through a network of Learning and Skills Councils (LSCs) which cover England and are co-ordinated by the National LSC. In Wales, the relevant body is Education and Learning Wales (ELWa), in Northern Ireland it is the Department for Employment and Learning Northern Ireland (DELNI), and in Scotland Local Enterprise Companies (LECs). However, there are many other agencies and bodies which have an impact on training and workplace learning.

The Departments for Education and Skills (DfES) and Trade and Industry (DTI), the Qualifications and Curriculum Authority (QCA), Regional Development Agencies (RDAs), all have an influence. There are also Sector Skills Councils (SSCs) which are independent UK-wide organisations developed by groups of influential employers in industry or business sectors of economic or strategic significance. SSCs are employer-led and are licensed by the Secretary of State for Education and Skills, in consultation with Ministers in Scotland, Wales and Northern Ireland, to tackle the skills and productivity needs of their sector. They are co-ordinated by the Sector Skills Development Agency. Examples of SSCs are the Financial Services Skills Council, Skills for Health, and Skillsmart Retail.

Investors in People

Perhaps one of the most well-known government initiatives with relevance to training is the Investors in People (IiP) Standard which is administered by Investors in People UK. The Investors in People Standard is described as a business improvement tool designed to advance an organisation's performance through its people. It was inaugurated in 1990 and aims to help organisations to improve performance and realise objectives through the management and development of their people. Since it was established the Standard has been reviewed every three years to ensure that it remains 'relevant, accessible and attractive to all'. In essence, an organisation that wishes to gain the IiP award must, with help and guidance, design and install a framework that links the performance of the organisation to the learning and development of individuals. The framework involves:

- *Plan* – developing strategies to improve the performance of the organisation
- *Do* – taking action to improve the performance of the organisation
- *Review* – evaluating the impact on the performance of the organisation.

In many ways, IiP is a mechanism to put a comprehensive training and development system in place which links the training function to the achievement of organisational objectives. The fact that IiP has been established as long as it has and covers almost 40 per cent of the UK workforce (go to the IiP website to check statistics: www.investorsinpeople.co.uk) shows that it has been very successful. Of course, there are always costs and downsides involved with a system like this. An organisation seeking the IiP award will have to pay for the consultants who assist them, and for the ongoing inspection process. This requires that comprehensive records and written reviews are maintained – and some line managers see this as burdensome bureaucracy. It is possible to put in a similar system to IiP without accreditation and gain all the business benefits without the hassle of periodic inspections by outsiders. But the IiP award confers status on the organisation and raises the profile of the training and development processes – giving a big signal from the top that these things are regarded as important. It also gives the training function leverage to get systems up and running. You may get much more response from saying: 'If your department does not submit the agreed documents by the end of the month I will have to tell the Managing Director that we will not be awarded IiP status,' than simply by pleading that you need them to be able to do your job properly.

National Vocational Qualifications

National Vocational Qualifications (or Scottish Vocational Qualifications) (NVQs/SVQs) were developed to address a number of problems.

- The UK qualification scene was very fragmented, with a plethora of awarding bodies. It was (and to some extent still is) very difficult to compare qualifications awarded by one body with those awarded by another. Also, qualifications would come and go. Older people could find that their hard-earned qualifications were no longer recognised because they had been discontinued.

- Some sectors of the workforce had no way at all of gaining meaningful qualifications in their particular field.

- Most qualifications were, at least to some degree, academic. Traditional apprentice-ships were in decline. People with lots of experience in practical skills but who had not completed an apprenticeship had no way to show a prospective employer that they were competent.

The first NVQ award was made in 1988, and NVQs are now firmly established within the UK. The central feature of NVQs is the National Occupational Standards (NOS) on which they are based. NOS are statements of performance standards which describe what competent people in a particular occupation are expected to be able to do. They cover all the main aspects of an occupation, including current best practice, the ability to adapt to future requirements and the knowledge and understanding which underpins competent performance.

QCA
On 1 October 1997 the National Council for Vocational Qualifications (NCVQ) merged with the School Curriculum and Assessment Authority (SCAA) to form the Qualifications and Curriculum Authority (QCA). QCA has a wider remit than any previous education or training body, including pre-school learning, the national curriculum for 5–16-year-olds, national tests for 7-, 11- and 14-year-olds, GCSEs, A-levels, GNVQs, NVQs and higher-level vocational qualifications.

SQA
The Scottish Qualifications Authority (SQA) was set up in April 1997 following the merger of the Scottish Vocational and Education Council (SCOTVEC) and the Scottish Examining Board (SEB). Unlike QCA, it has both accrediting and awarding body responsibilities.

Definitions of NVQ/SVQ levels
NVQs and SVQs are organised into a classification system based on the competence levels required. The definitions in Table 3 provide a general guide and are not intended to be prescriptive.

Table 3 *Definitions of NVQ/SVQ levels*

Levels	Definitions
Level 1	Competence which involves the application of knowledge in the performance of a range of varied work activities, most of which may be routine and predictable.
Level 2	Competence which involves the application of knowledge in a significant range of varied work activities, performed in a variety of contexts. Some of these activities are complex or non-routine and there is some individual responsibility or autonomy. Collaboration with others, perhaps through membership of a work group or team, may often be a requirement.
Level 3	Competences which involves the application of knowledge in a broad range of varied work activities performed in a wide variety of contexts, most of which are complex and non-routine. There is considerable responsibility and autonomy and control or guidance of others is often required.

Level 4	Competence which involves the application of knowledge in a broad range of complex, technical or professional work activities performed in a variety of contexts and with a substantial degree of personal responsibility and autonomy. Responsibility for the work of others and the allocation of resources is often present.
Level 5	Competence which involves the application of a range of fundamental principles across a wide and often unpredictable variety of contexts. Very substantial personal autonomy and often significant responsibility for the work of others and for the allocation of substantial resources features strongly, as do personal accountabilities for analysis, diagnosis, design, planning, execution and evaluation.

Please note that this may be changed in the near future. Further information about NVQs may be obtained from your local Learning and Skills Council (or equivalent).

ANALYSING ORGANISATIONS

As previously mentioned, there are many ways in which organisations can be analysed and described. One well-known method is PESTLE analysis, which is a way of examining the many different external factors (sometimes just risks) that affect an organisation.

The acronym PESTLE stands for the following:

- *Political*
  The current and potential influences from political pressures, such as local or national government or EU decisions.

- *Economic*
  The impact of the local, national and world economy – including interest rates, inflation and unemployment.

- *Social*
  The ways in which changes in society affect the organisation. This can include fads and fashions, demographic changes such as age or ethnicity profile and life-style changes.

- *Technological*
  The effect of new and emerging technologies – including consumer goods, new materials and medical advances.

- *Legal*
  The effect of national, European and world legislation and its interpretation in the courts.

- *Environmental*
  Local, national and global environmental issues.

PESTLE analysis is usually conducted in a group – often with the use of a whiteboard or similar. It can be a first step towards looking at the changes necessary to cope with the impact of the external factors. Many issues will be thrown up, particularly when the environment itself is changing rapidly. Some of these issues will require a contribution from the training function.

Note that you may sometimes find a slightly shorter version of this technique, leaving out 'environmental' and combining 'political' with 'legal' – this can be abbreviated to PEST, STEP or PETS.

EXAMPLE OF PESTLE ANALYSIS

Political

There is the real threat of terrorist attacks on air travel which would affect consumer confidence.

Economic

The economy is strong and consumer spending is likely to increase.

Fuel prices could increase.

Social

Many people are buying properties overseas and will wish to visit them regularly.

People are increasingly travelling abroad for short breaks as well as main holidays.

Technolgical

The proportion of customers booking on-line is currently 40 per cent but is likely to rise.

A failure of the on-line system could be very damaging.

Legal

Forthcoming EU legislation may increase the compensation payments due in the event of cancellation.

Environmental

Changing weather patterns could make air travel more hazardous as they may result in an increased frequency and severity of highly destructive weather events.

Another technique is SWOT analysis:

- Strengths
- Weaknesses
- Opportunities
- Threats.

Again, these are usually identified in a group situation. The actions needed to build on strengths, capitalise on opportunities and minimise threats and weaknesses are then identified. Training will usually play an important role in these actions.

EXAMPLE OF SWOT ANALYSIS

Strengths

No.2 brand in this market sector

Strong customer loyalty to the brand

Further product improvements due for launch within next three months will offer real competitive advantages

Weaknesses

Brand not very appealing to youth (under 25 years) market

The production process is complex and we have a long lead time (five months) to change the specification

Opportunities

Government legislation about to be introduced will require competitors to increase their costs to comply

New materials have been offered to us which could give us a unique selling-point

Threats

Competitors are moving to cheaper production facilities in the Far East

The increasing compensation culture means that any product defects could be costly

SUMMARY

In this chapter the concept of 'a training need' has been explored with reference to other reasons for wanting to improve performance. The model developed by Tom Boydell has been outlined – that is, distinguishing between individual, group, and organisational training needs. The differences between maintenance needs and development needs have also been considered, as has the difference between needs identified proactively and reactively. The ways in which these concepts interact have also been explored.

Some terms relating to organisations have been introduced and defined, and the concept of a 'learning organisation' has been explored. The influence of legislation has been explored, as has the effect of various governmental initiatives on the UK training scene. This has included a brief introduction to NVQs and the Investors in People award.

Three models of motivation – those of Maslow, Herzberg and Vroom – have been described.

Finally, the techniques of PESTLE and SWOT analysis have been outlined.

FURTHER READING

Boydell, T. H. (1983) *A Guide to the Identification of Training Needs*, London, BACIE

Boydell, T. and Leary, M. (1996) *Identifying Training Needs*, London, Institute of Personnel and Development

Senge, P.M. (1990) *The Fifth Discipline. The art and practice of the learning organization*, London: Random House.

Toffler, A. (1981) *The Third Wave*, London, Pan Books

Useful websites

www.themanager.org/Knowledgebase/HR/Motivation.htm Lots of links to articles about motivation, including Maslow's 1943 text.

www.dfes.gov.uk/nvq/ The NVQ website

www.investorsinpeople.co.uk The Investors in People website

www.solonline.org Society for Organisational Learning

www.sqa.org.uk The Scottish Qualifications Authority

www.ssda.org.uk The Sector Skills Development Agency

ACTIVITIES – CHAPTER 1

1 SWOT analysis

A simple but powerful tool for analysing your current situation and how you might need to change is a SWOT analysis. This identifies your organisation's (department's/team's) **S**trengths, **W**eaknesses, **O**pportunities and **T**hreats.

The simple idea that lies behind SWOT is that your change strategy should

- take advantage of your opportunities *and*

- overcome or avoid threats *by*

- fully using your relevant organisational strengths *and*

- taking account of your organisational weaknesses.

SWOT analysis, part 1
Using the following template, write in your organisation's strengths, weaknesses, opportunities and threats.

	Strengths	Weaknesses
Internal		
	Opportunities	**Threats**
External		

Now select the two most significant items from each box.

SWOT analysis, part 2
Enter each item selected under the appropriate headings.

Write down what evidence you have to support each of the perceived strengths, weaknesses, opportunities and threats.

Strength 1	Strength 2
Evidence:	Evidence:
Weakness 1	**Weakness 2**
Evidence:	Evidence:

Opportunity 1	Opportunity 2
Evidence:	Evidence:
Threat 1	**Threat 2**
Evidence:	Evidence:

SWOT analysis, part 3
Now consider:

- How can you maximise and extend the strengths you identified?

- How can you minimise or overcome the weaknesses?

- How can you seize the opportunities?

- How can you deal with the threats?

2 Organisational objectives

The following is an example of company objectives for a fictional UK retail chain. Look at each objective statement in turn, and determine what – if any – the training implications are.

Company objectives

- *To conduct our trade with complete integrity, carrying out our work to the highest standards, contributing to the quality of life in the community and endeavouring to systematically reduce the effect that our business has on the environment.*

- *To provide outstanding value to our customers – meeting their needs in terms of product quality and reliability, and maintaining an unrivalled range of products.*

- *In our stores, to achieve the highest standards of cleanliness and friendly, efficient, customer service.*

- *To offer the people who work for us outstanding opportunities for personal career development while practising industry-leading equal opportunities policies.*

- *To work with our suppliers to ensure that ethical employment and environmental policies are applied in the production of the goods which we sell.*

- *To constantly invest in the structure and interiors of our premises to maintain as attractive a shopping experience as possible.*

- *To generate sufficient profit to enable continued development and growth of the business, both in the UK and overseas, while providing our shareholders with a sound return on their investment.*

You can also undertake this exercise with your own organisation's objectives. Or select two organisations from the same sector, and compare their stated objectives (eg a publicly funded hospital and a private hospital; a national airline and a budget airline).

Techniques for the identification of training needs

CHAPTER 2

No one ever listened themselves out of a job.

Calvin Coolidge

CHAPTER OBJECTIVES

When you have read this chapter you should be able to:

- describe a range of methods for identifying learning needs

- identify sources of information relevant to learning needs

- use a variety of methods for information-gathering, including interviews, discussions and questionnaires

- explain the way in which development centres are constructed and operate.

There are many approaches to the identification of training needs, some of which are described here. Unfortunately, waving a magic wand isn't one of them! They all involve hard work and the adoption of an analytical and diagnostic approach to try to determine what is required. Some trainers prefer the term 'training needs analysis' (TNA) to 'identification of training needs' (ITN), but it is the same thing. As mentioned in the previous chapter, many people in the training profession prefer to use the term 'learning needs' rather than 'training needs' because it seems to be more inclusive of the wide range of learning methods that exist, and because it is less trainer-centred. Use whatever terms you like, bearing in mind the possible reactions from the people affected.

JOB AND TASK ANALYSIS

There are many reasons for analysing jobs and tasks. One common reason is to provide a basis for job evaluation; another is to be precise about requirements in a selection situation. There are also many different systems of analysis. Some seem to generate a multitude of documents; others use highly involved and sophisticated methodology. In their book *Job Analysis*, Pearn and Kandola (1988) describe 18 different analytical techniques. The process described below is a simple and traditional approach.

Background

'An analogy of digging a hole can well be applied to the task of job analysis. Both the area to be covered and the depth are arrived at by knowing the purpose of the hole. This analogy

> **goes further in that the task can be both tedious and messy. The area of a particular job to be analysed and the depth are arrived at by knowing the purpose of the analysis exercise.'**
>
> Malcolm Craig, in Truelove (ed.,1995)

Job analysis

I am using the term 'job analysis' to describe the level of analysis which takes us to the stage of writing a job description. This is a collection of statements regarding the functions performed in a job grouped in a way which helps a reader to get 'the big picture' of what is involved. The most widely used methods of gathering information to prepare a job description are:

- interviewing the job-holder(s)
- interviewing the boss of the job-holder
- direct observation
- asking the job-holder to keep a record of what is done (time-sheet or diary).

Whichever method or combination of methods is used, the aim is to provide a descriptive document which clarifies understanding of the functions performed in the job. To further aid understanding, certain key facts are usually inserted at the front of the description. The format and contents of the front section will vary from one organisation to another, but may typically comprise:

Job title
The official title as noted on employment (Personnel) records. Take care to avoid any terms which imply sex discrimination (eg tea lady, repairman).

Reports to
The position which has line responsibility for the job being described.

Responsible for
A list of any subordinates.

Purpose
A short, often single-sentence, description of the main objective of the job.

Location
Relevant information regarding site or department.

General
Any other relevant information.

Other commonly included pieces of information relate to pay grade, hours of work, and working conditions. These are not particularly useful from the trainer's viewpoint, but may be required for other purposes.

The job description then proceeds to list what is done in the job. There is some confusion in the terminology used in job analysis. I find the use of the term 'responsibility' unhelpful, and prefer to use the term 'duty' for a chunk of work described at this level. Later on, a duty may be broken down into smaller 'tasks'. Note that in the (very simple) example below several activities have been clustered together under relevant headings. Each of these duties starts with a present participle ending with an 'ing'. The key to describing what is done in the duty is to start each sentence with an active verb – 'answers', 'places', 'assists', etc.

EXAMPLE JOB DESCRIPTION: TELEPHONIST

Reports to: the Administration Manager

Responsible for: no subordinates

Purpose: to provide a prompt, efficient and courteous telephone service for a Regional Operating Centre

Location: Main Building, Northern ROC

General: the post-holder is one of two operating a modern switchboard serving 340 extensions

Duties:

Receiving calls
Answers incoming calls promptly and courteously. Ascertains the nature of the call and directs it to the most appropriate person. Takes messages accurately when required

Outgoing calls
Places calls for senior staff, and may assist other staff with difficult or overseas calls

Dealing with emergencies
Implements set procedures to deal with fire or other incidents

Operating fax machine
Sends and receives messages by fax

Other duties:

Assists with various office duties from time to time, including covering on reception

Once a job description has been completed, we can then proceed to analyse the components of the job further. This is done by clarifying in more detail the stages involved in each operation through task analysis.

Task analysis

Many training situations do not require the in-depth breakdown of tasks into small component parts. However, some complex tasks must be painstakingly analysed in order that an accurate and detailed picture is created which will form the basis of a training manual or programme. One of the consequences of the widespread use of Information Technology is that many people have to learn to find their way around software packages. These are becoming increasingly large and versatile, and whereas some people cope well by trial and error and using the manual, many others get stuck and give up. Even those who cope well may remain ignorant of some of the facilities available to them in the software, or may have found a laborious way to accomplish a task that has a much quicker solution available. The purpose of structured training is to ensure that everyone learns the most effective methods of performing the required tasks, and learns them faster than by trial and error.

The process of analysis is one of breaking down operations into component parts. How small these component parts should be is a matter of judgement which should take account of the existing knowledge of the learner. Will he or she already know the procedure for 'Open File Manager'? If so, it would be a waste of time analysing that operation further. On the other hand, if the learner does not know what is meant, then right at the beginning of the training you will have needlessly created a feeling of inadequacy and confusion. It is usually best to analyse in full detail and skip unnecessary explanation at the time of training if it is clearly not required. The analytical process itself is good preparation for instruction; it makes sure you know all there is to know before you start trying to teach someone else.

To continue with the example already given for a telephonist, the duty of 'Sends messages by fax' could end up as:

1   Loads document

2   Dials number of destination

3   Returns document and confirmation of transmission to originator

and so on.

This depth of analysis may be adequate for training purposes – that is, to act as a sequential series of prompts for a competent person to use in the instruction of someone else. If more depth is required, the analysis may be more detailed:

1   Loading documents

1.1   Place the document face down on the tray

1.2   Adjust the document guide to match the width of the document

1.3   Slide the guide to ensure that the document is centred on the feeder

1.4   Gently insert the leading edge of the document into the loading slot until you hear a beep

1.5   Select desired resolution

and so on.

Even now, more detail may be required. In the above example, 1.5 might be expanded to:

1.5   Select desired resolution

1.5.1   Press TX.MODE to cycle through FINE, SUPERFINE, or STANDARD modes

1.5.2   Press PHOTO if sending photographs

and so on.

It can also be appreciated that the above, although giving a sequence of operations, does not give the trainee any information about when it is appropriate to use different modes, or the consequences of each action (for example, that 'fine or superfine modes are slower and therefore more costly').

Often extra information is useful. There are many approaches to presenting the information from task analysis. One is to use the four headings shown in Table 4.

Table 4 *Checklist of task analysis*

What is done?	How is it done?	Points to ensure	Extra information
List the stages in a task starting each one with an active verb	Describe briefly how the operation is performed	Register factors that will affect performance List pointers that will show the trainee whether the operation is proceeding correctly Use sensory words like 'see' or 'feel' to describe signals which must be recognised	Note any other information which may be helpful or necessary
Example:			
Set up directory defaults	*Select 'Setup' from the main menu Select 'Defaults' Press Tab Type 'C:\' and the name of the directory containing your spreadsheet files*	*Save any work in progress before commencing The Default Settings screen should now appear (see Fig.5)*	*Using the arrow keys and pressing 'Enter', or using the mouse and clicking on either side*

Another way is to incorporate all the information into discrete steps:

1   Select 'Create New Chart' from the main menu.

2   Select 'From Gallery' from the Create New Chart menu to display the Chart Gallery.

3   Select the chart type by pressing the number in the upper left …

and so on.

> Always remember to include any necessary information regarding safety, whatever format is used. This is necessary to do a good and complete job. If you do not do so and someone is injured following your instructions, then not only could you be liable for prosecution, but you will have failed someone who had put their trust in you.

Faults analysis

The key skill in many jobs is recognising when something has gone wrong and knowing what to do to put things right. Fault-finding procedures can be analysed systematically and a faults analysis chart produced (see Table 5, overleaf). Good examples of these can be found in popular car manuals.

Table 5 *Faults analysis chart*

Fault	Causes	Remedies
File name invalid	Space, comma, or other character used	Remove the character and replace by letter or number
	More than 8 characters	Rename with 8 or fewer characters

Skills analysis

Once the task breakdown has been completed to the required depth, each operation may be examined to determine what skills or background knowledge are necessary for its successful completion. In the examples given under *Task analysis* above, the operations are mainly procedural and do not require particular skills or knowledge. However, if we look at an aspect of the job of the telephonist such as 'Receiving calls', this could be considered to require a number of skills and considerable knowledge (see Table 6):

Table 6 *Knowledge and skills breakdown*

Task	Knowledge	Skill
Answers incoming calls promptly and courteously	Company procedure for greeting callers	Switchboard operation Assertive and courteous telephone manner
Ascertains the nature of the call and directs it to the most appropriate person.	Functions within the company Extensions	Questioning and listening techniques
Takes messages accurately when required.	Company procedure for recording messages	Judging when to offer to take messages Memo-writing proficiency

When completed for all tasks, this stage is sometimes referred to as a 'job specification'. It may form the basis for the design of a training programme which will be discussed later in the book.

Otherwise, the completed task analysis or job specification may be used as a yardstick against which to assess current performance. If someone cannot do all the required tasks, then a training need is indicated. This approach has been developed extensively in the UK in the National Vocational Qualification system.

SKILL MATRICES

A quick and effective way of identifying training needs at an occupational level is to construct a skill matrix. For example, if we were to look at a workshop involved in the modification of light vans for a specialist purpose, we might arrive at a list of operations (perhaps at the 'duty' level) such as:

- cut off roof
- cut out windows
- cut out vents

- fit high roof

- fit windows

- fit vents

- fit panelling

- thread wiring.

We might have nine employees in this workshop whom we know well enough to be able to ascertain whether or not each one is capable of doing each operation. A matrix (Table 7) may in that case be constructed.

Table 7 *Skill matrix*

Name	Cut off roof	Cut out windows	Cut out vents	Fit high roof	Fit windows	Fit vents	Fit panelling	Thread wiring
R. Amos	✓	✓	✓	✓	✓	✓	✓	
B. Borg					✓	✓		✓
D. Cox							✓	
H. Dawes	✓	✓	✓					
M. Earl								✓
F. Fry					✓			
G. Grant						✓	✓	
S. Hunt				✓	✓	✓	✓	
J. Joyce							✓	

From this matrix, it can readily be seen that we have some possible problem areas.

There are many operations which can only be performed by two people.

The line manager may or may not be aware of this situation. Often the problem will be overlooked until, say, Dawes goes sick while Amos is on leave. On the other hand, this may not be an issue if 'roof cutting' is a once-a-month job and we can always get a subcontractor to do it if stuck.

But Cox, Earl, Fry and Joyce can each only perform one operation.

Again this may or may not be a problem. Perhaps they are all new to the job, or perhaps have some limitation which stops them learning other operations. The reasons must be investigated.

If there is not an acceptable reason, what should the desired skill situation be? If we discuss the matter with line management, they might say: 'We want everyone to be able to do at least three operations. We want at least three people capable of doing each cutting operation, and four people capable of doing each of the other operations.'

Our matrix can now be amended (see Table 8, overleaf).

Table 8 *Skill matrix with gap indications*

Name	Cut off roof	Cut out windows	Cut out vents	Fit high roof	Fit windows	Fit vents	Fit panelling	Thread wiring	Total	Need	Gap
R.Amos	✓	✓	✓	✓	✓	✓	✓		7	3	-
B.Borg					✓	✓		✓	3	3	-
D.Cox							✓		1	3	2
H.Dawes	✓	✓	✓						3	3	-
M.Earl								✓	1	3	2
F.Fry					✓				1	3	2
G.Grant						✓	✓		2	3	1
S.Hunt			✓	✓	✓	✓			4	3	-
J.Joyce							✓		1	3	2
Total	2	2	2	2	4	4	5	2			
Need	3	3	3	4	4	4	4	4			
Gap	1	1	1	2	-	-	-	2			

We are now in a position to discuss how the various gaps should be addressed and develop a training plan accordingly. However, so far we have only considered the question 'Can he or she perform the operation?' and have answered that question by using a tick or not. In other words YES or NO. Often, the position is more complex. Grant *can* do wire threading, but is very slow. Borg *can* fit panelling, but the quality of her work is not up to standard. A variety of ways of adding detail to the picture are possible. In Table 9 below, grades are given:

A = Quality to required standard

B = Quality below required standard

1 = Speed to required standard

2 = Speed below required standard

Table 9 *Skill matrix showing gradations of competence*

Name	Cut off roof	Cut out windows	Cut out vents	Fit high roof	Fit windows	Fit vents	Fit panelling	Thread wiring
R. Amos	A1	A1	A1	A2	A1	A1	A1	B2
B. Borg					B1	A2		A1
D. Cox							B2	
H. Dawes	A1	A1	A1	B2	B2	B2		
M. Earl								A1
F. Fry		B2			A1			B2
G. Grant						A1	A1	
S. Hunt		B1		A1	A1	A2	A1	
J.Joyce							A1	B2

A more complex picture has now emerged. Other coding possibilities include the use of percentages to indicate speed, or more sophisticated definitions of competence such as:

A = Fully competent, including fault rectification

B = Fully competent for straightforward operations

C = Competent to deal with straightforward operations with assistance

D = Competent to assist others

E = Not yet competent

One retail organisation I know of developed a system whereby competence was denoted by the use of red, silver and gold stars. This positive and motivating approach was made 'user-friendly' by the skill matrix being displayed in the staff room at each branch. Not only were the training needs easily determined by the line manager, but achieving competence was rewarded by a certification system which was in turn linked to pay.

INTERVIEWING

Interviewing is a technique that can appear to be very simple when used by an experienced practitioner. Although some people are naturally better at interviewing, the key skills of a good investigative interviewer are all capable of being learned. The first two skills are common to all types of interview – questioning and listening.

Questioning and listening

These two investigative skills are inseparable; one supports and reinforces the other. For trainers these skills are crucial not only at the stage of identifying training needs but also during instruction and evaluation. Many trainers who recognise that the ability to talk well is vital often underestimate the importance of questioning and listening. Hearing, which is an ability that may be difficult to improve, is not the same as listening which is a skill that can be significantly enhanced by training. Questioning is something that everyone can do, but which some people learn to do much more effectively than others.

In an interview to determine training needs, the interviewer may be delving into very emotive and sensitive areas. To ensure that the interviewee feels comfortable in talking about these issues, the interviewer must appear to be listening. To ensure that full understanding is attained, the interviewer must not only appear to listen but must actually do so with real concentration.

We let people know we are listening in two major ways: non-verbally and verbally.

Non-verbal cues

- eye contact
- smiling and nodding
- responding facially
- attentive posture.

Verbal cues

- encouraging inputs such as 'Yes', 'I see,' 'Then?', and so on
- asking for repetition of any word or name that has been missed
- checking understanding by paraphrasing what has been said and asking if the interpretation is correct
- making notes
- asking questions which show that previous replies have been absorbed.

Questioning appropriately may involve using a number of types of question. Some questions will be prepared in advance, but others must be constructed during the interview in response to what has been said. There are a number of different types of question which may be used:

Types of question

Open questions leave an 'open' field for the person to answer:

> 'Tell me about ...'
>
> 'What kind of work do you like?'
>
> 'How do you see the future?'

Probing questions fill in details from generalised replies:

> 'What exactly caused that?'
>
> 'You referred to an unpleasant incident a few moments ago; can you tell me exactly what was involved?'
>
> 'Who was it caused these problems?'

Reflective questions repeat what has been said *or implied* to encourage further disclosure. They show an awareness of feelings:

> 'You sound frustrated about that ...?'
>
> 'Does dealing with customers often upset you?'
>
> 'You say he actually made you cry?'

Closed questions are used to establish specific facts:

> 'Did you ask to be transferred?'
>
> 'How old were you?'
>
> 'Which machine was that?'

Comparisons are useful as a preliminary to more probing questions:

> 'Which do you prefer – writing or selling?'
>
> 'Which did you find easier, WordPerfect or Word?'
>
> 'Who is the better manager?'

Some questioning approaches are not appropriate, particularly:

Leading questions

> 'You'd like that, wouldn't you?'
>
> 'You'll need training in that, won't you?

Other aspects of the interview

- Ensure that interviews are conducted out of earshot of other people.
- Maintain confidentiality.
- Make good use of silence, allowing the other person time to think and reply.

- Maintain an appropriate distance from the interviewee.

- Make lots of notes.

You will also need to plan the interview, to some degree, in advance. It is sometimes worthwhile to prepare a standard list of questions to use with a group of people. Clearly the questions will vary according to the organisation and the types of job in question. Some possible questions are:

- What aspects of your job do you find satisfying?

- What would you change about your job if you could?

- Which aspects of your work interest you least?

- Which aspects of your work do you find most difficult?

- Have you sometimes found it difficult to do your job because of a lack of technical knowledge?

- What training have you had?

- What training do you think would be useful in your present position?

- What training do you wish you had received in the past?

- Have you any skills or knowledge that are not being used in your job?

- How do you know if you are doing a good job?

- What do you think other people think about your performance?

- When do you feel most pressured?

Another possible approach is to concentrate on the anticipated changes in the job. An example of this approach is given in the exercises following this section.

SURVEY METHODS

Surveys can be very useful in the gathering of data, including information on attitudes. People usually participate willingly if the completion of a survey form is not too complex or lengthy and if they think some good will come out of the exercise.

When designing a survey you must decide on:

- the size and nature of the sample

- the format of the questions

- exactly how the survey is to be conducted.

Sample

How many people will you ask? All of them or just 10 per cent of them? If not 100 per cent, how can you ensure fair representation? Make sure that you do not end up only asking grade 4 people, or only those in Scotland, if you are going to present the results as applying to the whole organisation. Political considerations often mean that it is better to survey everyone so that nobody feels left out.

Question format

The main formats available are:

Freeform
'What do you think of the training in this company?'

Multiple-choice
Which best describes the current position?

    a.   Excellent

    b.   Satisfactory

    c.   Unsatisfactory

    d.   Awful

Yes/No
Do you think training has improved over the last two years?Yes/No

How

Certain decisions have to be made in terms of how the survey is to be conducted. If you are just trying to get a global picture, you may choose to make the responses anonymous. More often, you will want to know the job or name of the person concerned so that any identified needs can then be met. If the survey says it is anonymous, but then asks for grade, age and length of service, people will assume that they will be identified from these particulars anyway. Make it clear when and how the form should be returned.

An alternative approach is to 'walk' the survey round. Delivering and collecting by hand will improve the response rate, but at a time cost. You may even want to ask the questions orally and write down the responses, as market researchers often do in shopping centres. Again, this is a slow method best suited for low numbers.

In order to get continued co-operation from people, publish the results and ensure that there is no negative comeback on participants.

A sample extract from a survey form constitutes Table 10.

Table 10 *Extract from a training needs survey*

Training Needs Survey
This is a survey to determine how well your manager communicates with you. The results will be used to help us determine training needs for managers. All responses will be treated as confidential and no attempt will be made to identify either respondents or their managers.
1 How well does your manager keep you informed of what is going on within your own division? Very well ☐   Fairly well ☐   Not very well ☐   Not at all ☐
2 How well does your manager keep you informed of what is going on within other divisions? Very well ☐   Fairly well ☐   Not very well ☐   Not at all ☐

3 How often does your manager organise team meetings?

Daily ☐   More than once a week ☐   Weekly ☐   Twice a month ☐

Monthly ☐   Quarterly ☐   Every six months ☐   Less than every six months ☐

Never ☐

---

4 How effective are the team meetings?

Very effective ☐   Fairly effective ☐   Not very effective ☐   Ineffective ☐

Please add any comments that you feel would be useful:

---

5 How often does your manager discuss objectives with you before you undertake any training or development activities?

Always ☐   Usually ☐   Sometimes ☐   Rarely ☐   Never ☐   No training ☐

APPRAISAL SYSTEMS

Many organisations see performance appraisal schemes as an integral part of their employee development strategy. Schemes vary considerably from one organisation to another, and nowadays may have a variety of names, but almost all of them include the identification of training needs as a key component. Most also consider the longer-term career options available to employees, and allow them to express their preferences. It follows that anyone with responsibility for training and development should influence the design of the scheme and ensure that notice is taken of the information generated by it.

This is not always readily achieved. Sometimes the scheme will focus on short-term performance issues, and line managers may not regard the consideration of developmental issues as important. The appraisal may also be considered to be confidential within the department concerned. Sometimes the section covering training and development needs is detachable, so that the training function only gets to see the appropriate information. This approach has its merits, but excludes the underlying performance issues which contribute towards identifying the training and development needs.

There are many issues to be addressed when designing and implementing an appraisal scheme, and some of the aims of the process may conflict with each other. For example, a scheme linked to the determination of pay increases may inhibit the appraisee from being honest about aspects of the job that he or she finds difficult, whereas it is precisely these aspects that must be discussed to identify training needs. Care is required to minimise these conflicts.

Who should be involved?

By far the most common arrangement is that employees are appraised by their immediate bosses, but there are many variations on this. In some organisations a second appraisal is conducted by the next-higher level in an attempt to ensure that any personality conflicts are overcome, and to promote improved contact between senior and junior staff. There is a noticeable trend to include inputs from both peers and subordinates in the appraisal process. Each option has implications for the appraisal process as a whole, but also for training needs identification in particular. Senior management are looking at performance from their perspective, whereas peers and subordinates may be much more concerned with the 'softer' aspects of performance, such as performing as a team member, motivating others, or being receptive to other people's ideas.

Incorporating the identification of needs into appraisal

There are very many different forms in use in very different organisations. Sometimes there is a separate section which looks something like Table 11.

Table 11 *Training and development within appraisal*

Please indicate the most important training and development needs that have been identified		
Learning need:	*Method:*	*Date:*

An alternative approach is to link each assessment of performance and the achievement of objectives to the identification of needs, as in Table 12.

Raising expectations

One very real problem with the introduction of appraisal schemes which include the identification of training needs as a core part of their purpose is that expectations are raised. On first introducing a scheme, hundreds of needs may be revealed which were previously hidden. Typically, the training budget cannot cope with all these needs in one go, and so many remain unsatisfied. The result of this is that profound cynicism quickly sets in. Should the same disappointment be repeated the following year, the reputation of the scheme as an effective and meaningful process for dealing with needs and aspirations will be permanently damaged. Accordingly, appraisers should be encouraged to:

- prioritise needs

- advise appraisees that some requests may not be met, and why

- actively seek out low-cost or no-cost solutions, such as coaching or reading.

Table 12 *Training and development linked to performance*

Performance area	Assessment	Training and/or development implications
1		
2		
3		
etc		
Next year's objectives	**Measure of success**	**Training and/or development implications**
1		
2		
3		
etc		

There are many other issues to be addressed in the design and implementation of an appraisal scheme. A number of good books are available which give help to someone who has to manage this task. The work by Anderson (1993) also includes advice on managing the relationship between performance appraisal and career development.

DEVELOPMENT CENTRES

The use of assessment centres for selection has continued to increase to the point where students approaching graduation now expect to undergo them routinely as they search for a suitable position. Somewhat less common, but growing in popularity, is the use of centres to assist in identifying developmental and training needs.

One of the reasons that the use of development centres has increased is that many organisations now base many of their employment practices on the idea of 'competencies' (or similar terms). Having identified key competencies for each job, it is comparatively easy to see how to make an assessment on that competency and compare it with the level of competency required. Following participation at development centres (or workshops), people can be informed how their performance was rated compared with the standard required for progression or movement into another role. This can be extremely helpful to them. Some organisations may also use these assessments to decide who should be given training and experience – and, of course, who should not be. It must be remembered that development centres do not function in isolation. The centre is just part of a bigger performance-enhancing process which may include appraisals, 360-degree feedback, mentoring schemes, etc.

There is no single 'right' way for a centre to be run. The design adopted will depend upon the competencies being investigated and, ultimately, how much the organisation wants to spend. Some centres run for several days but most commercial organisations cannot afford the resources to do this, and the pressure is usually on to reduce the duration to a minimum. The most common duration is one full day – perhaps with a follow-up feedback session.

Various elements can be combined within the time available. These are usually:

- exercises
- psychometric tests
- an interview.

Exercises

The most common types of exercises are:

- job-specific exercises
- case studies
- in-tray exercises
- group exercises
- role-plays
- individual presentations.

Job-specific exercises

For example: ask someone who is applying for a job as a website designer to design a website for a given scenario in a limited amount of time.

Case studies

For example: project managers may be asked to plan for the release of a new product. The plan may incorporate scheduling, budgeting and resourcing. This type of exercise may require the individual to display analytical thinking, planning and organising skills, etc. A case study exercise may be done by people working alone. More commonly, they are asked to work in teams. In that case, interactive skills, teamwork, leadership and persuasion might be assessed. Often there is a requirement to present the findings and the agreed plan.

In-tray exercises

Someone undertaking an in-tray exercise is asked to assume a particular role as an employee of a (perhaps fictitious) company and work through a pile of correspondence in an in-tray. These exercises commonly look at the ability to organise and prioritise work, analytical skills, communication with team members and customers, written communication skills, and delegation (if a higher-level position). Often participants will work on their own for a time before discussing their priorities and decisions as a member of a group.

Group exercises

Group exercises involve participants working together as a team to resolve a presented issue. These exercises commonly focus on interpersonal skills, leadership, teamwork, and problem-solving skills. They may be presented as a 'leaderless group discussion', or people may be assigned a particular role. Sometimes a problem-solving scenario may be used.

Role-plays

Participants may be asked to assume a fictitious role and handle a particular work situation. Customer service supervisors may be asked to respond to a number of phone inquiries, including customer queries and complaints, or managers may be asked to provide a staff member with feedback, or to conduct a counselling interview.

Individual presentations

Participants may be required to bring an 'about me' presentation with them. This can be very revealing – not only about the individual's personality as indicated by the content, but also about how much thought and effort has gone into the presentation. An alternative is to ask participants to prepare a brief presentation on the spot – perhaps around a topic such as 'my role model'.

Psychometric tests

If you want to measure somebody's aptitude at, for example, verbal reasoning, then using a properly designed psychometric test is the way to do it. Such tests are quick, accurate, objective and cheap. The only real problem is that you have to be qualified to buy and use them. They are dealt with in some depth in the final chapter of this book.

Interview

Interviews may be conducted on the same day as the rest of the centre or separately. It can be useful to give the individual a chance to air his or her perceptions of the activities undertaken, and questions are often tailored to probe why someone performed the way he or she did. Otherwise, the usual objectives of an interview are addressed, with questions selected to provide further information in relation to the relevant competencies.

DIY or ready-made?

It is possible to buy a range of assessment centre activities, including case studies, in-tray exercises and group exercises. However, you may prefer to write or design your own activities specific to your requirements. Some of these can be created quite simply: 'Discuss this problem as a group and recommend a course of action' – whereas the creation of a really good in-tray exercise may well take many hours of work. Ideally, use real-life (perhaps current) business problems, possibly presented by senior managers. Exercises perceived as irrelevant tend to be regarded as less valid by both participants and line management.

Who should assess?

Assessors must have good observational and analytical skill. They must also have some credibility with the participants. Often, relatively senior and/or experienced members of the line function concerned are used as assessors. Otherwise, trainers or recruitment specialists from within HR assess. Sometimes one or more outside consultants are brought in. An outside consultant can help to add expertise and credibility. Also, he or she is performing his or her core job and will not, therefore, be pulled off onto other tasks as line management might. One problem that bedevils development centres is scepticism from line management. Their involvement should quickly convince them of the merits of this approach. Participants will also value development centres more if they see that one or two respected managers have given up some time to be involved in them.

Whoever is going to assess, training is vital. This must include the development of clarity and consistency about the meaning of competencies, the need to back up assessments with evidence, and the need to maintain as objective a view as possible. Observing, recording and classifying behaviour is not easy, and requires practice. The training may be done by a consultant or internally, but should be specific to the organisation involved.

Writing up

At the end of the centre assessors should discuss their observations as a group, taking into account all views. Often, someone will have seen something that the appointed assessor missed, or will put a different interpretation on it. Final decisions should be made on a consensual basis. It is important that the instances of behaviour that were used as the basis for the assessment are recorded. You may need to justify your feedback to a participant: 'You were aggressive' is judgemental. 'You talked over Clive when he tried to explain his view, and told Marie that she was an idiot' is a statement of observed behaviour. Non-verbal behaviour (eg head in hands, arms folded, laughing) can also be recorded and fed back.

If too many competencies are being considered at any one time, assessors get confused. 'When he said that, was it customer focus or concern for accuracy?' It is best to limit the number of competencies in any one exercise to three or four.

Feedback

All participants should have access to feedback. Anything you say must be substantiated with examples. Feedback about psychometric test results should be given by a qualified person. Feedback is best given face-to-face.

Feedback from development centres is all-important. It can develop into an in-depth discussion about what actions the individual can take to address his or her development needs, and can become a career counselling exercise. In some instances you may want to ask the individual to make notes and to write up the feedback so that you can be certain he or she has taken it in correctly. The assessors become coaches and advisers, helping individuals to draw conclusions and think through implications. The individual may also write a report and agree it with his or her manager.

CRITICAL INCIDENT TECHNIQUE

Critical incident technique (CIT) was developed by John Flanagan, an American psychologist, during World War II. He wanted to know why errors were being made in bombing missions over Germany, and to improve flight-crew training.

The underlying basis for CIT is that most jobs contain a lot of padding – routine operations that don't matter that much. The things that distinguish someone who is particularly good in the job from someone who is average or poor are what they do in situations which may be fairly rare, but which are important in terms of outcome – critical incidents. People tend to talk about work in generalities. Asked what makes a good bar manager, they may talk about needing a good sense of humour, good judgement, and a customer-focused attitude. This may be true, but how do we train these qualities?

Using CIT we ask (for example): 'Give me an example of when having good judgement was important.' The person may then describe an incident involving a group of people who entered the bar but looked under-age, and tell how he or she politely asked them to leave. This can then produce a list of critical behaviours which can be taught to someone to ensure that they can cope in a similar situation. Of course, a whole range of incidents may be described which required good judgement, a good sense of humour and customer focus. It is important to get as wide a range of incidents as possible, preferably from a number of people, so that the important skills are identified. Instances where things have gone wrong can be extremely useful in identifying the difference between effective behaviour and ineffective behaviour.

For a fuller description of CIT, refer to the contribution by Malcolm Craig in Truelove (1995).

SUMMARY

Methods of identifying needs have been considered under the following headings:

- Job and task analysis
- Skill matrices
- Interviewing
- Survey methods
- Appraisal
- Development centres
- Critical incident technique.

All of these methods are resource-intensive. Seldom can the trainer operate without the agreement and co-operation of the line management, and often the analysis of training needs must be devolved to the line management. The trainer must then act as the co-ordinator of information, as an adviser, and as the instigator of training activity. Time spent identifying training needs is wasted unless those needs are subsequently addressed.

FURTHER READING

Anderson, A. H. (1993) *Successful Training Practice: A manager's guide to personnel development*, Oxford, Blackwell

Anderson, G. C. (1993) *Managing Performance Appraisal Systems*, Oxford, Blackwell

Bartram, S. and Gibson, B. (1994) *Training Needs Analysis*, Aldershot, Gower

Goodge, P. (1997) Assessment and development centres: practical design principles, *Selection and Development Review*, Vol.13 No.3, June

Pearn, M. and Kandola, R. (1988) *Job Analysis: A practical guide for managers*, London, Institute of Personnel Management

Truelove, S. (ed.)(1995) *The Handbook of Training and Development*, 2nd edition, Oxford, Blackwell

Woodruffe, C. (1990) *Assessment Centres*, London, Institute of Personnel Management

Useful websites

http://adulted.about.com/od/trngneedsasst/a/needsassessment.htm Adult   www
continuing education – a part of the New York Times Company

http://www.businessballs.com Some free material and exercises

www.cipd.co.uk/subjects/training/trnneeds/ Useful information from the CIPD

ACTIVITIES – CHAPTER 2

1 Case study: The interview

Mary arrived at the factory in ample time for her interview with Clive Roberts, the human resources manager. She had answered the advertisement for a training officer a few weeks before, and was keen to join the Parmell team. She approached the gatehouse and noticed the two security officers chatting in the corner of the room over a copy of a newspaper. She tapped on the window, but the men ignored her. She tapped again, and this time one of them looked up. He sauntered across to the window, still chatting to his colleague as he did so.

'Yes, dear?' he enquired.

After Mary had explained that she had come for an interview, the security officer directed her to reception, and then resumed his chat with his colleague.

'Didn't think we were taking any women on,' she heard him say.

It was a difficult job finding reception, but Mary did so eventually. As she signed in, Mary noticed that the telephone was allowed to ring for ages before, eventually, a young woman picked it up.

'Hello?' Pause. 'No, this is reception. No. No, I can't transfer you, I don't know how. Sorry. Bye.'

'Been here before?' asked the receptionist. Mary replied that she had not.

'Well, just be careful as you walk across the yard – some of the delivery drivers go at quite a lick! Anyway, I'll point out the Personnel's door to you.' The receptionist propped open the side door with the fire extinguisher and directed Mary across the yard.

As she waited for her interview, Mary overheard one of the office workers calling someone on the internal telephone.

'Ken? Thank goodness. The photocopier's jammed again. Could you come and have a look? Thanks.' The office worker returned to her keyboard at the computer.

Mary noticed that she was copying a handwritten manuscript of several pages and commented: 'That looks a lengthy job.'

'Yes. I keep telling the safety officer he should write his reports directly onto the computer, but he says it takes him too long.'

During her interview, Clive Roberts said: 'Well then, Mary, you seem to know a lot about identifying training needs in theory – how about in practice? Have you spotted any here at Parmell?'

What training needs might Mary comment on?

2 Task analysis

Introduction

This activity is most suitable for use with a group of between six and twelve people, but can be adapted for smaller or larger numbers.

Aims

To give practice of the process of task analysis and of the writing of instructions. Precise objectives may be determined by the course tutor.

Method

Divide the class into three teams. Assign each team a task to analyse with the following brief:

'You will be assigned a piece of equipment. Analyse all the steps necessary to take the equipment from the state it is in when given to you to the state required. From this analysis, produce a written set of instructions. This set of instructions will be handed to a member of another group who will read them out to a colleague from the same group who will attempt to follow them precisely.'

Suggested equipment

The actual equipment for analysis may have to be carefully selected in order to balance out the difficulty of the tasks according to the nature and usability of what is available. But see examples in Table 13.

Table 13 *Task analysis exercise*

Equipment	Initial state	Final state	Safety notes
Flipchart stand	Completely folded down with the pad removed.	Fully erected with the pad properly positioned.	Involves bending and lifting.
Overhead projector and screen	Overhead projector as folded down as possible, facing the wrong way. Screen folded down or out of position.	Image correctly projected onto screen.	Care with electricity – also avoid turning on the projector when the mirror is down.
Video recorder and monitor	Leads disconnected and monitor/TV not tuned in. Video cassette in case.	Showing a video tape with correctly adjusted volume, etc.	Care with electricity.

Timings

Allow 40 minutes to perform the task analysis and prepare the instructions. Allow about five to ten minutes for each activity to be demonstrated, with a similar time for discussion of the learning points that arise.

Variations

Specifically allow or forbid the use of diagrams. The activity is more difficult if diagrams are banned.

3 Training needs identification by interviewing

Introduction

This is a self-generated role-play exercise. It may be conducted in pairs or with observers.

Aims

To provide an opportunity for interviewing techniques to be practised.

Method

Every participant produces an outline job description and an interviewer's brief. These are then swapped and the interviews are conducted either in pairs or in threes, the participants taking turns to observe, be interviewed, or interview.

Timings

About 20 minutes to prepare the briefs, followed by about ten minutes for people to study the briefs received. The interviews will typically last about ten to 15 minutes. Feedback, discussion and analysis will take a further ten minutes after each interview.

Training needs exercise

Think about some of the people where you work. Select someone who has one major or several minor weaknesses which must be addressed in order to improve performance. Some of these may be due to training needs, some to poor attitude or motivation. If necessary, exaggerate the problem(s) or combine a few individuals' faults.

1   Prepare a *brief* description of the job.

2   Prepare an interviewer's brief – as if you were looking at the situation from outside and were briefing yourself for the encounter. Use a fictitious name, please. Do this using the format below.

3   You will play the character that you have described. Someone else will conduct the interview.

Interviewer's brief

You are going to talk to someone whose performance is less good than required. His/her manager has left you some notes, but is away from work for some time and can not be contacted. Try to identify any training needs, but also note any non-training issues.

The interviewee's name is: ....

(use a fictitious name)

He/she has been employed ....

He/she works as ....

His/her performance is :

4 Skill matrix exercise

Introduction

Learners prepare a skill matrix.

Aims

To consolidate learning, and to raise issues for further discussion.

Method

The group selects a suitable area for study and a list of tasks or duties generated. If they are all from the same organisation, it may be appropriate to select an actual department. If from different and diverse organisations, then some fairly common activity is selected to use as a simulation. For example, operations concerned with basic car maintenance may be analysed to produce a list ranging from 'Fill up with petrol' through 'Change wheel' to 'Replace clutch'. Participants' names are then listed and the individuals identify themselves as competent or not. If required, they may use a more sophisticated assessment system. Issues related to problems of assessment and the definition of competence will arise and may be discussed. Other possibilities for matrix generation are 'Using office equipment', 'Looking after babies', and 'Preparing a Sunday lunch'. Note that it does not matter if some of the participants have a lot of knowledge whereas others have only a little – the matrix will be more interesting if that is so.

Timings

About 30 minutes for the whole activity.

Agreeing learning needs within the organisational context

It isn't the incompetent who destroy an organisation. It is those who have achieved something and want to rest upon their achievements who are forever clogging things up.

Charles Sorenson

CHAPTER OBJECTIVES

When you have finished this chapter you should be able to:

- describe the contribution that training and development makes to organisational success, and the factors that influence its effectiveness

- prioritise and agree learning needs with individuals and groups

- recommend learning and development opportunities relevant to identified needs

- explain organisational roles and relationships with reference to personnel and development

- describe a variety of influence techniques relevant to the role of the trainer.

Having conducted a training needs analysis, it may be that you will be able to progress straight on to the next stage of determining solutions and organising for them to be implemented. Very often, though, you will need to gain agreement from other people in the organisation. In this chapter we explore organisational roles and relationships and the contribution that training and development makes to organisational success and the factors that influence its effectiveness before considering tactics to gain agreement.

THE TRAINING FUNCTION

We must appreciate that the training function is a relatively recent addition to organisation structures compared with other functions such as production, accounts and sales. In their book *Training Interventions*, Reid, Barrington and Kenney describe some of the factors that have affected its emergence. Before the 1960s hardly any companies in the UK had training units in operation. Then the 1964 Industrial Training Act introduced a financial system with levies and grants which effectively forced many companies to appoint training officers for the first time. Often this was someone from the existing personnel department who then took on training as a part-time role or who was, for instance, an engineer nearing retirement. In some organisations, therefore, training was seen as a peripheral activity involving some fairly low-status individual 'going through the motions' to minimise the amount of money to be paid over to the relevant Industrial Training Board (ITB).

Some organisations did appreciate the value of training, and the financial 'sticks and carrots' in place resulted in training departments of high status and influence emerging. However, the removal of the levy/grant system and the abolition of most ITBs at the start of the 1980s, coupled with an economic downturn, saw many training functions shut down or substantially cut back. Even where they did survive, they were sometimes dispersed to other functions as line managers reasserted their control over matters affecting their departments.

Since the end of the1980s, however, a different picture has emerged. One of the influences has been that writers such as Tom Peters and Charles Handy have stressed the importance of training for organisational success. This is linked into the bigger picture of constant organisational change and developments in quality systems. In the book *Thriving on Chaos*, which Tom Peters published in 1987, there is a chapter entitled 'Train and retrain'. The main thrust of this is that successful companies train their employees – unsuccessful companies don't. To pick out a few sentences:

- 'Workforce training must become a corporate (and indeed national) obsession.'
- 'You can't overspend on training.'
- 'Don't cut the training budget when crises come; increase it!'

At the same time, Peters, Handy and others were looking at how well Japanese companies were doing in comparison with US and UK companies. What did they do differently? Peters reported that when Nissan opened a plant in Tennessee, they spent $63 million training about 2,000 workers before it even opened. That's more than $30,000 per person.

So the link between training and organisational success gradually began to sink into the minds of the senior people, and a new wave of training functions began to emerge in progressive organisations. Although in some organisations training is now seen as high-status and core, there are some where the old low-status peripheral view remains. What you are expected to achieve, what you can achieve, and how you can achieve it may be determined in large part by this perception.

Another point that Peters made was that all training should be line-driven. He wrote that the line must take the lead in developing programme input *and again* in the teaching – assigning people temporarily to training to work out course content. The 'training department person' is the pedagogy (teaching methodology) expert, but not the content leader. Peters feels that it is better to have conservative training 'owned' by line management than an innovative programme written off as 'the training department's fantasy after they consulted with academics'.

FACTORS THAT INFLUENCE ITS EFFECTIVENESS

There are very many forces at work that affect the training function's effectiveness. Reid, Barrington and Kenney identified three main conditions which must be satisfied if the function is to secure a relatively stable place in the organisation:

1   The management team should accept responsibility for training.

2   The training function should be appropriately structured within the organisation – with roles that are perceived as relevant to such aspects as boundary management, organisational culture, operational strategy, management style, and the organisation's geography.

3   Specialist training staff should be regarded as professionals – trained, with clearly defined roles.

These three conditions are discussed below.

Management's responsibility for training

All managers should accept personal responsibility for the training and development of their own staff. Of course managers have lots of other responsibilities and they have to make decisions about their priorities. Anyone who has attended a time management course will appreciate the difference between *urgent* work (which must be done now or ASAP) and *important* work (which directly contributes towards the accomplishment of the goals of your job and thus the goals of the organisation): see Figure 2.

The problem is that training and development is very rarely urgent but is often time-consuming. So although many managers appreciate that it is important, it is easily displaced by tasks of more immediate urgency (production line down, sales under budget, waiting times for operations increasing, etc). Indeed, managers can be actively discouraged from attending to their staff's training and development by a performance appraisal system that does not value time spent on this activity. I remember someone telling me that as a retail manager he had voluntarily adopted the role (which he enjoyed) of an on-the-job trainer for the region – spending time developing assistant managers in his shop so that they could be given shops of their own. But that resulted in slightly lower sales figures in his shop – for which he was admonished. So he stopped doing it. All performance review systems ought to include the training and development of a manager's staff as a core objective against which his or her performance is measured.

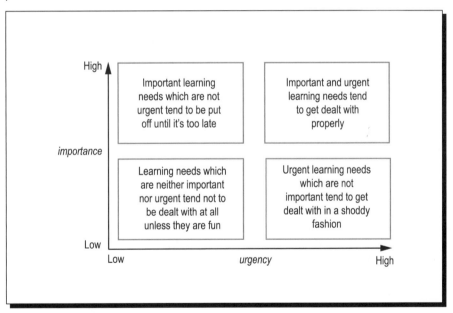

Figure 2 *Urgent or important*

Another barrier to managers spending time on training and development is that some of them find it difficult. Someone who has been promoted to a managerial position, perhaps because of his or her exceptional technical expertise, may have a lot of trouble mastering the people management side of the job. He or she is busy having to recruit, motivate teams and individuals, allocate tasks, and influence other people within the organisation. When people are promoted to roles which involve responsibility over others, part of their preparation for these roles should include being taught how to train and develop their staff.

There is also the matter of the manager's own experience of learning. In some instances, there is the 'Nobody ever taught me anything – I had to learn the hard way' attitude – which is understandable, if regrettable. The benefit to the manager of helping his or her staff to learn and develop as well as possible must be demonstrated. In other cases, the manager may have very negative memories of the learning process. He or she may not have done particularly well in formal education, and may thus remember the learning process as uncomfortable and unpleasant. This may also apply to training he or she has received while at work – with memories of embarrassing role-play exercises, or a team-building exercise which finished with his or her weaknesses being discussed insensitively for 20 minutes at the end. Any involvement with someone else's learning will therefore be avoided, even if it is done subconsciously. Helping such a manager to overcome this negativity will be a complex and lengthy process – and will require some understanding.

The structure of the training function

There is, of course, no single 'one-size-fits-all' answer to the question 'How should we structure the training function?' Back in the days of the ITBs, the philosophy that was imposed on companies was that there should be a centralised training function staffed by specialists who 'knew better' than the line managers and who would ensure that all training was done properly and was fully documented. This structure can still be found in some organisations. Sometimes the training function is independent of the rest of the human resources function; sometimes it is part of it.

In other organisations there is no central training function at all. Training is carried out independently in each department or division – and there may be training officers (by whatever name) scattered about the organisation who report to the functional head. There may be no attempt to ensure a consistency of approach across all areas. This is sometimes referred to as an 'integrated' training function.

In many organisations there is a combination of these two approaches. Each department has its own technical trainers, but there is a central co-ordinating function. Thus the finance department will have a finance trainer who will identify needs and design and conduct training within the department. The customer services department may have a team of trainers, perhaps with a team leader, who do the same in that area. So too in sales, purchasing, maintenance, IT and distribution. But there is also a small central training function. This may have direct responsibility for some aspects of training (eg induction), but also act as a source of training expertise for the departmental trainers. This central function will, most likely, be staffed by people who regard themselves as career trainers – training professionals who have, or intend to get, certificates and diplomas in their chosen professions, and who want to stay in the profession. The departmental trainers may or may not want to be trainers. It may be a role they have accepted as a temporary, developmental, step in their careers, or it may be that they have been selected for the role because they are not particularly valued in their core profession.

Training staff seen as professionals

To begin to examine this third condition, let us first of all consider the concept of 'role'. We all play many roles in life, such as those of parent or friend, and it is not difficult to see how this sense of the word 'role' is related to its meaning in the theatre. Apparently, this French word originally meant 'a roll, as of parchment', particularly with reference to a rolled manuscript (or scroll). It came to refer to the script from which an actor learned a part – 'Here is your *role*.' This use in the world of the theatre has spread to everyday language. It broadly means 'function'. So if you are taking your aunt from abroad around town, your role may be guide, interpreter, bodyguard, companion, bag-carrier, nurse, banker, or any combination of these or other functions. In large part, your role would be determined by what your aunt wanted or needed it to be, and by events that might occur along the way. If she were fluent in English, the interpreter role would not be required. If she has already mapped out in detail which museums and sights she wants to see, then the guide role is not required.

The same applies at work. To a large extent – but not entirely – the role(s) that you perform will be determined by the other 'players' within, and to some extent outside, the organisation. Events will also determine what role you are required to perform at any given time as well as by your own decisions about how you want to function at work. Whether you want to challenge other people's expectations of your role, or accept them, or to gradually develop a new role, may be a matter of personality, ability and determination. But the more you know about your chosen profession, the more you can do, then the more likely you are to be able to take control of your own work role.

Charles Handy, in his book *Understanding Organizations*, has a chapter called 'On roles and interactions' which goes into some depth about role theory and makes interesting reading. One of the concepts which he explores is that of 'role ambiguity'. Role ambiguity relates to the feeling of uncertainty one may have about one's role. This can happen for a trainer who responds to a wonderful advertisement for a job as a 'dynamic proactive agent for change' – only to find that the environment expects a 'plodding reactive bureaucrat' just like the one they've always had. Developing the role you want when other people's expectations of the role are so different requires considerable strength of character and perseverance, but some people do succeed.

To be seen as a professional thus very much depends on the way in which the role as a whole is perceived. Certainly, qualifications and membership of an appropriate professional body, such as the CIPD, helps to enhance the perceived professionalism of the training function. It is also important that training is recognised as a possible career rather than as just a temporary interruption in a line career or as a sinecure for long-serving has-beens. Above all, the training function must operate in a professional manner – relating its objectives to those of the line managers and the organisation as a whole, and demonstrating that it adds value through its activities.

It is also worth acknowledging that, to be effective, the training function must be adequately resourced. I have met many trainers whose remit has covered so many areas and with such a small budget that they are hardly able to keep up with the reactive side of the job – let alone spend time being creatively proactive.

THE CHANGING ROLES OF THE TRAINER

The context in which organisations operate is in a constant state of change. Just as organisations must adapt to the shifting economic, technological, social and political environments, the training function must, in turn, respond to the ever-evolving needs of the parent organisation. There has probably never been a more exciting time to be involved with training. Training is increasingly being seen – by line managers – as a powerful force in their efforts to keep the organisation ahead of the game. To be really effective, the training function must become as proactive as possible – anticipating the changing shape of the organisation and having solutions available even before they are asked for. It must become a function to which the key line managers turn for advice before major decisions are taken. In this way, the strategic role of training will become strengthened and its contribution maximised.

There have been various attempts to categorise the roles that trainers perform in organisations. Generally, they distinguish between:

- *direct trainers* whose main role is actually training or instructing people
- *training managers* who plan, organise and administer an organisation's training
- *consultants* who advise line managers on training matters, or who are asked to work as change agents.

Some writers add further roles. For example, Bennett mentions the role of 'provider' (designing training, maintaining and delivering programmes, training needs analysis) and the role of 'innovator' (heavily involved in the change process).

Obviously, these roles can be mixed to a greater or lesser extent – and there are also many people for whom training is a part-time role. These can be line people who also train, human resource or quality assurance managers with responsibility for training as well as other matters, and even outside trainers or consultants who come in and perform a variety of roles for the organisation. The role that is increasing in prominence is that of the internal consultant who has expertise which the line managers can tap into.

As with all consultancy, the role is one which has little or no direct power. Rather, the consultant has to exert influence through his or her expertise and ability to analyse complex situations. He or she must persuade rather than direct, and must work with and through the line management rather than taking independent decisions. So even when you are sure that you know what the problem is, and how to tackle it, you must think in terms of persuading others that you are right.

AGREEING LEARNING NEEDS

Having conducted some kind of identification of training needs exercise, and having thought about the organisational context, then, you will (usually) need to get other people to agree with you. In some circumstances this is extremely easy and straightforward; in other circumstances it is extremely difficult. Whatever you may read in books about training or influencing, some of the people that you may have to deal with are likely to be stubborn, hostile, indecisive, unstable or otherwise difficult. The good news is that the majority of people are open-minded, friendly, rational and generally in favour of training and development. But they are also under pressure to achieve results. They must be convinced that if you are proposing to make their people attend a three-week residential course, at great expense, it will be a good investment.

Prioritise and agree learning needs

Very often, you will have uncovered a large number of learning needs. In most cases there may be no realistic prospect of tackling *all* of the issues that have been identified in the immediate future. It is therefore necessary to prioritise the needs and to agree which will be dealt with now, and which will be set aside for future consideration. This must be done, of course, in conjunction with line management. Sometimes how this is done will be obvious; on other occasions a little ingenuity may be required – so we will look at a couple of useful techniques. One method is to look at the consequences of taking action.

Look at the consequences

1   What are the consequences, in *operational* terms, of tackling or not tackling the identified need?

2   What are the consequences, in *process* terms, of tackling or not tackling the identified need?

Let us distinguish these two concepts with an example.

EXAMPLE OF PROCESS CONSEQUENCES

Imagine you are the training officer for a trendy pub chain. You have recently visited one of the establishments, and talked to the manager and all her staff.

An employee, Mark, who has been with the company for three years, has expressed a desire to obtain a 'personal licence' – which is something that someone is required to have if he or she is to be in permanent charge of licensed premises. It takes a short course, costing less than £300. It is not essential for this pub, because the manager and her assistant are already personal licence holders. But it is a long-term aim of the company to assist all permanent employees to gain the licence to ensure good practice and to make sure there is always someone on the premises with such a licence – even though it is not strictly necessary. The manager regards Mark as someone with great potential.

There is a course running locally next week. The manager looks at the staff roster, and realises that to grant the leave would cause operational difficulties. There are various possible solutions that could be explored, but these will take time and incur overtime costs. If you decide not to put Mark on the next course, there will be no significant operational consequences.

On the other hand, by not arranging the training, you may be causing Mark to lose some motivation (consequence 1). Also, Mark may ask you about the issue every time he sees you. Each time he does this, he puts more energy into explaining to you why he feels he should undertake the training. You may end up spending a long time talking about why you have not yet organised the training – and you have still got this to do (consequence 2). Finally, you may decide not to respond to this pressure and harassment because you want Mark to realise that this is an inappropriate and ineffective way of working (consequence 3). Mark feels rather resentful about this, and starts to consider whether his long-term future should lie elsewhere (consequence 4). These four are *process* consequences that impact on the relationship between the training officer and operational staff, current and future job performance by the individual, and possibly the way in which other employees behave.

The importance of process considerations is often understated in textbooks. The focus is on evaluating the problem in terms of organisational goals – cost-benefit analysis or return on investment. In the example given above, a big factor is the importance to the employee of his *personal goals* in this situation.

Now, if the situation were that the manager was about to be relocated to a different area in two weeks' time, and the assistant manager has asked for extended leave to visit relatives in Australia for six weeks, then the training need is obviously a high operational priority.

Deciding on priorities is therefore often not as straightforward as we would like. It requires a subjective assessment of the consequences of action or inaction as well as an objective assessment. Even apparently simple situations may involve complex issues. Practicality is often a major influence in deciding which needs should be addressed first: needs A, D and F can be sorted out quickly and simply, whereas B, C, and E will require a lot of planning and further investigation.

Recommend learning and development opportunities relevant to identified needs

Again, this may be a straightforward or highly complex situation. The first thing to do is to consider all the possible options, including:

- on-the-job training
- distance learning
- interactive computer-based learning
- planned experience
- coaching
- external courses
- in-house courses
- directed reading.

Then, each possible solution must be considered against a number of factors:

- cost
- acceptability
- timing
- likely success.

This can never be a wholly 'scientific' exercise. No commercial training provider is going to market programmes with the promise that they 'may or may not' produce the desired learning. Nor can you fully assess the effectiveness of an interactive programme before purchasing it. However, you can ask for references, seek out reviews, and use a variety of other approaches to make your judgement. Acceptability can include considerations such as the personal preference of the learner – 'I don't like learning with computers' – or domestic considerations. I have known more than one person who has not wanted to go away for a training course because of domestic commitments or because of pressure from a spouse. Some learning is better done in-house; some is better done on a public (open) course. For example, attending assertiveness training where personal fears and weaknesses are explored can be much more comfortable and effective in the company of strangers from other organisations than in the company of colleagues from within one's own organisation.

INFLUENCE TACTICS

There are a variety of models of influence tactics. The following is adapted from the model developed by Gary Yukl. In this context, the 'target' is the person or group to whom the influencing effort is addressed – which may be the individual or group with a training need, or may be a line manager.

Rational persuasion

The influencer uses logical arguments and factual evidence to persuade the target that a proposal is viable and likely to result in the attainment of task objectives. This is the strategy that should work when dealing with logical people – but be sure that you have done your homework and thought through all the possible questions that may be raised.

Inspirational appeals

The influencer makes a proposal that arouses target enthusiasm by appealing to target values, ideals and aspirations. For example, someone concerned with status may be influenced by the thought of gaining a certificate. Someone who is concerned about job advancement may be influenced by a reference to previous learners who have been promoted.

Consultation

The influencer seeks target participation in planning a strategy, activity, or change for which target support and assistance are desired, or is willing to modify a proposal to deal with target concerns and suggestions. Many people automatically react negatively to proposals which they see as attempts to force them into a particular course of action. Involvement is much more acceptable to them.

Ingratiation

The influencer uses praise, flattery, friendly behaviour or helpful behaviour to get the target in a good mood or to think favourably of him or her before asking for something or suggesting a course of action. This tactic can backfire if it is seen through – but works surprisingly well with many people.

Exchange

The influencer offers an exchange of favours, indicates willingness to reciprocate at a later time, or promises a share of the benefits if the target helps accomplish a task. For example, 'If you agree to let me take your team away for a weekend residential course, I'll see if I can get you on the senior management programme.' This is negotiating – and only works if the target wants what you have to offer.

Legitimating tactics

The influencer seeks to establish the legitimacy of a request by claiming the authority or right to make it, or by verifying that it is consistent with organisational policies, rules, practices, or traditions. This is most often by reference to senior management, but can also be by reference to strategies such as Investors in People.

Pressure

The influencer uses demands, threats, frequent checking, or persistent reminders to influence the target to do what he or she wants. As we all know, nagging can work – or can produce an unwanted backlash.

Whatever approach is adopted, it is important that whatever is agreed is recorded so that no misunderstandings arise. Often a simple email memo will be adequate – detailing the identified need, the agreed action, who will take the action and when. Sometimes a written report will be more appropriate. A written, formal, record of the identification of training needs process, together with documented reasonings and factual evidence supporting any recommendations lends authority and conviction to the whole process.

SUMMARY

This chapter has considered the historical development of the training function, and some of the factors which affect both its effectiveness and its permanence. One of the key factors identified is that the management team should accept responsibility for training.

A variety of training roles has been discussed – direct trainers, training managers, and consultants. Within the organisation, it is important to identify which of these roles you perform and in what proportion and to relate this to other people's perceptions of these roles.

The process of obtaining agreement has been considered, and a variety of persuasive approaches has been examined.

FURTHER READING

Bennett, R. (ed.)(1988) *Improving Trainer Effectiveness*, Aldershot, Gower

Hamblin, R. (1995) National training policies in Britain, in Truelove, S. (ed.) *The Handbook of Training and Development*, 2nd edition, Oxford, Blackwell

Handy, C. (1985) *Understanding Organizations*, 3rd edition, Harmondsworth, Penguin Books

Peters, T. (1987) *Thriving on Chaos*, New York, Alfred A. Knopf Inc.

Pettigrew, A. M., Jones, G. R. and Reason, P. W. (1981) *Organisational and Behavioural Aspects of the Role of the Training Officer in the UK Chemical Industry*, Staines, CAPITB

Reid, M. A., Barrington, H. and Kenney, J. (1992) *Training Interventions*, 3rd edition, London, IPM

Yukl, G. (1994) *Leadership in Organizations*, Englewood Cliffs, NJ, Prentice Hall

Useful websites

http://changingminds.org/ A very large site about change and persuasion www

http://www.tompeters.com/ The website of Tom Peters

ACTIVITIES – CHAPTER 3

1 The structure of the training function

In groups, consider and prepare a presentation about:

- the advantages and disadvantages of having:
  - a centralised training function
  - an integrated training function

- the advantages and disadvantages of having:
  - training as a part of the larger human resources function
  - training completely separate from human resources.

2 Agreeing training needs: role-play

Ideally, this should be conducted in groups of three or four.

Group A:
You are members of the training function who have been interviewing people across the organisation to determine training needs. Nearly all the members of one particular department have complained of a lack of team spirit, poor communication and feeling undervalued. Prepare a strategy for a 15-minute meeting – possibly, but not necessarily, including a presentation – to persuade the management team of that department of the need to address these issues. Decide what options you might put forward for consideration should the needs be agreed. You have 30 minutes to prepare.

Group B:
You are the management team of the department concerned. You are aware of the poor morale within the department, but are under pressure to meet targets. The training team want to meet you to discuss its findings. Decide what kind of influence strategy you will respond to (eg are you only going to be persuaded by factual evidence, or are you more interested in increasing your own profile) and how you will respond to perceived criticism (eg acknowledge and accept it, or react with some anger). If possible and appropriate, base your decisions on the personalities of managers that you know (or have known) in your own organisations. Think about what questions you will ask the training team. You have 30 minutes to prepare.

Plenary
Discuss how the meeting went.

- To what extent was it realistic?
- Which influence tactics worked?
- Which influence tactics did not work?
- How satisfied were you with the outcome?
- If you were to repeat the exercise, what would you do differently?

Design

The learning process

CHAPTER 4

Creative minds have always been known to survive any kind of bad training.

Anna Freud

CHAPTER OBJECTIVES

When you have finished this chapter you should be able to:

- **prepare learning objectives, and relate them to Bloom's taxonomy of educational objectives**

- **describe some of the key processes and models of adult learning, including Kolb's experiential learning theory**

- **explain the principles of self-directed learning.**

LEARNING OBJECTIVES

The purpose of training is expressed through the use of stated *aims* and *objectives*. Words such as 'aim', 'objective', 'goal', 'target' and 'purpose' are used in different ways according to the context. There has long been controversy about exactly how 'objectives' should be defined. The current consensus favours the views of those who believe that objectives are meaningless unless they describe terminal behaviours in very precise, measurable and observable terms. I shall start by describing that viewpoint, which is widely held, before considering different attitudes. With regard to training, we can consider the following as usable definitions:

- aim: a general statement of the purpose of a programme of training

> **'To train journalists to be more effective in the way they manage their time'**

- objective: a definition of the behaviour that the person will be able to display at the end of the training.

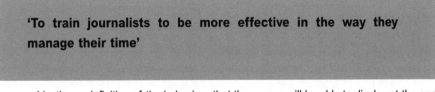

> **'The trainee will be able to locate, activate and operate the widget machine so as to produce widgets to the company standard at the rate of 100 units per hour.'**

This approach to writing objectives has been refined and extensively written about by Robert F. Mager. Objectives following his rules are sometimes labelled 'Mager-style' objectives and sometimes 'behavioural' objectives. Mager believes that an objective should have three components:

- a definition of the behaviour/act

- a definition of the important conditions under which the behaviour is to occur

- a definition of the criterion of acceptable performance.

In the United Kingdom the third component 'criterion' is more usually expressed as 'standards', but the effect is the same.

Obviously, it is easier for precise objectives to be set in terms of speed and accuracy for readily measured outputs (eg typing) than for sophisticated behavioural outputs (eg motivating people). Nevertheless, statements can be made which give a reasonable indication of what the training is meant to achieve:

> **'The trainee will be able to initiate conversation with the customer in a friendly and businesslike way which will create a positive impression of both the trainee and the Company.'**

With such a statement, whether or not the objective has been met will still be a subjective decision – but at least there is a guideline to judge against.

Note the use of the definite 'will be able to' followed by an active verb. This clearly expresses the required behaviour. Phrases such as 'should be able to' are considered to be too imprecise. Similarly, words such as 'know', 'understand', or 'appreciate' are considered to be too open to differences in interpretation for use in objectives. Also, they are not observable. How can you tell if someone 'knows' something? Well, you can ask them to state or write what they know. If this is really what is required, then we should say so. Words like 'state' or 'write' should therefore form part of the objective. It can be seen that if so written, the objective will give us a clear idea of how to approach the measurement necessary to confirm the achievement of the desired learning.

If a lot of detail is required for a training programme to be constructed, objectives must be stated for each component part of the programme. These are sometimes termed 'learning unit objectives' and can be expressed with whatever precision is required in terms of standards and also with reference to the conditions under which the performance is required. They may be written in three-column format as shown in Table 14.

Table 14 *The components of an objective*

Performance	Conditions	Standards
Mow the lawn	An electric mower in good condition Square or rectangular flat lawn Initial grass length 3cm to 5cm Dry grass	No areas missed No cuttings left Clear straight line pattern No scalping At the rate of 600 square metres per hour

An alternative is to combine the conditions and standards into a test of performance that will indicate whether the desired performance outcome has been achieved: see Table 15.

Table 15 *Test of performance*

Performance	Test of performance
To type a business letter	In an office situation using Word for Windows from a handwritten original of 400 words at 40 words per minute or faster with no more than 10 errors before spell-checking, and no more than 2 errors after spell-checking

The objective must

- state what the trainee will be *doing* when demonstrating his or her achievement, and how you will know when he or she is doing it

- define the important conditions

- define the standards of performance required.

Write as many separate objectives as are needed to achieve clarity and let the learner know the objectives.

Different views

Some jobs are very complex, and the time spent writing Mager-style objectives can be enormous. Educational research reported by Ivor Davies (1976) suggests that specific behavioural objectives are no more effective than general objectives. Other writers believe you should include the learning process as part of a well-written objective. The following quotations are taken from *The Adult Learner: A neglected species* (4th edition) by Malcolm Knowles (1990), who explores the topic more fully than is possible here.

Taba (1962) says:

> 'Objectives should also be so formulated that there are clear distinctions among learning experiences required to attain different behaviours.'

> **'Objectives are developmental, representing roads to travel rather than terminal points.'**

Schwab (1971) says:

> **'I do not intend or expect one outcome or one cluster of outcomes but any one of several: a plurality.'**

These views emphasise both the unpredictability of learning and the importance of considering the processes which lead to learning outcomes.

The ultimate limitation of Mager-style objectives is that they may lead us to take a trainer-centred approach. We control what will be learned as precisely as possible. I believe that this approach is wholly valid when considering the training of tasks such as operating a photocopier or using a lathe. However, more complex and 'softer' skills such as counselling or leading a group discussion benefit little from such attention to detail – and may even be harmed by it. If the trainer is taking a facilitative approach and drawing upon the skills and knowledge present in the group, and responding to the issues that arise from the group, then the precise learning outcomes must be different on every occasion, if only to a small extent. To reject learning simply because it does not fit in with a preordained prediction seems rather limiting.

A balance must be struck. It is possible to become very vague about what will be learned, or to use phrases such as 'a voyage of self-discovery'. Busy line managers tend to be impatient with that approach. Not unreasonably, they want to know what the objectives of the programme are before committing their time or that of other people. Accordingly, the declared objectives of a training event often represent the *minimum* learning that will take place and can act as a reminder to the trainer that this has been promised. Whatever promises you make in the declared objectives, you must try to ensure that these promises are kept.

SMART objectives

The above text specifically relates to learning objectives. For the sake of completeness, and to avoid confusion, let us briefly consider objectives which are set for performance. Setting and agreeing objectives is generally seen as an appropriate way for a manager to agree performance criteria with a subordinate. Poorly set objectives, however, make later evaluation of achievement difficult. To be effective, objectives should be SMART:

- Specific – as clear and as precise as possible. This is sometimes given as 'simple'.

- Measurable – quantifiable, as far as is appropriate. Note that some very important objectives (eg to improve teamwork) may be hard to measure, but quantification may be helped by the use of an indicator (eg to reduce the number of transfer requests).

- Agreed – the process by which objectives are set is very important. The more an employee participates in setting goals, the more likely he or she is to show commitment to their achievement. This is sometimes given as 'achievable' – but that means much the same as 'realistic'.

- Realistic – challenging, significant, but not impossible. An unrealistic objective produces despair and no extra effort. Too easy an objective may actually *lower* effort.

- Timed – make it clear by when the objective should be accomplished.

When agreeing objectives with others, focus on meaningful issues. It is best to confine the number of objectives to between three and six key areas of the job.

Revise the objectives as and when circumstances change. If an objective is set but then not mentioned for months, the person who is supposed to meet the objective may well conclude that it does not really matter. Schedule periodic progress reviews for maximum effect.

BLOOM'S TAXONOMY OF EDUCATIONAL OBJECTIVES

Benjamin Bloom's work on objectives was linked to his perception that education was overly concerned with teaching pupils to regurgitate facts rather than how to think clearly about what they had learned. Bloom was heavily involved (with others) in formulating a classification system (or taxonomy) of 'the goals of the educational process' from the end of the 1940s.

Bloom's taxonomy is a useful tool because it allows teachers or trainers to decide what level of cognitive skill they would like their learners to attain. It is the basis for the concept of higher- and lower-order thinking. This scheme emphasises that learning is hierarchical – that learning at the highest level is dependent on the achievement of lower-level learning first. Bloom's levels from low to high are:

1 *Knowledge* – the remembering and recall of previously-learned material. This may involve the recall of a wide range of material, from specific facts and terminology to complete theories – but all that is required is the bringing to mind of the appropriate information. Knowledge represents the lowest level of learning outcomes in the cognitive domain.

2 *Comprehension* – the ability to grasp the meaning of material. This may be shown by translating material from one form to another, by interpreting material (explaining or summarising), and by estimating future trends (predicting consequences or effects). These learning outcomes go one step beyond the simple remembering of material, and represent the lowest level of understanding.

3 *Application* – the ability to use (ie to apply) learned material in new and concrete situations. This may include the application of such things as rules, methods, laws and theories. Learning outcomes in this area require a higher level of understanding than those under Comprehension.

4 *Analysis* – the ability to break down material into its component parts so that its organisational structure may be understood. This may include the identification of the parts, analysis of the relationships between parts, and recognition of the underlying principles involved. Learning outcomes here represent a higher intellectual level than Comprehension and Application because they require an understanding of both the content and the structural form of the material.

5   *Synthesis* – the ability to put parts together to form a new whole. This may involve the production of a unique communication (eg a speech or poem), a plan of operations (eg a proposal to tackle a complex problem), or a set of abstract relations (eg a scheme for classifying information). Learning outcomes in this area usually stress creative behaviours, with emphasis on the formulation of new patterns or structures.

6   *Evaluation* – the ability to judge the value of material (essay, novel, poem, research report) for a given purpose. The judgements are to be based on definite criteria. These may be internal criteria (organisation – how well something is constructed) or external criteria (relevance to the purpose), and the student may determine the criteria or be given them. Learning outcomes in this area are the highest in the cognitive hierarchy. They contain elements of all of the other categories, plus conscious value-judgements based on clearly defined criteria.

The taxonomy above is concerned with the *cognitive* domain, which deals with the knowledge and understanding of concepts or ideas. Later work introduced discussion of the *affective* domain, which involves the attitudes and feelings that result from the learning process.

Bloom's taxonomy is often used as a framework in the formulation of objectives, teaching methods, and assessment criteria. In doing this, it is possible to find lists of verbs which may be used to prepare objectives at each level. For example, the following verbs may be useful when constructing objectives for (level 5) Synthesis:

arrange	compose	design	manage	plan	set up
assemble	construct	develop	modify	prepare	write.
collect	create	formulate	organise	propose	

Bloom's work has had a lasting effect on education and training practice. In particular, the taxonomy links in with the concept of the 'learning organisation' – which requires that all employees are able to apply knowledge, solve problems and evaluate information.

ADULT LEARNING

The process of learning is a highly complex one and many theories have been put forward to help us understand it. Knowles (1990) lists some 61 propounders and a further 33 interpreters of learning theory. For the training practitioner, an understanding of one or two theories or models of learning can be very useful.

Although there is no single, unequivocally accepted definition of precisely what the word 'learning' means, most authorities agree that learning is about 'changing behaviour'. We will firstly consider a well-established model of learning that can be very useful in some situations.

Conditioning theory

Although developed from observations of animal learning, the process termed 'conditioning' has been demonstrated to apply to human learning in very many instances. Its most eminent advocate as a theory was B. F. Skinner (1968) who conducted research into the process over many years. The principle by which conditioning works is that behaviour that is rewarded (or 'reinforced') is more likely to recur. Behaviour that is punished (or 'negatively reinforced') tends to occur less. The desired behaviour is *conditioned* to occur as a result of a particular stimulus.

This is the principle used to train a dog to bark in response to a particular blast on a whistle. At the beginning, considerable patience is needed because the dog does not understand what it is supposed to do. If the trainer blows the whistle and the dog barks, it receives a reward, such as a biscuit. No bark, no reward. No whistle, no reward for barking. Eventually, the connection is established. The reward may now be given only intermittently, but the behaviour will tend to persist. Also, the reward may change to a pat on the head or verbal praise. The behaviour will persist – assuming that the dog regards the new reward as a positive experience.

Human beings can learn in the same way. Small children are rewarded with praise for the desired behaviour, and punished by being told off, or possibly smacked, for 'bad' behaviour. Immediately a problem arises when dealing with adult learners. Being praised inappropriately is not rewarding: it is irritating. Being told off is often not acceptable, and being smacked certainly is not! So great care must be taken in this process. The frequency and style of praise must be geared to the individual learner. Often the reward can be self-administered. Provided that the learners are given the information to know whether or not they have done something well, they can give themselves a notional 'well done'. The reward process can also be built in to a learning task. Study any good computer game aimed at children. Success *at learning the game* is periodically rewarded by points, secret levels, progress, fanfares, passwords, or whatever other device the creators have dreamed up. The motivational effect of these on *some* players is very powerful. The fact that others seem not to respond demonstrates that the reward must be a reward *to that individual learner*.

The other limitation of a conditioning approach is that it is best suited to the teaching of simple operations or sequences of operations. It is not an adequate approach when dealing with situations that require an understanding of complex concepts, underlying principles, or problem-solving (other than to predetermined formulae). Before considering other models of learning, it is worth considering a simple but valuable way of looking at the ways people learn.

Three ways of learning

A system developed by Sylvia Downs in the 1980s is to arrange learning into one of three categories (see Truelove, 1995; Downs, 1995). This is the memorising-understanding-doing (MUD) taxonomy. The basic concept is that all learning tasks are comprised of one, two, or all three of these components. Identifying the ways in which things are learned is an important first step in the design of training programmes, activities and materials. The MUD system distinguishes three different groups of things to be learned, each of which uses different methods:

- *facts* which have to be *memorised*
- *concepts* which have to be *understood*
- *physical skills* which have to be experienced by *doing*.

If the nature of the learning is misunderstood, the training method applied will be inappropriate. For example:

- You can get someone to repeat a phrase from a textbook until it is word perfect – but there may be no understanding.
- You can explain in detail to someone the process of juggling, perhaps using slow-motion video, until he or she understands what is happening – but it does not mean that that person will be able to juggle.

- You can teach someone how to operate a microwave oven – but he or she may not be able to name the component parts of the oven.

There are various ways to help people cope with all three types of learning.

Memorising

The main mechanism for straightforward memorisation is through repetition. It is the trainer's task to organise repetition so that it is not boring. Exercises can be devised which repeat information in new ways and require the learner to use the new information. However, it can be very helpful to think of memory aids which assist this process. For example:

- *Link or group items*: 'This is another way of affecting the appearance. So, as with 'character', 'paragraph' is found under Format.'

- *Break into parts*: make sure no one item is too big for comfortable memorisation. Teach part 1, then part 2, and then combine them before moving to part 3.

- *Mnemonics*: special aids such as acronyms or rhymes. These can be incredibly helpful in some instances – for example, the way in which most British people remember how many days there are in each month: 'Thirty days hath September ...', or the order of the spectrum: 'Richard of York Gave Battle in Vain' (red, orange, yellow, green, blue, indigo, violet). If you can think of a nice easy-to-learn mnemonic, you can help people to memorise lists or sequences much better.

People memorise best when they concentrate. Concentration is crucial to the memorisation process. Concentration can be impaired by tiredness, and improved by a feeling of commitment to the learning task. People must also be allowed time to reflect on what they have learned. Resist lengthy training sessions, therefore – particularly after the trainee has been hard at work for some hours.

Understanding

Helping people to understand something is not always easy. We cannot understand for them. What we can do is to explain carefully, and to encourage analysis by asking questions. Downs (1995) gives us four keys to understanding, which are:

- *purposes* – why something is as it is; what it is trying to do

- *comparisons* – comparing and contrasting with other experiences; identifying similarities and differences

- *viewpoints* – imagining things from other directions, or from others' viewpoints

- *problems* – what could go wrong; how we would overcome that.

We can also aid understanding by ensuring that the use of unfamiliar jargon is minimised, and by relating the learning to what the trainee already knows and understands. Understanding is the most difficult form of learning to assess. Whereas memory can be checked by asking for facts to be repeated, and doing can be checked by observation, understanding requires a variety of checking processes. The keys to understanding given above can also serve as the keys to checking understanding. One approach that does *not* work is to ask: 'Do you understand?'

Learning to do something

Learning to do something is easier if you are clear as to the *purpose* of what you are trying to achieve, know relevant *procedures* or rules, and are allowed adequate *practice* of the skills involved.

Because *unlearning* can be difficult, it is important to get the movements right from the start. Often professional sports coaches prefer to teach people who are absolutely new to the sport, rather than people who have picked up bad habits already.

Learners often get to a stage where they do not seem to improve much. This is termed a *learning plateau*. Trainers may need to support and encourage learners through this stage. When someone begins to learn a piece of skilled behaviour, he or she has to concentrate on memorising a series of movements, perhaps linking them to sensory cues. Eventually, these conscious actions become automatic, and this is how people 'get off the plateau'. This is often the stage when people are unconsciously learning to use information from muscles as well as from eyes and ears. Using this muscle information is much quicker than using other cues.

EXPERIENTIAL LEARNING

It is common for training courses to be described as 'practical', perhaps workshop-based, or 'theoretical', probably classroom-based.

However, we know that the good workshop instructor will relate the practical to the theoretical, and the good academic teacher will illustrate theoretical points by reference to practical examples. Similarly, we have probably all experienced training which we thought was very good, but which was quickly forgotten. Or when we came to use the learning, we found that it did not seem to apply to our situation. Among many theorists who have studied human learning, the work of David Kolb has been widely adopted as the most useful way of helping trainers to design learning events. Kolb developed a four-stage cycle to describe the ideal sequence for effective learning to take place.

The four stages should always follow the same sequence, but the process may start at any one of the stages:

- concrete experience
- reflective observation
- abstract conceptualisation
- active experimentation.

Concrete experience

This is where the learner is personally involved in carrying out a task, and gains feedback on how well or how badly he or she has done it. To be useful as a learning experience the learner must be aware of what is happening. The trainer may help by pointing out various cues: 'The steering may feel less responsive now.'

Reflective observation

It is not enough simply to have an experience in order to learn. Without reflecting on the experience it may quickly be forgotten or its learning potential lost. It is from the feelings and thoughts emerging from this reflection and analysis that generalisations or concepts may be generated. If this does not happen, the learner may become skilled at the *specific* task being taught, but cannot generalise from one situation to other situations. This is the stage of the cycle that may benefit from a trainer asking questions to stimulate thought, and from discussion.

Abstract conceptualisation

It is only from generalisations and conceptual understanding that new situations can be tackled effectively. This stage involves learners developing a deeper understanding of what they have learned. It is often helped by a 'teacher's' input about a theory or a model which can be applied in a variety of situations. If the learner does not understand the connection between the theory and the practice, he or she will be unable to make use of the theory in the work situation.

Active experimentation

For learning to result in changed behaviour it is not sufficient to learn new concepts and develop new generalisations. The implications of the newly learned concepts must be tested out in new situations. The learner must make the link between theory and action by planning for that action and carrying it out.

Figure 3 illustrates the cycle.

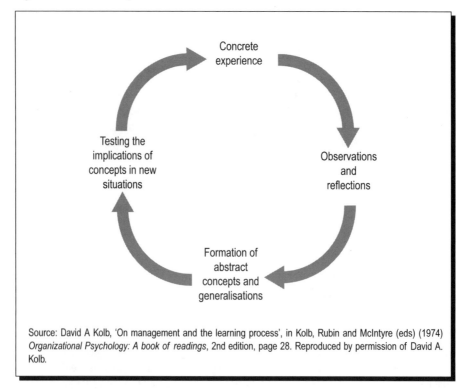

Source: David A Kolb, 'On management and the learning process', in Kolb, Rubin and McIntyre (eds) (1974) *Organizational Psychology: A book of readings*, 2nd edition, page 28. Reproduced by permission of David A. Kolb.

Figure 3 *The Kolb learning cycle*

Example

1   A trainee nurse might start learning to lift a patient by trying to lift a dummy out of a wheelchair (*Active experimentation*).

2   She finds this difficult and fails (*Concrete experience*).

3   The instructor encourages reflection by questioning: 'How did that feel? Was it hurting your back?' (*Reflective observation*).

4   The nurse then reads a manual about lifting techniques (*Abstract conceptualisation*).

5   The nurse now *tries out* one of the techniques on the dummy (*Active experimentation*).

6   The nurse notices how much more effective the new method is (*Concrete experience*).

7   She discusses her experiences with some other trainees (*Reflective observation*).

8   The instructor now asks the group to look in the manual and to identify all possible methods suitable for lifting an unconscious patient (*Abstract conceptualisation*).

and so on.

The important point about experiential learning theory is that experience alone is not enough. We must think about what we have done, and what we are going to do, to maximise learning. We must also understand the underlying principles concerning whatever we are learning if we are to be able to work out appropriate courses of action for ourselves.

The other implication from Kolb's concept is that learning actually requires more than one skill from the learner. The four stages of the learning cycle require us to operate in a different learning mode. Kolb found that people differ in their comparative ability to operate in each of the four modes. He developed a questionnaire, the Learning Styles Inventory, which allows individuals to look at their own preferences and profiles. This may be found in the book by Kolb, Rubin, and Osland (1995) which is listed in the *Further reading* section.

In the United Kingdom, the concept of learning styles is more usually associated with the work of Peter Honey and Alan Mumford (1986). Honey and Mumford took Kolb's learning cycle and developed a questionnaire which produces scores for four learning styles. This is a different set of styles from that produced by Kolb, and the interested reader should refer to the *The Manual of Learning Styles* by Honey and Mumford for an explanation of their reasoning for adopting this different approach as well as a thorough description of how the concept of learning styles may be used. I will not attempt to give an explanation here, but many trainers find the concept extremely useful for tailoring course designs to suit particular groups of learners. Once the manual has been purchased, the Learning Styles Questionnaire may be reproduced 'as often as you wish', which is very helpful.

Using the cycle

Of course, 'theoretical' ideas like those of Kolb can very easily be seen as irrelevant to practical training. The learning cycle is a useful starting point in the design process. If it is borne in mind, the process of producing worthwhile learning experiences is more likely to occur. In general, the trainer will often find that his or her greatest contribution is in ensuring that sufficient reflection takes place for the fundamental aspects of the learning to be internalised. De Geus (in Kolb *et al*, 1995) states that:

'Research on learning styles has shown that managers on the whole are distinguished by very strong active experimentation skills and are very weak on reflective observation skills.'

The challenge for the trainer is to make such managers reflect without alienating them. If they see the trainer as an 'ivory tower' thinker, they may react negatively to the whole process of reflection. They will become impatient to get on with the next activity. As in many things, a balance must be struck.

SELF-DIRECTED LEARNING

Most adults spend a considerable time acquiring information and learning new skills. Much of this learning takes place at the learner's initiative, even if available through formal settings. A label given to such activity is 'self-directed learning'. Self-directed learning is seen as any study form in which individuals have primary responsibility for planning, implementing and evaluating the effort.

Self-directed learning has always existed, but has only recently been researched and analysed. Many important historical figures were self-directed learners (such as Socrates, Alexander the Great and Abraham Lincoln) as were (and are) many unknown ordinary people who have striven to improve their skills and knowledge.

Much has been written about self-directed learning. One fairly early and highly influential contribution was made by Malcolm Knowles. In his 1975 publication *Self-Directed Learning* he provided definitions and assumptions that guided a great deal of subsequent research. He describes 'self-directed learning' as a process:

> **'in which individuals take the initiative, with or without the help of others, in diagnosing their learning needs, formulating learning goals, identifying human and material resources for learning, choosing and implementing appropriate learning strategies, and evaluating learning outcomes.'**

Knowles puts forward three key immediate reasons for self-directed learning:

- People who take the initiative in learning (proactive learners) learn more things, and learn better, than do people who sit at the feet of teachers passively waiting to be taught (reactive learners).

- Self-directed learning is more in tune with our natural processes of psychological development. 'An essential aspect of maturing is developing the ability to take increasing responsibility for our own lives – to become increasingly self-directed.'

- Many of the new developments in education methods and learning technologies put a heavy responsibility on the learners to take a good deal of initiative in their own learning. Those who have not learned the skills of self-directed inquiry will experience anxiety, frustration, and often failure, and so will their teachers.

Knowles, and others, developed the concept of self-directed learning as an instructional process centred on such activities as assessing needs, securing learning resources, implementing learning activities, and evaluating learning.

This can be simplified to a four-stage systematic model:

1   What areas of knowledge and skills do we need to gain in order to get something done (our learning needs)?

2   What specifically do we intend to know or be able to do at the end of this process (our learning objectives)?

3   What resources or learning opportunities can we use to reach these objectives (learning activities)?

4   How we will know that we've gained the required knowledge and skills (learning evaluation)?

So it is essentially the same as any other learning – except that the learner is determining his or her own learning needs, deciding how they will be met, and deciding for himself or herself the extent to which they have been met. The trainer who is helping someone to become an active self-directed learner becomes a facilitator – helping to formulate objectives, identifying resources and options, and helping with study skills such as using a library or critically reflecting on learning experiences.

When this approach is used on a training programme, it involves 'letting go' to a large extent. For example, instead of a course tutor setting an assignment that has to be submitted in two weeks' time, the course tutor might say:

■   You decide what you need to learn.

■   You decide how you are going to learn it.

■   You make sure that happens.

■   Write it up – including your evaluation of its effectiveness.

SUMMARY

This section has examined some aspects of the learning process. First, the writing of objectives was considered with reference to the work of Robert Mager. The preparation of precise behavioural objectives is considered to be very important by many people involved in training, although others see limitations in this approach. Being *able* to write precise objectives is a fundamental requirement of the modern trainer, even if he or she sometimes prefers not to do so. The writing of SMART performance objectives has also been covered, and Bloom's taxonomy of learning objectives has been introduced.

Learning processes were further considered – conditioning theory was outlined, as was the MUD taxonomy developed by Sylvia Downs. Experiential learning theory, as developed by David Kolb, has also been described. Finally, the process of self-directed learning has been examined.

FURTHER READING

Davies, I. K. (1976) *Objectives in Curriculum Design*, Maidenhead, McGraw-Hill

Downs, S. (1995) *Learning at Work*, London, Kogan Page

Honey, P. and Mumford, A. (1986) *The Manual of Learning Styles*, Maidenhead, Peter Honey

Knowles, M. (1990) *The Adult Learner – A neglected species*, 4th edition, Houston, Gulf

Kolb, D. A. (1974) On management and the learning process, in Kolb, Rubin and McIntyre (eds) *Organizational Psychology: A book of readings*, 2nd edition, Englewood Cliffs, NJ, Prentice-Hall

Kolb, D. A. (1984) *Experiential Learning: Experience as the source of learning and development*, Englewood Cliffs, NJ, Prentice-Hall

Kolb, D. A., Rubin, I. M. and Osland, J. S. (1995) *Organizational Behaviour: An experiential approach*, 6th edition, Englewood Cliffs, NJ, Prentice-Hall

Krathwohl, D. R., Bloom, B. S. and Masia, B. B. (1964) *Taxonomy of Educational Objectives: The classification of educational goals. Handbook II: Affective domain*, New York, David McKay Co.

Mager, R. F. (1990) *Measuring Instructional Results*, 2nd edition, London, Kogan Page

Skinner, B. F. (1968) *The Technology of Teaching*, New York, Appleton-Century-Crofts

Truelove, S. (ed.)(1995)*The Handbook of Training and Development*, 2nd edition, Oxford, Blackwell

Useful websites

http://coe.sdsu.edu/eet/Articles/bloomrev/index.htm   www
About Bloom's taxonomy

http://adulted.about.com/cs/coursedesign/a/Objectives3_3.htm About objectives

http://www.trans4mind.com/learning/ About self-directed learning

ACTIVITIES – CHAPTER 4

1 Training objectives: exercise

The following are attempts to write the performance elements of training objectives. Indicate which ones describe an observable and measurable behaviour.

		YES	NO
1	Name six motor insurance companies operating in the UK	☐	☐
2	Know the principles of fire prevention	☐	☐
3	Be aware of how viruses are introduced into computers	☐	☐
4	List the ten biggest selling cars	☐	☐
5	Understand the way a laser printer operates	☐	☐
6	Load and fire a pistol	☐	☐
7	Speak clearly on the telephone	☐	☐
8	Appreciate the factors affecting trainee motivation	☐	☐
9	Recall the names of the main board	☐	☐
10	Apply paint as required	☐	☐
11	State how to trigger the alarm	☐	☐
12	Restore antique furniture	☐	☐

2 Learning cycle exercise

Think about a training course which you are involved in as a trainer. If you do not currently run any training courses, think about a programme you have attended as a learner. Analyse the programme, or a section of the programme, in terms of Kolb's learning cycle. If any parts of the cycle are missing, what could be done to correct this?

3 MUD analysis exercise

Introduction

A simple exercise designed to show how MUD can be used in practice.

Aims

To allow learners to appreciate the way in which MUD can be used in the early stages of programme design.

Method

Divide the group into teams of three or four people. Ask them to select a job for analysis which they all have some knowledge of – for example, the job of a bartender or waiter/waitress. They should first of all generate a list of activities within the job. These must then be categorised as requiring learning primarily by memory, or understanding, or doing. Answers are then compared and discussed in a plenary session.

Timings

Twenty minutes in small groups. Then about 20 minutes' discussion and analysis in a plenary session.

Designing learning events and strategies

That is what learning is. You suddenly understand something you've understood all your life, but in a new way.

Doris Lessing

CHAPTER OBJECTIVES

When you have finished this chapter you should be able to:

- list the factors that affect the design of learning events

- structure a training and development session

- incorporate sound principles relating to health and safety, equality and non-discrimination in the design process

- distinguish between the concepts of education, training, and development

- describe the concept and practice of continuing professional development.

WHAT IS DESIGN?

Tony Earl (1987) defines design as:

> '**the plan, structure and strategy of instruction used, conceived so as to produce learning experiences that lead to pre-specified learning goals.**'

In turn, the term 'learning experience' may have to be considered. Earl gives a definition by Tyler (1949):

> '**A learning experience refers to the interaction between the learner and the external conditions in the environment to which he can react. Learning takes place through the active behaviour of the student; it is what he does that he learns, not what the teacher does.**'

This is an important point. Although giving people information through presentations and handouts has its value, it is getting people to *do* things that is really effective.

First stages of design

- Assess learning needs and from these determine objectives. Simultaneously, consider practicalities concerned with time and the resources available. Although many texts will encourage you to define the objectives precisely at this stage, most trainers leave the detailed writing of objectives until later. The questions that follow will all influence what will be achievable.

- Consider who the learners will be. What are their individual differences? What are their expectations? What are their learning styles, and what style of training will they respond best to? What are they used to?

- Assess the nature of the learning. Is it a matter of memorising, understanding or doing? What activities or resources are needed?

  - *Memorising*
    Lists, handouts, presentations, activities that require memorisation, etc
  - *Understanding*
    Lessons, discussions, case studies, role-playing, exercises, etc
  - *Doing*
    Demonstration, skill practice, role-playing, dismantling and reassembly, etc.

We are now in a position to consider what resources exist to meet these needs and what must be created or modified. It is very often possible to find good commercial activities which can be used as they stand. On other occasions, you can take the idea and modify it to suit your particular purpose. A decent library of books and commercially produced exercises and case studies can be invaluable as a starting point. Sometimes, though, it is better to start from scratch and think up your own ideas and write your own material. The old saying that 'Necessity is the mother of invention' applies as much to the origination of good training ideas as it does to anything else. Do not underestimate your own ability to be creative.

When a good solution has been identified, subject it to the 'three Es test' (as adapted from a four-part model by Earl – see *Further reading*).

Ask yourself whether the activity will be:

- effective – will it work?

- enjoyable – will it get a positive response, or be seen as tedious?

- efficient – even if effective and enjoyable, is it worth the time taken? Or could a shorter activity achieve the same results?

Ideally, try out or *pilot* the activity in a non-critical situation, perhaps with colleagues, before using it with 'real' learners. Also be prepared to revise and refine the activity in the light of experience, suggestions from participants, and as a result of the formal evaluation system.

This process is summarised in Figure 4.

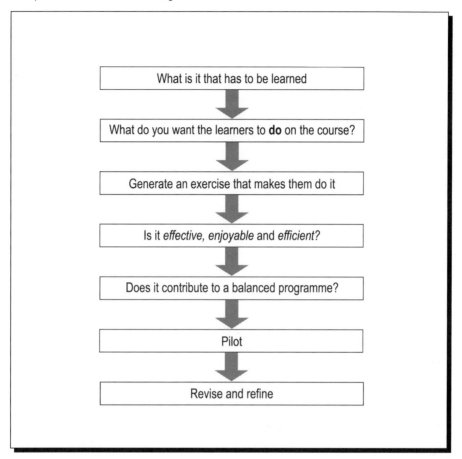

Figure 4 *Designing learning activities*

Scheduling

Begin with the fixed elements – meals, normal working hours, etc. These considerations are especially important if there is little chance of changing them.

Consider what needs to be learned first. Start with small units and build up to more complex activities. Later elements should consolidate earlier learning in a cohesive way.

Mornings are generally better for theory; afternoons for activity.

We all have a limited attention span – some more limited than others. Break up 'heavy' input sessions into smaller chunks, and use other media between these chunks.

Balance

The aims and objectives should be used to determine how much time ought to be devoted to each topic. In part, the time spent will be perceived as an indication of the topic's importance. Thus a two-day selection interviewing course which devoted only 15 minutes to the topic of sex discrimination might give the impression that sex discrimination was not considered an important topic – even if it were possible to put across the key points adequately within that time.

There should also be a mixture and balance of training methods. Too much input is tedious. Too much action with little time for discussion or reflection is not good for learning. Too many self-analysis questionnaires, videos, case studies, role-plays or games can all give a feeling of monotony to the programme. Many of the methods available to trainers are discussed later in this book.

Facilitating group formation

Unless a course consists of an existing fully coherent group, a process of group formation will occur. The longer the course, the more important this is. Even on short courses the group will develop. Its capacity to tackle exercises increases, as does its confidence to challenge and question. Early activities should be relatively short, should not be too difficult, and should not promote animosity between group members. Activities should help people to identify with each other, rather than cause conflict or embarrassment.

Timings

Although this has already been considered, the design will have to be modified as the material is developed. If time is short, long exercises – even if effective – will have to be discarded in favour of shorter ways of achieving the learning. If you are struggling to fill the time available, the best solution is to shorten the course. There is a tendency to think that a course must be either (say) three days or four days. Could it be three days and three hours? Is a three-hour session likely to be unacceptable? If so, could each day be extended by an hour to fit in the learning? What would the reaction to that be?

A good test is to refer back to the objectives. Decide which of them is essential, which less so, and which could be left out altogether. A common way of doing this is to prioritise the objectives as:

- must know

- should know

- nice to know.

Training is often a compromise between three factors: the range of learning which will be covered, the depth to which the coverage will go, and the time which will be taken. This may be likened to a balance (Figure 5). If more range is required, either the time must be increased or the depth be reduced. Similarly, if more depth is required, either the range of coverage must be decreased or the time must increase.

Finally

After the design has been produced, modified, and refined, leave it for a few days. Go back to it and think it all through again. Very often, good ideas take time to filter through, or ideas that seemed great at the moment of inspiration look rather lame a few days later.

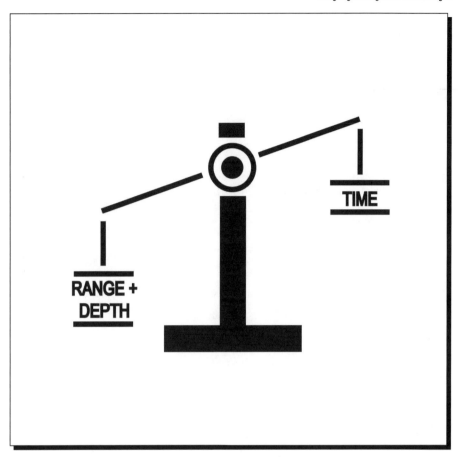

Figure 5 *Balancing the range and depth of learning with available time*

Once the course has been run, revise it and amend it further. Of course utilise the feedback from participants, but your own feelings and perceptions will also be important in assessing what ought to be changed. Many experienced trainers find that it usually takes about three courses before they are happy with a design.

More guidance on how to tackle the writing of material is given later in the book.

SESSION PLANS

The purpose of a session plan (or lesson plan) is to guide the trainer through the training event. A session plan is an outline of what you intend to happen, in the required sequence, and a reminder of what is required to make it happen. It is particularly important when more than one trainer is delivering the same session or course. If things are not written down, then it is likely that people will end up receiving different messages or that 'version A' of one course overlaps with 'version B' of another. Even if you are the only person to be delivering the training, it is still good practice to write down what you intend to do. Consider also that in months or years to come you might want to hand over the course to someone else. It is so much easier if a good session plan is available.

The first part of the session plan is primarily administrative. A sample is shown below.

SESSION PLAN

Course title: ... ...

Lesson title: ... ...

Code: ... ... .Prepared by: ... ... Date: ... .

Learning objectives:

Target audience:

Maximum class size: ... ... Minimum class size: ... ...

Essential prior knowledge:

Learner preparation:

Learner materials:

Handout list:

Equipment:

Duration: ... ...

Evaluation/validation:

Comments:

After the administrative details are completed, some sort of 'session outline', 'training brief', or 'tutor guide' is required. This is prepared to the degree of detail necessary. It should not be a 'script', but a reminder of what to do and when. A sample format is given in Table 16.

Table 16   *Tutor guide to a lesson/session*

TIME	SESSION	OBJECTIVES	METHOD	MATERIALS
9.00	Welcome and introduction	To gain commitment to the course To create appropriate climate	Paired interviewing (15 mins) Report back (*c*.20 mins) Tutor gives own details (5 mins) Domestics (5 mins) –fire/ toilets/ first aid/ smoking/ timings/ lunch (5 mins) Course outline (5 mins)	OHP of fire procedure
9.55	Clarifying objectives	To enable learners to influence the course content with regard to their own perceived needs	Split into 2 or 3 groups (*c*.5 in each) Groups to discuss course outline. To identify any points apparently not covered, and any aspects of particular interest to them and any aspects not interested in. Groups to make notes on flipchart and feed back to plenary. 20 mins syndicate 20 mins plenary	TM1-Programme Flipchart paper + pens
10.35	Coffee			
10.50	What is a leader?	To identify the skills and characteristics of successful leadership	Split group into 3s/4s Ask: Think of 4 successful leaders from politics, sport, warfare, work List qualities on flipchart Report back in 15 minutes	Flipchart paper + pens

Although a detailed guide like this is highly important when preparing for delivery, many trainers find it easier to work with their own handwritten notes as simple prompts. These can be highlighted with colour, or appropriate symbols can be used. A rough working plan may look like this:

9.00	Intro
→Do	Paired interviewing
9.25	Input on new policy (OHP 1–4)
9.45	
→Do	Syndicates to discuss
9.55	Plenary
	Chart and discuss
10.10	
*Video	*Tomorrow today*
10.40	Discuss
10.50	Coffee
etc	

This example shows how a full day could be noted on a page of A4, which is how I prefer to work. Other people use cards, or work from the full guide. There is no right way: develop whatever way suits you or your team.

STRUCTURING PROGRAMMES

We have looked at some of the ways in which training needs can be identified, and we have looked at the way in which the design of 'learning events' is approached. I am using the term 'programme' to design a series of learning events. These may follow on from each other one after the other, or they may be separated in time. The key thing about a programme is that it is designed as a coherent whole. The process of preparing a programme to address needs at the occupational level may be thought of as comprising ten stages.

Stage 1

Enlist support and gain commitment from the key people. These may be the job-holders, but will always involve the line management. Do not embark on a lengthy analytical and design process before enlisting such support.

Stage 2

Examine and describe the job as previously explained in Part 1 of this book, or using whatever other method you prefer.

Stage 3

Prepare a knowledge and skill breakdown, again as explained in Part 1. If you prefer, you may use MUD analysis or any other system that is suitable for the kind of work you are dealing with. Sometimes an extra category of 'attitude' is added to the knowledge/skill breakdown.

Stage 4

Produce a syllabus. A training syllabus is simply a composite list of the learning identified as necessary at Stage 3. It may be helpful to divide the list up under the headings chosen (eg Memorising, Understanding, Doing). It may also be found that certain areas of learning are present in a number of different tasks. These may be considered as 'basic' to the job, and it may be useful to separate these out at this stage so that they can be given special attention.

Stage 5

All of the learning identified in the syllabus must now be defined more closely. Objectives should be written with as clearly defined standards and conditions as necessary for this stage. Alternatively, use 'competence criteria' if that is the language your organisation prefers.

Stage 6

It is also useful to prepare a statement of pre-entry requirements for the training programme. This has two components:

1   What skills, knowledge, or experience must someone have before they can start the current training? (eg Must have held a full driving licence for at least six months)

2   What personal qualities or abilities must they possess before they can start the current training?(eg Must have normal colour vision)

The purpose of doing this is so that you can be fairly clear in your own mind about what you can assume learners will already know and what their minimum existing capabilities will be.

Ensure that no requirements have the effect of causing either direct or indirect discrimination (eg Must have been a Boy Scout).

Stage 7

The various objectives or syllabus components can now be 'played around' with. A rough idea of the methods to be used and the duration of the learning activity can be assigned. As more thought is given to this process, it may become apparent that one activity will serve more than one learning objective or that more than one activity will be required to achieve the level of learning required.

Thought must also be given to sequencing the learning. Some things must be learned before others can be. There will also be considerations to do with practicalities:

1   room availability

2   equipment availability

3   optimum group size

4   taking people away from their existing work

5   how large a group of newly trained people can the operational areas absorb?

You may also want to consider various formats for the programme. If the programme looks as if it should last for six days, it may be more sensible to break it into two three-day, three two-day, or six one-day sessions. There are always advantages and disadvantages with whatever format is chosen, so think all the options through and discuss them with the people who matter – line managers and/or the learners.

At some point the 'learning events' which have been designed to produce the desired outcomes must be designed in detail. The process is still interactive at this point in that the precise content of one session will affect and be affected by the content of other sessions. Constant rethinking will occur as the design is worked on until a sound programme is reached. The objectives may have to be revised to more closely reflect what you now think will be possible. This may seem to be doing things the wrong way round, but it is in fact what most trainers actually do.

It is often useful to produce an 'outline programme' for issuing to learners or their managers. This does not need all the detail found in the tutor guide, and is not so precisely timed. An example is given in Table 17, which also has a code referring to the appropriate session plan and tutor guide.

Table 17 *Sample outline training programme*

Week 1	Session title	Code	By
Day 1	Data lists	K1	AS
	Sales leads and market coverage	K2	AS
	Demonstrations	S1	GH
Day 2	List management	K3	AS
	Pricing policies	K3	AS
	Marketing materials	K4	GH
Day 3	Job costing system	K5	JP
	Credit verification	K6	AS
	Telephone skills 1	S2	GH
	etc		

Stage 8

Discuss the design with those people whose support you sought at Stage 1. Be prepared to amend your design to keep their support, but try to defend the points you think are important.

Stage 9

Produce the materials.

Stage 10

Agree and publish dates a reasonable time in advance. Book the room(s), venue, catering, equipment, and videos in good time and in writing. Good luck!

EMPLOYEE DEVELOPMENT

Most of us use the phrase 'training and development' without much thought. But the terms, although they have some overlap, have quite different meanings – and so too does the term 'education'.

- Education is a process of which the prime purposes are to impart knowledge and develop the way mental faculties are used. Education is not primarily concerned with job performance.

- Training endeavours to impart knowledge, skills and attitudes necessary to perform job-related tasks. It aims to improve job performance in a direct way.

- Development is a process whereby individuals learn through experience to be more effective. It aims to help people utilise the skills and knowledge that education and training have given them – not only in their current jobs, but also in future posts. It embodies concepts such as psychological growth, greater maturity and increased confidence.

Obviously, many 'educational' courses include elements of training, and some training courses have educational components. Development can happen during courses – especially when we think of something like a three-year degree course – but for the most part, development happens through real-life in-the-workplace experiences. To give an example, you might send someone, Jenny, on a short course to learn about disciplinary procedures. This might include some role-play exercises in which Jenny has to sack someone. She will learn useful rules about the law and how to conduct the interview, and so on.

But it is not the same as actually looking someone you have known for three years in the eye and saying 'Your employment will be terminated with immediate effect. I have arranged for you to be escorted off the premises and we will forward any monies due ...' This contains an element that no education or training programme can – reality. No matter how hard we try, as trainers, to make our exercises realistic, they are not real. The emotional stakes are not as high as in real life, and the consequences are usually fleeting or trivial.

So when we are looking at trying to help someone's development, we may think in terms of training or education courses to help them, but we must primarily think in terms of arranging experiences for them. Thus, a really high flier may be given a succession of jobs (or roles) which promote development. Typically, each position will have responsibility for more people than the one before, and/or a bigger budget to manage, and/or more important customers to deal with. Gradually, he or she gains experience of motivating staff, hiring and firing, planning and organising, etc, all the time putting into practice the theories and techniques taught on training courses (but don't expect any credit for that!).

This may be a process best thought of as a development strategy rather than a plan. Very often the learning opportunities will arise in an unplanned way – perhaps due to someone else's illness or because of unforeseen crises.

If people at work complain of a lack of development opportunities, you can always point out to them that they can gain many of these experiences outside work. For example, working as a volunteer for a charity, writing a book or joining the local Junior Chamber of Commerce can provide developmental experiences. The same applies to self- or personal development. If you can't gain the experience you want at work, see how else you can develop your skills.

CONTINUING PROFESSIONAL DEVELOPMENT

Continuing Professional Development (CPD) is described by the CIPD on its website as:

'CPD is a mandatory requirement for all levels of membership. It is a personal commitment to keeping your professional knowledge up to date and improving your capabilities throughout your working life. It is about knowing where you are today, where you want to be in the future, and making sure you get there.'

There are other definitions. The Professional Associations Research Network says:

'CPD is defined as any process or activity that provides added value to the capability of the professional through the increase in knowledge, skills and personal qualities necessary for the appropriate execution of professional and technical duties, often termed competence.'

The origins of CPD appear to be in the medical, legal and scientific professions. It may be found with some variations – particularly where the word 'development' may be replaced by 'learning' or 'education', or the word 'continuing' by 'continuous' – and it may be specific to a particular discipline (eg continuous medical education). There was once a time when, having completed your formal professional training as, for example, a doctor, you were regarded as qualified. You did not have to undertake any more learning prior to retirement. At a time when medical advances were few and far between, this was not a major problem. But as the pace of development of new drugs and treatments increased, it became more and more important that doctors kept themselves up to date. Of course, the best had always done so – particularly through reading relevant publications, but also by attending lectures and seminars. *The Lancet* first appeared in 1823. It published transcribed medical lectures from the London teaching establishment so that doctors in any part of the country could keep themselves informed.

Eventually, it became obvious that although many professionals were actively keeping them-selves well informed about current best practice, some did not bother. Gradually, professional bodies began to require members to demonstrate CPD in order to maintain their membership grades. In particular, the old practice of moving through membership grades as a result of, for instance, having spent ten years in a professional role began to be replaced by a requirement to demonstrate appropriate CPD during that time.

Unfortunately, CPD has a built-in bureaucratic requirement – but it is not too onerous. Although the good news is that those of us in 'soft' professions such as training are able to select our own learning topics and methods, it is still necessary to provide evidence of our learning and that we are planning for the future. The CIPD gives a guideline of 35 hours as an annual minimum requirement for CPD.

There are two parts to the CPD process. Both parts must be satisfied to meet the criteria for upgrading. These are:

- CPD development record

    This lists the activities that you've carried out during the last 12 months, with an explanation of why they were undertaken, what was learned and how this learning was or is to be applied.

- CPD development plan

    This sets out your aims and objectives and your proposed action for the next 12 months. It must include resources required, success criteria, and target dates for review and completion.

The CIPD website includes all the information you need about CPD, including examples of CPD records and plans which have been provided by CIPD members.

Remember that virtually all professional bodies now require some form of CPD – in some instances much more prescribed than for the training profession – and you may sometimes be asked for help and support in producing evidence. Because of the need to keep individual records, many organisations now routinely issue attendance certificates after all training events.

HEALTH AND SAFETY, EQUALITY AND NON-DISCRIMINATION IN THE DESIGN PROCESS

Health and safety

Always remember to incorporate good health and safety practice into your course and programme designs. The first session that you put down in your planning might well be to do with emergency fire procedures. Also remember that anything involving lifting, climbing or operating equipment can carry some risk, as can contact with hazardous materials. You could find yourself held accountable, or even prosecuted, if you fail to take adequate precautions. This could include a preliminary training session on, for example, manual handling or emergency shutdown procedures. I have seen classroom-based team exercises in books that I would never use because they carry, in my opinion, too much physical risk. For example, one involves a team having to carry a 7.25-kilogram (16-pound) bowling ball across the room by making a 'cat's cradle' with ropes – one held by each participant. There is a photograph showing the bowling ball precariously suspended about a metre (3 feet or more) in the air above the toes of one of the team!

Another activity in the same book has the objective to 'Blow gelatine through a clear plastic tube into your opposite number's mouth.' Preparation instructions include: 'Clean the tubes with bleach water and allow them to dry and look clean.' Perhaps I am over-cautious, but the dangers seem to me to be obvious and not worth the risk.

- Carry out a risk assessment on each activity.
- Provide protective equipment where appropriate.
- Never force people to do something that they feel is risky.
- Ensure that safety is included in all instruction.

Equality and non-discrimination

You have a responsibility to ensure that you, both as an individual and as a representative of your employer, comply with the law regarding equal opportunities and discrimination. First introduced in the 1970s, legislation affecting these issues has been steadily refined and made more comprehensive as time has passed. The original legislation had many gaps. For example, discrimination on the grounds of race was illegal when recruiting – but not when training. Discrimination on the grounds of religion was, at best, a vague area. Not any more. And the Disability Discrimination Act of 1995 and a number of other pieces of legislation since have introduced a further set of responsibilities for everyone.

It is easy to think that 'We're good people; we don't discriminate,' so we don't have to worry. But it is very easy to discriminate inadvertently. In the passage above regarding health and safety, I gave an example of a game involving the use of gelatine. Gelatine is most commonly made from animal by-products, including pig-skin. So the exercise would not be suitable for vegetarians (including Sikhs), Muslims or Jews. I am certain that the author of the exercise had no intention to discriminate or cause distress – but imagine the effect on a training session.

The use of outdoor activities can add a great deal to a training programme, but could also exclude a large number of people with disabilities such as mobility problems, back problems, or even hay fever. Great care must be taken. If in doubt, ask the participants for their views – and listen to them. Another issue is the actual location of a training event. Some years ago I was running an in-house programme for a local council's social services department. We were allocated training rooms in various locations, and I was not involved in their selection at all. One of the learners was quite a large man in a wheelchair. On one occasion we all turned up to find that the training room, at a residential home for people with severe disabilities, was up a flight of stairs with no lift. On another occasion the allocated room was fine for him, but the door to the coffee lounge was too small for his wheelchair to pass through. Eventually the problems were resolved – but they were distressing, could have had serious consequences, and were avoidable.

The main areas of law that you should be conversant with relate to:

- race discrimination
- sex discrimination
- sexual orientation discrimination

■ disability discrimination

■ religious discrimination.

In addition,

■ age discrimination, although not directly covered by UK legislation at the time of writing, will be in the near future.

Individual instances of discrimination are often hard to spot. Did the manager fail to nominate Jane for the course because she was female? Or because she wasn't very good? The manager will say it was for the second reason. But if he never nominates females for training, then perhaps there is systemic discrimination at work. To avoid a situation in which systemic discrimination prevails, training patterns must be monitored so that problems can be spotted and dealt with.

The law is changing constantly. For an authoritative and up-to-date overview on any aspect of the law regarding discrimination visit the CIPD website.

SUMMARY

This chapter has set out the processes involved with the design of training events. The topics of scheduling and achieving balance in the design have been discussed, and guidance on the preparation of session plans and structuring has been given.

The 'three Es test' for deciding whether or not an approach is appropriate has been introduced. Will the acitivity be *Effective, Enjoyable and Efficient*?

The concepts of Employee Development and Continuing Professional Development have been introduced. Finally, there is guidance on how to incorporate sound principles relating to health and safety, equality and non-discrimination in the design process.

FURTHER READING

CIPD (2004) *Discrimination and the Law*, London, CIPD

Earl, T. (1987) *The Art and Craft of Course Design*, London, Kogan Page

Rae, L. (1995) *Techniques of Training*, 3rd edition, Aldershot, Gower

Useful websites

www.astd.org The American Society for Training and Development

www.cipd.co.uk Information about CPD, employment law, and much more

www.parn.org.uk Information about CPD

www.trainerslibrary.com Resources for trainers

ACTIVITIES – CHAPTER 5

1 Programme design exercise

Introduction

This is a substantial exercise which consolidates many of the learning points covered in the book up to this point.

Aims

To allow learners to apply the techniques in a real job programme design exercise.

Method

This activity works best in groups of four to six people. All instructions are given below.

Timings

Depending on the complexity of the job, the degree of detail required, and how the programme is presented, between two and five hours.

Programme design exercise

From within your group, select a volunteer from an organisation which recruits into a particular job category on a regular basis. This should be a job which typically takes between two and six weeks for new starters to learn to a reasonable level of proficiency. It is better if no formal training programme currently exists. The volunteer must be familiar with the operations within the job.

- As a group, use interviewing techniques to analyse the skill and knowledge that must be learned within this initial period to attain proficiency.
- Prepare a syllabus.
- Write objective statements for three of these syllabus items.
- Decide on appropriate training methods and prepare an outline training programme which includes timings and methods for the whole syllabus.
- Present your programme, being prepared to justify the decisions taken with regard to the content, timings and methods used.

2 Exercise: equal opportunities

Part 1

An analysis of a company's workforce is undertaken to determine ethnic origin. An analysis of the amount of training received by everyone is also undertaken. The results are as follows:

Category	Number in category	Average number of days training
UK European	300	5.2
Afro-Caribbean	100	2.7
Asian	70	7.3
Oriental	15	4.8
Other European	10	2.0
Other	5	5.3

What queries should these figures raise?
How would you set about determining if the company was discriminating in any way when making training available?

Part 2

A series of programmes entitled 'Preparation for management' is offered to non-managerial grades. The people who run the course are asked to grade the participants. When analysed by gender, the following picture emerges:

Grade	Male (%)	Female (%)
A (Highest)	10	3
B	20	12
C	40	30
D	20	30
E (Lowest)	10	25

How might you investigate whether this is evidence of bias in the trainers or a fair reflection of the capabilities of the participants concerned?

Develop

Preparing presentation material

The secret of teaching is to appear to have known all your life what you learned this afternoon.

Anon.

CHAPTER OBJECTIVES

When you have finished this chapter you should be able to:

■ list the advantages and disadvantages of a variety of equipment used to present material

■ prepare material for use with low-technology equipment, or be able to locate further guidance on the preparation of material for use with technology-based equipment.

VISUAL AIDS

Although the presentation of information is not always the most important task of a trainer, it is often a key part of a training event, and it is certainly a part by which the overall quality of the trainer may be judged. The delivery of information is dealt with in Chapter 8. In this section, we consider what is involved in the preparation of visual aids.

Why bother?

■ Visual aids make it easier for people to retain information. In most (but not all) classroom learning the two main senses used are hearing and vision. To fail to make use of the sense of vision as a way of getting information across is unnecessarily limiting.

■ Visual aids are often time-savers when putting across certain concepts. A diagrammatic representation of a process is often much more readily understood than a verbal explanation.

■ They add emphasis, variety, and humour to a learning session.

■ They help the trainer to remember what to say! You can use prepared visual aids to guide yourself through a session.

■ They take people's eyes off you. If you feel nervous at the start of a training session, put up a visual aid and stand back. They will not be looking at you now, and this will help you to relax.

Although the range of possible aids is quite extensive, and new technologies are continuing to evolve, I will concentrate on the five most widely available formats for the delivery of visual information:

- the flipchart
- the whiteboard
- the overhead projector
- the projected computer screen
- the interactive whiteboard.

One or more of these items are found in nearly every training room, and the flipchart and overhead projector are readily available in most hotels or other venues used for training. First, we will consider the advantages and disadvantages associated with each of these aids.

Flipchart

Advantages

- They can be used anywhere. There is no need for a power point or special lighting conditions. Apart from the ones which hang from rails, they all have reasonable portability. They can be moved around the room, taken onto the lawn, or turned away from the group.
- They are easy and straightforward to use.
- They often have a whiteboard surface, useful if the paper runs out.
- They are cheap to buy, usually last for years, and have little to go wrong.
- The information written on them can be retained for future use or reference.
- They are good for 'live' use. Pages can be turned quickly backwards or forwards. They can be torn off and stuck on the walls or on special rail systems.

Disadvantages

- Unless prepared very carefully, flipcharts prepared in advance can look rather scruffy and amateurish.
- Prepared flipcharts are bulky to carry and are easily damaged in transit. Once rolled up they are hard to get flat again.
- The stands are quite heavy and difficult to carry – even the portable ones.
- They consume a lot of paper. Although not very expensive, this is still a cost (as are the marker pens), and an ample supply must always be kept in stock. Some people are upset at heavy paper usage for environmental reasons.

Whiteboard

Advantages

- They are usually much bigger than flipcharts, which can often be a major advantage.
- They are inexpensive to buy, and have very low running costs.
- Some expensive whiteboards have a built-in photocopying facility and 'wind-on' mechanism.
- Some have a flipchart section built on.

Disadvantages

- You have to stop and clean them when they are full. You often get your hands dirty doing this.

- If you use the wrong (permanent) marker pens on them you are in trouble.

- Writing neatly on a large whiteboard is not easy.

- Most are fixed to the wall, and although some are mounted on framework with castors, they are usually quite heavy.

Overhead projector

Advantages

- The slides are very portable if travelling between sites. They are also easy to store.

- The projectors are fairly portable within a building, and some are truly 'portable' in that they fold down and are equipped with a carrying handle.

- They give a large and easily seen image.

- Slides can be prepared in advance. Modern software and colour printers mean that professional-looking results are available to most people at realistic costs.

- They can be really good for presenting graphical data and pictorial information.

- You can choose to sit down or stand when using an overhead projector.

Disadvantages

- You may be restricted by the need to be near a power point. Trailing flexes are a real safety hazard for trainers.

- They take up a lot of room because there must be space for the image to be projected. The screen may be fixed, reducing your room layout options, or the presence of doors and windows may mean limited choice of position for a portable screen.

- They are quite expensive to buy, and consume expensive bulbs. Spares must always be kept at hand.

- They get very dirty, and few people can be bothered to clean them. Some in use (particularly at hotels) are extremely old and battered, which can lead to problems with the projected image.

Projected computer screen

Advantages

- As for the overhead projector, but more so. Very attractive and professional 'slides' can be prepared using a variety of software, by far the most widely used of which is PowerPoint.

- Animation and video clips can be included, as can sound effects.

- Once prepared, presentations can be modified and updated without the need to reprint.

- A vast quantity of material can be carried on one CD, DVD or laptop hard drive.

- Presentations can be emailed to someone at a distant location.

Disadvantages

- The projectors and their lamps are very expensive, although becoming less so as usage increases.

- As with an OHP the location of power sockets is important and there must be adequate room to project the image.

- Laptop computers, projectors and leads are quite heavy to carry and are tempting to thieves.

- If the equipment goes wrong or becomes damaged, you are completely helpless.

- Changing versions of software can result in lack of, or incomplete, compatibility.

- Setting up the equipment, powering up a computer and locating the correct file can take a long time.

- There are occasions when a shared laptop is found to be out of the building or when a required password is not known.

Interactive whiteboard

Advantages

- As for the standard projected computer screen, but it can be written on live with special pens or even a fingertip, and what has been added can be easily saved.

- If the audience all have a touchpad or keypad, appropriate software allows interactivity by, for example, the trainer bringing up questions for which the learners can choose the answer. By displaying anonymous responses on the IWB the trainer can easily see the errors and misconceptions of a particular topic and correct them.

- Accessing online resources – for example, to show a university homepage – is possible.

- The instant preparation of graphs is possible using Excel.

- By using hand-held scanners you can display individual learners' work on the board.

- The software is controlled from the board, not from a computer.

Disadvantages

- The cost of the board, projector and possibly software is relatively high.

- Hard work is essential: a lot of preparation and practice is required to use it well.

- The user must have or develop expertise with both the hardware and the software.

- A variety of formats and software is in use.

- It is not very portable; to be permanently set up where needed is really best.

- It is subject to the same 'if it goes wrong' problems as a projected computer screen, plus issues like the special pens not being recognised.

PREPARING VISUAL AIDS

Flipcharts

In my view, flipcharts are at their best when used for 'live' recording of contributions from the group, or for writing up information as you go along. However, there are some occasions when advance preparation is appropriate. Although the following tips may be helpful, there is no need to regard such ideas as 'golden rules' never to be broken.

- Use every second page only. This will eliminate 'showing through'.

- Take the paper off the stand and lay it down flat on a table before you start. Use a T-square to get straight lines.

- Block capitals are usually easier to write neatly, and are easier to read than lower-case letters.

- Use colour for emphasis and variety – but don't overdo it because it can be visually messy and confusing. Avoid light colours: they are harder to read.

- Drawings can look very effective on flipcharts. If you are a poor artist, but have a picture you want to put on a flipchart, then you can cheat:
  - Trace the image onto an acetate.
  - Project the image onto the flipchart using an overhead projector.
  - Trace round the image with a marker pen.

- Make 'bookmarks' on the flipchart pad by marking pages with folded corners, paperclips or Post-It notes.

Perhaps have a second flipchart or a whiteboard to use as a scribbling pad so that you don't lose your place on your prepared pad.

Whiteboards

Unless the whiteboard can be turned around, any advance work will be immediately visible to the group. However, if this does not matter, it can be sensible to prepare in advance. Many of the points listed above for the flipchart apply to the whiteboard. Additional points are:

- Always clean the whiteboard as thoroughly as possible before you start.

- Take care to write in straight lines. Some whiteboards have faint lines or grids which are very helpful. Otherwise, try projecting a ruler onto the board with an overhead projector. As you finish a line of text, tilt the head of the projector down until the ruler is at the next line down, and so on.

- Use dry marker pens, not permanent pens.

- You can stick pictures onto whiteboards with tape or blu-tack. Some whiteboards are metal, on which magnets can be used.

Overhead projector

Slides used on the overhead projector are variously referred to as 'transparencies', 'acetates', 'viewfoils', or 'slides'. They may be prepared freehand using special pens, by photocopying onto special acetate sheets, or by printing directly onto acetates compatible with your computer's printer. The general rules apply whatever method is used.

- Transparencies should be concise. Do not project a full text, but rather key points which remind you of what you want to talk about. If a lot of words are necessary, consider putting them on a handout instead.

- Learners expect the *key* points to be put on a transparency for them. They do not want less important background information to be presented in this way.

- In general, limit the transparency to six or seven lines of text. Make sure it is large enough to be read by someone sitting at the back who has less than perfect vision.

- Colour adds impact and interest, and nowadays is considered to be standard.

- Most people think that a horizontal (landscape) orientation is better than a vertical (portrait) orientation; but do not feel constrained by this if your subject matter demands a portrait orientation.

- You can trace pictures directly onto acetates if doing them by hand.

- Settle on a format and font that you like and try to keep your transparencies consistent in appearance.

- Number your acetates as you make them. If generating transparencies by computer, link the numbering to your file name so that you can find the right image when you need it.

- Protect acetates by using plastic pockets or flip-frame sleeves.

- Always check the spelling. Remember that a computer's spell-check will, for example, pass the word 'manger' as well as 'manager'.

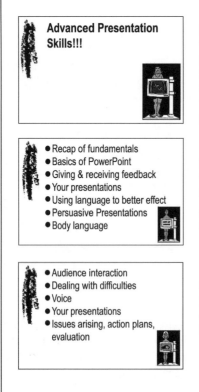

Advanced Presentation Skills!!!

Slide 1

You can use the drop-down menu from 'File' in PowerPoint to send your slides to Word. These can then be annotated, if required, and printed off in miniature for your audience to take away with them.

This is also a good – if not ideal – fallback should the projection equipment fail

- Recap of fundamentals
- Basics of PowerPoint
- Giving & receiving feedback
- Your presentations
- Using language to better effect
- Persuasive Presentations
- Body language

Slide 2

This slide is as full as it should be with text. Any more would require a second slide.

Annotation effects could bring in the lines of text one at a time.

- Audience interaction
- Dealing with difficulties
- Voice
- Your presentations
- Issues arising, action plans, evaluation

Slide 3

If you pick a background design that you like, keep it consistent through the presentation. If possible, do the same with the style of the clipart.

Figure 6 *Some sample slides*

Projected computer screen

In many ways, preparing PowerPoint slides for projection is the same as for when preparing for printed OHP slides. One of the biggest differences is that slides on an OHP show up best when dark ink is used on a pale or clear background. For projection, it is the other way round.

The other main difference is that lines of text or components of charts or diagrams can be introduced one at a time. This means that the presenter is able to build up the slide at his or her chosen pace without having people reading ahead or trying to 'mask and reveal' parts of the slide. For many people, creating slides using PowerPoint is readily learnt by trial and error. But certain features are not obvious and some tuition can be very useful. PowerPoint itself includes tutorials and features such as the 'AutoContent Wizard'. For in-depth tutorials, one good source is **www.presentersonline.com** – a free site provided by Epson America Inc.

Always remember that a slide that can look terrific on your computer screen can look drab and difficult to read when projected. Check out your presentation on the actual equipment that you will be using before showing it to your audience.

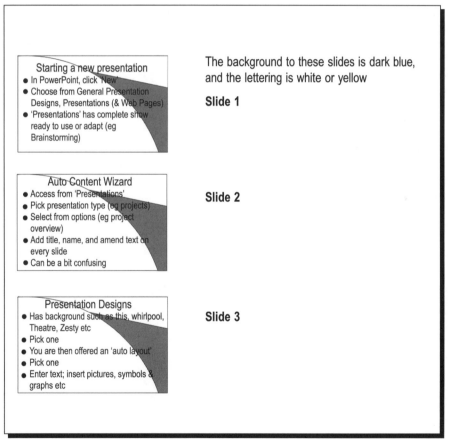

Figure 7 *Some more sample slides*

Interactive whiteboard

Again, a lot of the time you will be preparing slides as for other forms of projection. In addition, you will need to learn about whatever other forms of software are installed and what can be done with them.

The Internet has a lot of free information about the use of IWB software, because IWBs are extensively used in schools. Rather than attempt to talk through software which I am not completely familiar with, and which may change, I suggest that you visit the National Whiteboard Network website – **www.nwnet.org.uk** – which has tutorials dealing with Easiteach, Promethean and Smartboard, or visit the manufacturers' websites listed below.

Other relevant software includes the Hot Potatoes Suite of six applications, enabling you to create interactive multiple-choice, short-answer, jumbled-sentence, crossword, matching/ordering and gap-fill exercises for the WorldWide Web or for IWBs. Hot Potatoes is not freeware, but it is free of charge for those working for publicly-funded non-profit-making educational institutions which make their pages available on the web. Other users must pay for a licence. Check out the Hot Potatoes licensing terms and pricing on their website: **www.half-bakedsoftware.com** .

PICTURES

One of the nicest things about computer-prepared presentations is that we can all become artistic. The easiest way to incorporate pictures into a presentation is by using clipart. However, some of the clipart provided by the commoner programs has been overused, and has therefore lost its impact. For example, there is a nice picture of a man bending over to look at something with a magnifying glass. This is an excellent way of visually saying something like 'We took a good look at this' – but your audience has probably seen the picture before, and will be unimpressed.

So it is important to have some alternative images available. This can be achieved by buying clipart collections – I bought a collection of 45,000 images some years ago which has been very useful – or by looking on the Internet. As well as commercial sites, some private individuals have put together collections of clipart, photographs or other imagery that are either freely available or available at low cost. Figure 8 shows a few images available free from **www.horton-szar.net**.

Figure 8 *Some clipart images from the internet*

Apart from finding images in this way, it is nowadays easy (once you know how) to use a digital camera to take pictures of people, equipment and buildings which you might wish to incorporate into your presentation. These can be really effective. However, if you do not want to bother taking pictures yourself, again there are many websites which provide photographs that are either free or at a low price.

SUMMARY

This chapter has looked at a variety of equipment for use in delivering presentations, and has dealt with some of the fundamentals of preparing material. The advantages and disadvantages of a variety of media have been covered, and there has been some guidance on obtaining imagery from the Internet.

FURTHER READING

Atkinson, C. (2005) *Beyond Bullet Points: Using Microsoft PowerPoint to create presentations that inform, motivate and inspire*, Redmond, Microsoft Press

Fenwick, M. (1994) *Presentation Skills*, Ely, Fenman Training

Siddons, M. (1999) *Presentation Skills*, London, CIPD

Townsend, J. (1993) *The Instructor's Pocketbook*, 6th edition, London, Management Pocketbooks

Useful websites

www.arthursclipart.com Free clipart site

www.beyondbullets.com For PowerPoint users

www.clipart.com Clipart site

http://www.flickr.com/ Anybody can contribute photographs to a huge, searchable collection; see site for copyright information

www.horton-szar.net/clipart Clipart site

www.mayang.com Free pictures, especially textures

www.nutrocker.co.uk Free web graphics and pictures

www.presentersonline.com Very useful site run by Epson, the printer company

www.prometheanworld.com Interactive whiteboard manufacturer's site

www.smarttech.com Interactive whiteboard manufacturer's site

www.easiteach.co.uk Interactive whiteboard manufacturer's site

ACTIVITIES – CHAPTER 6

1 Preparing overhead projection slides

Introduction

A simple activity in which learners are required to design and produce a mainly pictorial overhead slide.

Aims

To allow practice of overhead slide production and to emphasise the importance of good visual design.

Methods

In pairs or singly, learners are asked to design and produce an opening slide for an imaginary presentation. Suggested topics are:

- My favourite television programme
- A sporting event
- A day in the country
- It's show time!

Participants should be provided with whatever materials are considered appropriate (eg acetates, pens), and may be encouraged to trace pictures out of magazines or newspapers. Alternatively, computer-based graphics packages can be used. The slides are displayed and judged by the whole group on whichever of the following criteria are deemed appropriate:

- impact
- relevance
- use of colour
- artistic merit
- creativity.

Marks out of 5 may be given, and discussion generated as to the importance of various aspects of slide design.

Timing

About 30 minutes to design and produce a slide. Allow a further three or four minutes for display and judging of each slide, followed by approximately 15 minutes for discussion.

2 Preparing PowerPoint projection slides

Introduction

An activity in which learners are required to design and produce a set of three PowerPoint projection slides each of which must contain a different sound effect, clipart image (one of which must be animated), slide transition effect, WordArt effect and text animation.

Aims

To allow practice of PowerPoint slide production using some of the capabilities of the software – and to emphasise the importance of not overdoing it.

Methods

In small groups, learners are asked to design and produce a set of three slides for an imaginary presentation. Suggested topics are:

- What I like most about presenting
- What can go wrong with computers
- How to irritate your audience with special effects.

Discussion should be generated on the importance – or otherwise – of various aspects of special effects in PowerPoint slide design and the time necessary to incorporate them into a presentation.

Timing

About 40 minutes to produce the presentation. Allow a further four or five minutes for display of each set , followed by approximately 15 minutes for discussion.

Preparing participative material

CHAPTER 7

Good teaching is one-fourth preparation and three-fourths theatre

Gail Godwin

CHAPTER OBJECTIVES

When you have finished this chapter you should be able to:

- **determine which of a range of participative training methods is appropriate**

- **prepare case studies, games, exercises, role-plays and handouts.**

CASE STUDIES

The earliest systematic use of case studies in management training is generally credited to the Harvard Business School, which published a collection as long ago as 1954. These involve the detailed examination of actual business cases researched in detail. Students analyse the cases individually, and the classroom discussions tend to produce highly competitive discussion corresponding to the quality and accuracy of each person's analysis. However, over the past 40 years the case study method has been used in many different ways from this, and cases take many forms.

Whatever the format, the purpose of a case study is to enable learners to analyse a situation. This process may involve the use of newly acquired knowledge to consolidate learning, or to give a practical illustration of a theoretical framework for analysis. Sometimes a case study is used to stimulate discussion so that, for example, learners are able to compare and contrast their own experiences with the situation described, and thus with each others' experiences. As a learning method, case studies are often challenging, stimulating, involving, and regarded as highly acceptable by learners.

Case studies may be based on real situations or on fictional situations. Very often, real situations are modified and fictionalised not only to preserve anonymity but also to focus the case on the particular learning points to be addressed.

Case studies may be useful for the practice of specific skills (eg financial analysis, interpreting statistical data, applying motivational models to situations) and also to practise generic skills including:

- analytical skills
- problem-solving
- decision-making
- presentation
- influencing.

Additionally, the case method may be a means of promoting teamwork and co-operation.

Although it is possible to provide cases for individual analysis, it is more usual for them to be analysed in small groups. This is generally popular with participants, and reduces the stress that less confident learners feel if required to act alone.

How long?

Some case studies may be 40 or 50 pages in length. Although these may be valuable on long postgraduate-level programmes, they are not appropriate for use on short courses. Management time is valuable, and activities should be as time-efficient as possible consistent with the intended learning. The designer needs to ask: 'Will a half-page case study bring out the learning points adequately, or is a three-page case really needed?' The shortest 'case study' I use is a single sentence. The longest is four pages. There must be sufficient detail to make the situation feel real and believable. On the other hand, long-winded and rambling cases irritate the readers.

On a practical note, people vary enormously in the rate at which they can read and assimilate written material. With a short case, this is seldom a problem. With a longer case, some learners will have finished reading long before others are half-way through. This leads to impatience or embarrassment, and does not produce the desired climate. However, complex situations require reasonably lengthy case material in order for the detail to be introduced properly. It may be better to break a long case into sections to improve its practicality, and this process will be discussed later.

Always remember that long case studies need a long time for analysis. Giving a group half an hour to analyse a case which takes them 20 minutes to read will not be appreciated and is a poor use of time.

Real-life cases

There are several good reasons why real-life cases may be preferred:

- They are more credible.
- They may be easier to produce than invented material.
- They can be followed by a 'What actually happened' input.

Some learners may attack fictional scenarios: 'That would never happen!', 'It's not realistic!', and 'Nobody would make that mistake.' If a case study is based on specific, real incidents, it is more readily accepted as something that might relate to the learners' own situations.

Finding real-life cases and producing a written document can be done in various ways:

- You may be able to write up a case based on your own experiences and recollections.
- You can interview other people and produce a case that details their experiences.
- You can find written material.

Whenever you write down a case based on either your own or other people's experiences, you should change the names of people and companies involved so as to preserve anonymity. Most case studies look at what went wrong, and the people concerned may not appreciate their actions being scrutinised. Changes should be such that identification is impossible. This is particularly important if the incidents described occurred in the organisation that the training is taking place in. Changing Reg White the warehouse manager into Ron Black the stores manager is not enough. But try to resist taking the opportunity to introduce humour into the case by the use of silly names. Calling the characters L. E. Fant, Michael Mouse or Jerry Attrick will simply detract from the learning process.

Written material may come from many sources. It may be possible to buy collections of case material to cover the learning points you want. It is usually more satisfactory to find articles in newspapers or journals that provide the detail you need. Lifting a complete article from a publication will, of course, breach copyright, but taking the *facts* from an article and writing them in a text of your own is perfectly legal. There are many journals which produce excellent source material in respect of such subjects as employment law and health and safety.

Other subjects, such as training and development, suffer from a 'whitewash' treatment in journals. Whereas it is easy to find cases of wonderfully successful training initiatives, nobody ever seems to write up the failures and disasters! With regard to the organisation as a whole, there are many books produced which look at successful and sometimes unsuccessful organisations, and again factual material can be extracted from them. Business biographies or autobiographies can also provide suitable material.

Fictitious cases

Fictitious cases may be preferred to real-life cases for a number of reasons. You can, of course, totally control a fictitious case. You can make your characters behave in the way necessary to illustrate the learning points you want, and you can control the environment in which they work. There are no problems with copyright if you prepare your own material. There are three basic strategies to preparing a fictitious case study:

- Create one from your own imagination.
- Create one which incorporates some elements from a real incident or a number of incidents, but which is substantially fictitious.
- Adapt an existing fictitious case study.

Being creative

We are all capable of writing creatively. The process comes more easily to some people than it does to others, but the main barrier to creative writing is a self-generated one. We often believe that to be inventive and creative is beyond us because we have not had occasion to put our imaginations to much use for a long time. When we need to generate an appropriate case study, the motivation level is high, and should stimulate our creative talents. There are five stages in the creative thinking process:

- preparation
- effort
- incubation
- insight
- evaluation.

Preparation

We must be clear about the learning point or points that we intend to cover. We must have some idea of the time that the case study should take to be analysed. We need to know what will come before and after in the training course.

As an example, suppose we wish to explore the options a supervisor has when giving orders to someone. We may anticipate a tutor-led discussion on this topic that will include 'requesting', 'suggesting', 'requiring', 'ordering', and so on. To consolidate learning, we may wish to include a case study that will require the course members to consider these options more fully in three syndicate groups. Perhaps half an hour seems appropriate. How will that time be spent?

- reading the case – 3 minutes

- discussing the case – 12 minutes

- presenting conclusions – 3 minutes per syndicate, ie 9 minutes

- tutor-led discussion – 6 minutes.

So we need to write something that will take no more than three minutes to be read by a slow reader. How much can a slow reader absorb in three minutes? This will depend upon the educational level of the group, the complexity of what you write, and how careful your course members are in their deliberations. However, as a starting point, let us assume that the *maximum* length we will let our case be is one page.

Effort

This is the stage where we must try hard to generate ideas. Idea-production and idea-evaluation must be kept separate, as in brainstorming. Do not expect a series of brilliant ideas to flow without any effort; rather, consciously try to associate ideas from as many angles as possible. In our example, we may think of possible scenarios such as:

1   There has been a disaster due to incorrect procedures – yet the supervisor was sure that the correct orders were given.

2   A new supervisor needs to get things done with a variety of people – inexperienced, mature, etc – how should he/she deal with giving instructions?

3   An industrial dispute arises because of insensitively-given orders.

4   A supervisor is failing to achieve targets because subordinates are (apparently) deliberately misinterpreting orders.

Having produced a few ideas, and *jotted them down*, it is usually best to turn our minds to other things. Perhaps a better idea will come later, or a half-formed idea will be stimulated by something we see or hear. This is the stage of:

Incubation

It often seems that the unconscious mind can continue to examine the problem for us without much effort, and that our conscious minds can return to the issue refreshed after an interval. Always allow time for ideas to incubate, therefore, rather than try to produce material in one solid slog. If no firm idea seems to be absolutely right, return to the original list and consider the ideas further. Again, jotting thoughts down can be very helpful. Let us return to the list of ideas we produced before:

- *Idea 1:*

  What kind of disaster? A fatality? Could the case be based around an inquest? What do I know about inquests? Not much. Anyway, it's a bit morbid. What about a financial disaster? Or perhaps an opening ceremony going wrong? Do I have experience of organising an opening ceremony? Yes. Did anything go wrong? Yes – not much, but it could have been a lot worse.

- *Idea 2:*

  What kind of thing? Perhaps setting up a training room for an important visitor. Or it could be a production or sales or administration situation. But the trainees from Sales won't like a production situation, and vice versa. Could I generate an administrative example which would suit all of them? Or should I set the scene in an alien environment for all of them, such as in a hotel?

- *Idea 3:*

  What kind of dispute? A grievance, or a strike? Will they immediately take sides with the supervisor even if the orders were badly given?

- *Idea 4:*

  Again, in what area? Production or Sales? Or how about distribution? It is a more relevant scenario than some of the others.

Insight

Sometimes, during the 'mulling over' process, there will be the flash of insight that says 'Yes, that would work!'. More often, it will be a gradual warming to an idea, perhaps accompanied by a growing confidence. Bouncing possibilities off colleagues often clarifies thinking at this point. Some people find the 'mind mapping' technique extremely useful when trying to clarify complex situations (Buzan, 1989).

Evaluation

Now all the ideas previously considered must be returned to and examined, even if the 'insight' stage has left a clear favourite. Returning to our four ideas:

- *Idea 1:* Yes, a definite possibility.
- *Idea 2:* Possible, but on reflection, it seems somewhat unexciting. Hold.
- *Idea 3:* Not a good idea. Too many pitfalls. Reject.
- *Idea 4:* Possible, but care would be needed in the writing to make it equally relevant to them all. Hold.

Okay. We have now provisionally selected an idea – number 1. However, we have not totally rejected two of the others because they could work. In due course, we may find that our chosen idea does not work out well, and it is comforting to have something in reserve. Some trainers keep an 'ideas file' to be referred to when a different learning need arises. An idea rejected for this problem might well be useful for another problem.

Writing the case

Having settled on an idea, we must now actually start writing. Before we do, let us remind ourselves of what we want to get out of the case.

We want to stimulate the learners to discuss various ways of giving instructions in order to clarify when the various styles are appropriate and when they are not.

It would be possible to develop this aim into precise behavioural objectives if this were required, but because the content of the discussion will be different for each group, it is often more honest to accept that the learning outcomes are not totally predictable from a case study. If you want to be precise about the outcomes, it is often easier to write the objectives after the case has been written. This is what most trainers actually do, even though few of us admit it.

Developing the plot

Jot down some rough notes as to how the case can develop. Make notes for yourself as you go along, including points on which you have yet to decide:

A supervisor [Male, female, or unstated? Named?] is tasked with organising an opening ceremony for a new warehouse or office block. This instruction could either be given well or be given badly.

The supervisor has to work through other people *[Reflect the types of people found in the organisation]* to get the various tasks done. Things to be organised could include:
- catering
- photographer
- flagpoles
- inviting guests *[Royalty, chairman or chairwoman, celebrity?]*
- furniture
- transport.

Show four or five different styles of instruction. This could relate to the previous tutor input very directly.

Some aspects go well, some go badly. Some remedial action is called for.

This could be included – or it could be the basis for the group to make decisions about.

Now actually start writing. Word processors are marvellous for this kind of activity because they allow for continuous revision. However, to reduce your inhibitions, label the document DRAFT.

EXAMPLE DRAFT CASE OUTLINE

Pat Jenkins felt nervous as she approached the door of Clive Senior, the Northern Regional Manager. She knocked lightly on the mahogany door. 'Come in!' bellowed Clive. 'Nice to see you, Pat. I'm off to Paris in a few minutes, so I'll get straight to the point. As you know, the builders will be finishing the new office block in a few days' time. Lady Barwell will be visiting this site at the end of next week, and Sir Giles, the company chairman, has asked her to perform an opening ceremony for us. I'm sorry to drop this on you, but I won't be back until the day itself, so I'd like you to organise everything ...'

Once the first draft is finished, leave it. Put it away and forget about it for a few days; then re-read it. Amend it, develop it, and rework it as necessary until a usable case study has been produced. Then, as with all other material, try it out. If possible use the case with a group you know well. After the course, ask them for feedback. Evaluate the activity in isolation and in the wider context of the course.

As with all written material, you may want to consider whether any learner with visual impairment, dyslexia or other difficulty in reading might potentially be involved. If so, can a large-print version be produced, and would this solve the problem? Or should the material be read out to the whole group? It is often best to ask the individual(s) concerned what they would prefer.

GAMES AND EXERCISES

There is a lot of confusion between concepts such as 'games and exercises' when used in a training context. For the sake of clarity, therefore, let us first look at some key characteristics.

Games

- are competitive
- involve scoring or racing to produce winners
- have 'rules'
- have participants who are 'players'.

Exercises

- do not have roles
- maintain objectivity
- may be undertaken by an individual or a group
- are often about analysing situations that have been described rather than experienced.

Games

Games are introduced into training events for a number of reasons. One of the main benefits of using games is that they are (usually) fun. Given a task to accomplish in competition with others very quickly produces a buzz of excitement and energy that participants find invigorating. The purpose of a game will often be to provide an opportunity to look at teamwork, leadership, organisation or planning. The value of the game is in the lessons that can be drawn from the processes that took place during the activity, so that participants gain insight into the principles under consideration, or into their own behaviour.

There are some dangers with the use of games:

- Some people reject them as childish and either do not participate at all or do so without commitment.
- Some people get so involved with the game that they may get upset about losing, or believe that having won they have nothing to learn. Many people have a strong need to complete games and become frustrated and unhappy if they are not allowed to.

115

- The lessons to be learned from the way in which the game went may be difficult to translate into a 'back at work' model.

- Some games have tricks built into them that can cause resentment.

- Some games are so widely used that there is a chance that participants will have experienced them before.

- Some trainers use the games without ensuring that the appropriate learning takes place. Everyone has a good time – but that's all. It is important that learning points are fully brought out and recorded.

Exercises

In an exercise, participants remain themselves. They analyse and discuss situations which may be given to them in a variety of ways. Exercises can be co-operative, and may be open-ended. They may be brief, or fairly extensive. Types of exercise include:

- a case study
- problem-solving
- task completion
- a review of participants' experiences
- brainstorming.

As before, any exercise should be used with specific purposes in mind. During a long training course, as many different kinds of exercise as possible should be used to help maintain interest.

Case study exercises come in many different forms, and are dealt with separately.

Problem-solving exercises are often used to illustrate the necessity of teamwork or sharing of information, or, indeed, to look at the process of problem-solving itself.

Task-completion exercises are often used in general management or team-building courses as a vehicle for looking at leadership or the process of task accomplishment. They need not be competitive, but often small groups work in parallel so that everyone is involved and differences in approach can be studied.

Reviews of participants' experience can be extremely effective if not used too often. This type of exercise may start: 'Think of the worst training event that you ever attended. Why was it so bad?' and so on.

Brainstorming approaches can be useful to get ideas out very fast, followed by discussion. For example: 'In groups of three or four, list at least 20 types of insurance policy.'

Whatever type of exercise is used, timing is often crucial – too little, and some of the value is lost; too much, and the course begins to drag. Be prepared to modify timings with experience.

ROLE-PLAYING

Role-playing is one of the oldest techniques devised to assist learners by direct experience in a simulated setting. It can be used to promote learning for the active participants, and also for observers (if any). Role-playing is often very helpful in working on problems in a way that produces graphic illustrations of effective or ineffective behaviour that the participants have generated for themselves. They have not simply observed someone else act out a situation, as they do when they watch a dramatised training video, but they have had to put effort, and perhaps emotion, into the process.

Role-play ought to be an opportunity to practise behaviours in a risk-free safe setting. This is not automatically the case, and people can get upset if a role-play gets out of hand. Participants can get carried away with the situation, or use it to score points in an aggressive manner. For some people, the role-play method can be quite abhorrent, while others relish the chance to demonstrate their dramatic skills.

Starting role-playing

In a role-play, the trainer provides a clear definition of the situation in as much detail as is necessary. Often a very brief description will suffice, but some role-play briefs can be quite lengthy. Individuals are selected or volunteer to be characters to play the various roles in acting out the situations. They may be briefed publicly or privately. The brief may be verbal or written, or a mixture. Time to prepare may be allowed. The drama may take place with or without part of the group as an audience. Some people find role-playing in front of a large audience extremely stressful and it is often best to leave this to volunteers.

Role-plays can be left open-ended or subject to strict time limits. Sometimes they are interrupted for discussion after interesting points have emerged. They may or may not be recorded. In any event, the process must be analysed and discussed on completion so that learning points are fully absorbed.

The uses of role-play

1   To illustrate clearly a feature of some specific behaviour in a lively and direct way. This can include features of non-verbal behaviour that cannot be clearly illustrated otherwise.

2   To increase the involvement of the group. Effort is required from them and a well-performed role-play leads to a feeling of accomplishment.

3   To provide a common experience for the group to discuss.

4   To practise specific behavioural skills, such as interviewing, chairing a meeting or greeting customers.

5   To help people understand a situation from the viewpoint of others. Having to play the part of someone who has the opposite role to that usually performed in real life often produces a significant increase in empathy and understanding. For example, a manager who plays the role of a union representative defending a colleague from dismissal may achieve far more insight in this way than from simply discussing the situation.

6   To give insight into the role-players' own behaviours and the effect they have on others.

7   To make possible experimentation in a no-risk setting. Participants can try tactics that are new to them, or employ alternative behaviours to evaluate their effectiveness.

Points to watch

1   It is usually best to keep written descriptions as brief as possible. Very long, detailed scenarios are difficult for people to memorise, and items that have been inserted for background can end up dominating the discussion.

2   Sometimes it is better for the trainer to choose participants, sometimes to call for volunteers. You should aim to avoid anyone trying to perform a role-play that is beyond him or her. The participant may feel humiliated or inadequate, or may 'rubbish' the exercise, with reactions like, 'It's not real,' 'The brief was unclear,' or 'I would never do that.'

3   Avoid boss–subordinate pairings unless you have a good reason for them.

4   Watching too many role-plays one after the other can become boring for audiences.

5   Beware of the over-exuberant character who turns your description of a slightly disgruntled customer into a raving monster.

6   People find it hard to play characters who are of a different age-group or of the opposite gender. It is often possible to write roles which allow participants to project themselves into the situation. Rather than 'You are a 56-year-old transport manager named Norman who wants to tell Mandy, the 19-year-old typist, to cut down on private telephone calls,' try 'You are a manager who has decided to tell a subordinate to cut down on private telephone calls.'

7   If it is easier to use names, try to reflect the organisation's gender and cultural mix in the role-plays. But take care not to stereotype.

8   It is the trainer's responsibility to protect participants from role-plays which get out of hand.

9   It is sometimes possible to create role-plays on the spot from incidents described by course members. For instance, members of the group may be asked to describe situations which they have found difficult to handle. One or two of these may then be acted out to determine the best way to resolve the problems described.

10   Debrief. Ensure that the mistakes made by the role character are seen as such, not as those of the person playing that character. Role-plays often stimulate conflict. If the debriefing does not allow the participants to discard their roles, you may have created tensions and animosities between course members.

11   Review what happened. Make sure that anyone who has been designated as an observer is allowed to report what she or he has observed. In leading the discussion:
   ■ Determine what happened.
   ■ Identify what went well.
   ■ Explore the way in which the situation developed and the reasons the role-players behaved as they did.
   ■ Discuss how the situation might be better handled, or how real situations differ.

12   When the situation is appropriate, allow a second go to get it right.

EXAMPLE ROLE-PLAY BRIEF – 1

You are a storekeeper, Lee Martin.

You are conscientious in your duties. Your insistence on following procedures does not always make you popular; but it's your job to ensure that the rules are complied with. Recently, you have been subject to considerable pressure because you have refused to shortcut the rules. If the procedure requires a manager's signature before you release a part, then a telephone call is simply not good enough. If everyone else followed the rules, you would have few problems. Apart, of course, from the new computerised system.

Operating the system is no problem, unless you make a mistake. Then it is a real performance to correct it. Once or twice a week you have to ask Rachel from accounts to sort out problems. She used to help willingly, but now her boss is getting funny about letting her come to the stores so often – probably because she spends half an hour chatting to Wayne in the yard on the way back.

One grumble you have is that you used to get help to keep the stores clean and tidy, but now you have to do it all yourself. It isn't your top priority.

EXAMPLE ROLE-PLAY BRIEF – 2

You are preparing to appraise a storekeeper, Lee Martin.

Lee is conscientious in his duties. However, his insistence on following procedures makes him unpopular. On one recent occasion Lee refused to release a part because the system had not been followed correctly, and this led to some avoidable downtime.

Lee is having trouble learning the new computerised system. He has had a lot of help from accounts, but they have other things to do.

One matter you wish to tackle is housekeeping. Remind Lee of the importance of housekeeping. You expect he will harp on about the time when there were more staff, but there is nothing you can do about staffing levels.

As previously mentioned, you can also ask people to create their own role-plays. Although this may take more time and effort, the results may be much more relevant and therefore effective. However, people do vary in their ability to prepare such activities, so having back-up material is helpful. I also find it helps to give them forms to complete as they go along. An example set of forms is given as Table 18 on page 120.

Table 18 *Forms for self-generated role-play*

Disciplinary exercise
Form A Think about the people for whom you are responsible. Select someone who has one major or several minor weaknesses which need to be addressed in order to improve performance and who has not responded to subtle indications. If necessary, exaggerate the problem(s) or combine a few individuals' faults. Prepare an interviewer's brief – as if you were looking at the situation from outside and were briefing yourself for the encounter. Use a fictitious name, please. Do this on Form B. Form B will be given to someone else who will prepare and conduct the interview. You will play the character described.
Form B: Interviewer's brief Your name is .... (use a fictitious name) Your present position is: .... in .... department The interviewee's name is: .... (use a fictitious name) He/she has been employed for .... He/she works as a .... His/her performance is :

HANDOUTS

Most kinds of training benefit from the provision of appropriate reference material. It may serve two main purposes. Firstly, it may provide the learner with a reminder of what has been put across on the course. Some of the learners will read the material immediately, others may not. In many cases what will happen is that the folder will be put on a shelf, but in weeks or months to come it will be referred to as a particular need arises. Handouts should not replace the process of note-taking, which aids memory, but ensure that everyone has a full and accurate version of the information. A second purpose of handout material is to give more depth of coverage on certain points. It may not be a good use of time to go into a lot of background information on a course, but the handout material can do so. Case examples can be given for the learner to read about.

When preparing a training session, you will be collecting a lot of information about the subject in question. Writing a handout is a good way of clarifying your own understanding, and also helping with the structure of the input. As you write the handout, you can spot key points which will form the basis of a visual aid. Writing these in a handout will enable you to say 'yes' to the question 'Is this in a handout?' that frequently crops up when information is displayed on a visual aid.

It is often tempting to shortcut the process of writing handouts by using existing material, perhaps written by someone else for another purpose. This can result in the embarrassment of not being able to explain part of the text, or issuing something that directly contradicts what you have been saying. It is all too easy to find yourself talking about 'the four stages of problem-solving' and issuing a handout which lists 'the five stages of problem-solving'. You will lose credibility very quickly if you do this.

How long and detailed the handouts should be depends on your learners and their needs. Detailed and lengthy handouts will often not be read, and some trainers like to give handouts which are essentially a series of bullet points. I personally prefer to issue handouts which are fairly full because I have had feedback from some learners who say they prefer this.

Handouts can be enlivened by pictures and diagrams, and can be made as lively or serious as is appropriate. Again, bear in mind any special needs that may exist when selecting font, font size and colour combinations. (See Figure 9.)

SECURING AGREEMENT

When dealing with complaints, we should normally aim to acieve a settlement which both parties regard as fair and which brings an end to the complaint. We all have defensive emotional reactions which are basic and strong, and which tend to make us defend a position when complaint is lodged of turning it to our own advantage.

Normally, a complaint is valuable feedback that something has gone wrong. We should overcome our instincts, and thank the person who brings a complaint.

Figure 9 *Part of a handout with pictures*

Coding

At first you will remember every handout you write. Every exercise, case study and role-play will be clearly recalled. After a year or two, though, you may find that it takes hours to find a particular document. Questions such as: 'What course is the handout on leadership in? What role-plays have we got? Have we any good exercises on planning?' can become difficult to answer. Modern word processors help immensely, but can be rendered much less effective by the absence of a usable coding system. It is sensible to use the same system for the paper copies as for the word processing files. There are many possibilities. One simple one is:

Handouts: H1, H2, H3, etc.
Case studies: CS1, CS2, CS3, etc.
Exercises: E1, E2, E3, etc.

Another possibility is to add a second code to indicate contents:

H1qual   (quality)

H2lead   (leadership)

H3safe   (safety)

H4safe   (safety)

H5cust   (customer care)

Some people like to code by course:

EM1–1   (electrical maintenance, module 1, document 1)

EM1–2   (electrical maintenance, module 1, document 2)

EM1–3   (electrical maintenance, module 1, document 3)

EM2–1   (electrical maintenance, module 2, document 1)

MM4–2   (mechanical maintenance, module 4, document 2)

Whatever coding system is adopted, it will also be necessary to have a procedure for revising and updating material. This is particularly important where more than one trainer is involved. If an agreed procedure is not in place, it is easy to end up with two or three versions of the same handout title with the same code.

A coding system is also invaluable when assembling material for printing or photocopying. Instead of working to a list of titles, the person doing this works with a list of codes. This is much easier, and makes checking quicker.

SUMMARY

This section has dealt with the preparation of various kinds of training materials. There are many other kinds of training material – such as videos and computer-based learning systems – that are not dealt with here. These are specialised disciplines that require in-depth study, but with which many trainers will never become involved. Instead, I have concentrated on the most widely-used technologies and activities. The production of interactive materials has been considered under the following headings:

- Case studies
- Games and exercises
- Role-playing
- Handouts.

Inevitably, the topics of design and production have overlapped. The processes of preparation include creative thinking as well as applying a systematic and disciplined approach. What is sometimes overlooked is that these processes which lead to good-quality training materials also lead to a thorough understanding of the topic in the trainer. The best way for a trainer to prepare for the delivery of a training event is to write and produce the materials for himself or herself. It often, of course, requires background reading, investigation, and analysis. This is how a real depth of expertise is developed which is apparent in what the trainer says as well as in the material that he or she has produced.

FURTHER READING

BACIE (1970) *BACIE Case Studies*, London, BACIE

Buzan, T. (1989) *Use Your Head*, Revised edition, London, BBC Books

Cooley, K. and McEwan, K. (2004) *Games for Legendary Away Days*, Aldershot, Gower

Hackett, P. (2003) *Training Practice*, London, CIPD

Rae, L. (1995) *Techniques of Training*, 3rd edition, Aldershot, Gower

Rae, L. (2001) *Develop Your Training Skills*, London, Kogan Page

Useful websites

www

www.trainerslibrary.com Resources for trainers

www.businessballs.com Free articles and resources for trainers

www.caseplace.org Free case material

ACTIVITIES – CHAPTER 7

1 Structuring a presentation

Introduction

Learners are given a news report and asked to produce a slide showing how they would structure a presentation about that news. Reports may be torn from a newspaper. Alternatively, use the fictitious article 'Warning shot' which appears below.

Aims

To give learners the opportunity to decide how to structure a presentation.

Method

Split the group into pairs or threes. Provide a newspaper article of suitable length and interest. Brief them to produce a plan of how they would structure a five-minute presentation about the report given. It may be useful to specify that the presentation should contain, for example, five slides.

Timings

Twenty minutes to prepare. About five minutes to view and discuss each plan.

FICTITIOUS NEWS ARTICLE

Warning shot

The American vice-president, Harvey Hopkins, was involved in an incident in which Russian security police accompanying him fired a warning shot at a motorist. Mr Hopkins was being escorted in a six-car motorcade which was approaching the Kremlin when a motorist cut across the middle of the convoy and appeared to be about to pull alongside the car containing the vice-president.

A detective in the car behind produced a handgun and fired a single shot over the roof of the intruding car, believed to be a Lada, which then veered away. Police did not pursue the vehicle, and the official view is that the motorist had simply failed to appreciate the nature of the convoy.

A spokesman for the vice-presidential party stated: 'We do not believe there was ever any danger to the vice-president. This is the sort of incident that could happen anywhere, and we were very pleased with the firm and decisive way in which the possible threat was dealt with by the Russian escort.'

The vice-president is in Moscow on an official goodwill visit lasting ten days. It is not the first time he has been involved in a security scare. Last year, while in France for a meeting with European industrialists, a young woman was arrested attempting to enter his hotel carrying a concealed sub-machine gun. She later claimed to be a member of an extremist ecological group which blames the USA for much of the destruction of the world's rain forests.

In a more recent incident, a bomb was discovered in a Detroit conference centre three days before Mr Hopkins was due to speak there. Although several groups subsequently claimed responsibility for the bomb, police feel that it was most likely that an individual with a grudge had made and planted the device. No arrests have yet been made.

The recent increase in attempts to kill senior American politicians has alarmed the administration. It calls into question the proposed fact-finding tour of African states by a group of Senators and Congressmen scheduled for next year. One White House spokesman is reported to have said that the only way the trip would go ahead was in 'armoured cars escorted by helicopter gunships'.

2 Create a game

Introduction

This activity should follow on from input and discussion about the design process.

Aims

To give the opportunity to be creative in the design of an activity.

Method

Divide the group into pairs (or threes for a large group) and issue the following instructions:

During the next 30 minutes you must create a game which people from the other groups will play. The game should last about five minutes. Use only materials readily to hand (eg paper, coins, etc). The game must produce a clear winner, and should have the objective of enabling players to demonstrate their creativity. Please do not simply use a game you have already played, but be creative in the design process.

Timings

Thirty minutes to prepare, and about ten minutes to set up and run each activity. Also allow some time to discuss the difficulties of designing such an activity in such a short time, the difficulty of predicting time requirements, and other learning points as appropriate.

3 Role-play case study

Introduction

This activity relates to input and discussion about the use of role-plays.

Aims

To examine a situation in which a role-play exercise has gone wrong, and to discuss issues arising.

Method

A case study exercise suitable for individual or group analysis.

CASE STUDY

Jenny's solo run

Jenny had been rather nervous about running the negotiating skills course on her own for the first time. Still, she had thought, she had helped Sue run it twice before and it had always gone well. All the material was prepared to a high standard. 'Apart from some input at the beginning, it runs itself,' Sue had said.

It had been a reasonable morning, thought Jenny. No mistakes with the input and discussions, and they had all enjoyed the video. Now she would get the role-play exercise going, and that would provide a good afternoon's session. Just as she had seen Sue do, Jenny divided the course into two groups and issued the role briefings. The role-play was based around an industrial relations scenario, with one group playing the management team and one playing a trade union team. There were five people in each team. After she had issued the briefings, she sent the two teams away to prepare for the next half-hour. She would run the exercise just as Sue did, with no interference and without commenting until the end.

At the end of the preparation time, Jenny sent the management team back into the training room first to prepare for the negotiation. The union team, however, would not go back. Graham, a mid-thirties production manager, had been elected as the 'senior shop steward' by his group. He insisted that the management team should come and ask them politely to attend the meeting. Jenny went along with this, but the management side would not comply! It took her nearly ten minutes of persuasion to get Graham to lead his team back to the training room.

When they arrived back, the management team was seated behind a row of tables at the far end of the room. There were no other chairs left in the room for the union team to use. Another five minutes was wasted sorting that difficulty out.

When, at last, the negotiation actually started, Jenny was horrified by Graham's behaviour. He shouted and swore. He banged the table with his fist. At one point it looked as if he would actually throw the table over. Jenny was not the only one who was horrified. The management team had appointed Jonathan, a young manage-ment trainee from accounts, as their lead negotiator. He was no match for Graham, and quickly caved in to most of Graham's demands. Some of Jonathan's team objected to Graham's tactics. 'It's not fair,' said Alison. 'This is supposed to be a learning experience, not a slanging match.' Graham was in victorious mood, however, and simply stood his ground with the baying support of two of his 'union' partners. The other two, however, had not said a word. Eventually, one of them, Paul from management services, announced quietly that he had 'had enough of this nonsense' and left the room. He was closely followed by his colleague.

By now, Jonathan had completely withdrawn and was looking deeply upset. Alison was trying to counsel him while the other three team members continued to argue with Graham and his two cronies that the negotiation should start again. Alison glared across at Jenny. 'Do something!' she hissed.

- *What should Jenny do now?*
- *What should she have done in the first place?*

4 Role-play design exercise

Introduction

A design exercise in which people are asked to create a role-play, which is then tried out.

Aims

To give the opportunity to create a role-play exercise, and to see how it works in practice.

Method

Divide the group into threes and issue the following instructions (adapted as necessary):

During the next 45 minutes you must create a role-play which people from the other groups will perform. The role-play should last about 10 minutes, and should involve two or three people. The role-play should have the objective of allowing participants to practise some skill or behaviour that is relevant to their role at work – for example, dealing with a disciplinary problem, coping with a difficult telephone call from a customer, or asking someone to stop disrupting a course. Please do not simply use a role-play you are already familiar with, but be creative in the design process.

Once prepared, groups take it in turns to brief participants from another group to perform the role-play. They also analyse the learning points from the role-play *performance*, and debrief as necessary. The qualities and limitations of the role-play *design* are then discussed and learning points extracted.

Timings

About 45 minutes' preparation of the role-plays followed by a further 20 minutes per group for the performances and performance reviews. Allow a total of around 30 minutes for the design considerations to be discussed.

Conduct

PART 4

Presentation techniques

The devil's name is Dullness.

Robert E. Lee

CHAPTER OBJECTIVES

When you have finished this chapter you should be able to:

- **list the key aspects of delivering information by means of a presentation**

- **list the key aspects of presenting, with particular regard to voice, mannerisms, language (including the use of analogies, metaphors and humour), pace, and non-verbal delivery**

BEFORE PRESENTING

Good training and good presenting are not the same thing. It is possible to find excellent trainers who say that they never give a 'presentation' as such. Equally, some excellent presenters are not good trainers. Presenting information is only one aspect of training. Nonetheless, it is a very important aspect because a presentation

- is an effective way of giving information to a group
- may be necessary to gain commitment from a management team
- is how some people judge a trainer's competence
- can be useful to summarise learning points.

Delivering a presentation is a skill that people have to learn. Although it is true that some people find it easier than others, everyone is capable of learning presentation techniques to some degree. There are points of technique to be learned and practised, and all of us must evolve ways of presenting which suit our particular personalities. There is no single 'right way' to deliver a presentation in a training context. A good trainer will employ a range of styles that will vary according to the particular combination of subject matter, audience and other circumstances that he or she may encounter on different occasions.

Confidence

For many people, lack of confidence is the biggest single obstacle to delivering an effective presentation. It leads to nervousness and anxiety, and hence to a stilted and awkward performance. The individual thus becomes convinced that he or she is 'no good at giving presentations', and avoids doing them. This sets up a negative cycle (see Figure 10) which inhibits learning improvement. It is therefore necessary to break this cycle to increase confidence.

Lack of confidence is caused by:

- fear of looking foolish
- fear of the audience's reaction
- fear of drying up.

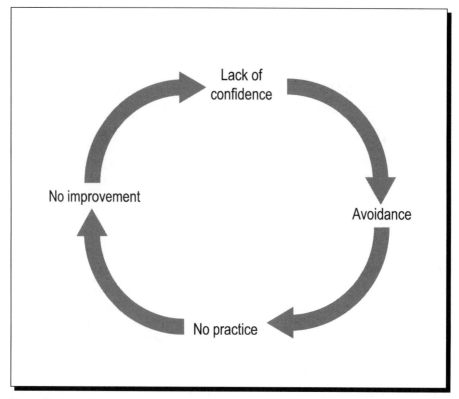

Figure 10 *A negative cycle in delivering presentations*

Fear of looking foolish

The fear that many of us experience when standing in front of a group can be intense. If we are not used to it, the psychological pressure of having people staring at us can be quite incapacitating. First, it can be reduced by thinking about what clothes you will wear, and your appearance in general. Usually, a smart conventional choice of clothes will be appropriate, but more casual clothing may be the right choice in some situations – although a very youthful style of dress can reduce your credibility. Think about your appearance in relation to the audience concerned.

Provided you have thought about it, you will get your appearance near enough right for the audience not to be affected by it and for you to feel psychologically comfortable. Make sure that you will be physically comfortable as well by avoiding new shoes, tight collars, etc. Wear clothes that will be warm enough but not uncomfortably hot. Jackets are easy and quick to take off or put on; sweaters are not.

Having thought about appearance, the second thing to think about is starting the presentation. This is the most stressful part of any event. Reduce the pressure on yourself by having a visual aid ready for use after the opening minute or two. As the projector is switched on, the audience's eyes will turn from you onto the screen. You will probably feel the tension diminish and as you relax you will be able to talk more fluently.

Third, remember that you don't have to be perfect! Your audience will forgive occasional stumblings and other signs of nerves. They too will have a fear of speaking to groups or will remember what it was like before they became experienced.

Finally, this fear will diminish with practice. Force yourself to 'stand and deliver' a few times and get beyond the feelings of fear and into the feelings of accomplishment and satisfaction that can come from this activity.

Fear of the audience's reaction

They are there to learn, and if they think you know what you are talking about they will respond naturally to your input. Try to anticipate their attitude. If you have pitched your presentation to their needs, then their reaction is likely to be appreciative and encouraging. Reduce your anxiety about the audience by meeting them in advance, if you can. Again, experience will reduce your fear of audiences. Most of them are kind and friendly.

Fear of drying up

Thorough preparation is the key. You know your subject and you know you know it. Reduce the fear by having notes so that you can remind yourself of what you were going to say. How to prepare notes will be dealt with later in this section, but it is important to stress that you must prepare your own notes. Using somebody else's notes does not commit the presentation to memory in the same way. Timing of an input session is difficult, so keep it flexible by having some material which can be left out if time is short or included if there is ample time.

Preparation

Before you can begin to prepare a presentation, it is necessary to ask yourself a series of questions:

- What is the purpose of the presentation?
- Who is the audience?
- What are the circumstances?

The purpose

There are three categories into which the purpose of most presentations falls:

- to communicate information
- to make a proposition
- to inspire and motivate.

In a training context, the presentation may serve all three of these purposes simultaneously. For example, the trainer may want to:

- outline an appraisal scheme
- persuade the audience to support the concept
- generate enthusiasm for the introduction of the scheme.

The commonest purpose of the trainer's presentation is to impart knowledge. When this is the case, it is usually simple to generate a concise overall objective statement such as: 'By the end of the presentation, the members of the audience will be able to list the four main stages in the selection and purchase of a new photocopier.' If more than one purpose is being served, then obviously more than one objective statement must be generated.

The audience

The members of the audience will influence the presentation in several ways. Before beginning to prepare, it is necessary to consider the following questions:

- Who will be present?
- How many will be present?
- What is the extent of their existing knowledge?
- What will be of interest to them?
- What attitudes, preconceptions or expectations will they bring with them?
- Do any of them have special needs – particularly with regard to vision or hearing?

The presentation must be pitched as accurately as possible for the audience. Explaining things at too elementary a level will leave the audience bored and frustrated; assuming they know more than they actually do can result in their losing the thread and failing to absorb the message. Either way, the audience will become irritated and will resent your lack of consideration for them. However, it is not always possible to obtain accurate information about the audience. Even when it is, the audience may turn out to be very mixed in terms of existing expertise, age, education, and so on. In this case, consider whether it is possible to reorganise the presentation to overcome these problems. It may be possible to provide background information for those that need it in advance. Otherwise, acknowledge the problem to the audience. Explain that some of them may find some aspects rather elementary, and ask for their forbearance. Plan to use their knowledge to support your presentation if possible.

The circumstances

Other factors that have to be taken into account at this stage are the general and specific circumstances in which you will be operating. They include:

- the venue
- equipment
- the time available
- the context.

You may have a wide choice of venue, or you may have none. The size of the room, the furniture, the position of power points, and other practical considerations, all need to be known. If they are not ideal, can a better venue be found, or must you make do, come what may?

You may have access to the full range of modern high-technology audiovisual equipment, or none at all. You must know what is available, and select the appropriate aids for your purpose.

Ideally, you should have as much time as you need to put across your message, and no more. In practice, you may be allocated a very specific time slot and have to make the best use of it.

We often underestimate the time needed to put across a complex message, so if time is limited, the message may have to be simplified.

The context in which a presentation is delivered is important. Is it at the start of the day with a group who are new to each other, or is it the fourth item in a crowded agenda? Are you being judged against others making similar presentations, or will they only see yours? Are you bringing good news that will be eagerly anticipated, or bad news that will provoke hostility? Only when all these questions have been addressed can the presenter move on to the detailed preparation, the planning, of the presentation.

Planning

There are various methods that people use to plan a presentation. One popular way is to jot down key words or phrases to cover all the points that might be included in the presentation. At all times, the objective of the presentation should be kept in mind. At this stage, do not worry about sequence or timing.

A good presentation, like a good story, has a beginning, a middle, and an end. That is:

- Introduction

- Development

- Conclusion.

Paradoxically, the introduction is best prepared after the other material. This is because the introduction will outline the content of the development section, and so that section must be prepared first. To do this, the points already noted down must be grouped under appropriate headings. Three or four major sections should evolve, and as you work a theme will probably suggest itself. Some of the points will fit best into the Introduction or Conclusion sections. Others may not fit well anywhere. Perhaps the section headings will have to be revised, or maybe the points should be dropped from the presentation altogether. If you get stuck or confused, leave it. Do something else for a while and let your mind clear. Often, when you return to the problem things will fall into place more readily.

Once you have decided upon the content, the next stage is to work out a logical sequence and timings. The sequence will depend upon the nature of the content. Sometimes it will be obvious (for example, historical development); sometimes less so. It may not even be important. Try different ideas until it feels right. Timing can be achieved either by speaking aloud what you intend to say, and noting the time taken, or by making the material fit the time you decide. Your broad outline may look like this:

Time available: 20 minutes

Introduction	2 minutes (10%)
Development	
Historical background:	4 minutes (20%)
Recent developments:	5 minutes (25%)
Case examples:	6 minutes (30%)
Conclusion	3 minutes (15%)

Then prepare your notes. Try not to write a speech; rather, write down key words or phrases to remind you of what you wish to say. Note down the points at which you might use a visual aid. Some people like to use cards as prompts; others are happier using a flat sheet of paper. Try different approaches until you settle on one which you are happy with.

Your notes may look something like this:

Welcome
Introduction   – Self
                  – Topic (equal opportunity policy)
                  – Reason for presentation and its scope

                                                              2 minutes

OHP1:   'The law'
                  Key points   – Sex Discrimination Act
                                      – Equal Pay Act
                                      – Race Relations Act
                                      – Disability Discrimination Act

                                                              5 minutes

OHP2:   'Why do we need a policy?'
                  Key points   – Codes of practice
                                      – Consistency
                                      – Moral arguments

                                                              6 minutes

and so on.

Rehearsal and practice

A rehearsal is an important element in the preparation of a presentation. If possible, use the actual venue where your presentation will be delivered. One of the key purposes of the rehearsal is to check the timing. Find out if your time estimates are near the mark, or way off. Your timings need not be absolutely precise: remember that an audience slows you down.

Even if you do not rehearse standing in front of an empty room, practise what you are going to say by using your notes as triggers. This can be done at home, and you can ask friends or relatives to give their reactions. Rehearse key points. If you are going to move around, practise this too, so that your movement looks purposeful and authoritative, instead of random and pointless. If you are using visual aids, practise their use as well. Knowing how to switch the projector on before you appear in front of the audience may sound obvious, but you will probably be able to remember an occasion when the presenter had to call for assistance!

Well before the day, decide what you are going to wear. Remember to choose clothes that make you feel both comfortable and confident. Make sure that your chosen outfit is clean and presentable.

DELIVERING A PRESENTATION

It is not really possible to learn much about the delivery of a presentation simply by reading about it, so I will be brief.

Project enthusiasm

Many of the most popular presenters would fail an assessment from a 'purist' presentation techniques expert. They are popular because they project energy, enthusiasm, and belief into their sessions. This projection comes across in the voice, posture, gestures, eyes and body movement. I would far rather listen to an enthusiast with poor visual aids than to someone who looked bored and tired with perfect visual aids.

Eye contact

Look at your audience from the beginning. Smile at them. Do not, however, fix on one 'friendly face', but rather scan the audience. This creates empathy, and also lets you read their reaction to what you are saying.

Non-verbal aspects and mannerisms

Appropriate facial expressions are an important part of effective communication. People watch a speaker's face during a presentation. When you speak, your face reveals your attitudes, feelings and emotions. It is usually best to start off by smiling. Later, you might want to look thoughtful, concerned or excited. The key thing is, of course, that your facial expression should match the words that you are using. When you are nervous, you may tend to look deadpan or to frown. This detracts from your message because it confuses the audience.

The same applies to other non-verbal aspects of delivery – such as body language. When you are tense, you may fold your arms and look negative. If nervous, you may clasp or wring your hands. Try to relax and allow yourself to respond naturally to your thoughts, attitudes and emotions. Your facial expressions and body language will be appropriate and will project conviction, and credibility.

Some mannerisms are a direct result of nerves. Others are present for some people even when they are not nervous. In fact, everyone has some mannerisms. For the most part, they are not important and do not get in the way of effective delivery. But if you are frequently told that people find your habit of hair chewing, adjusting your clothing or scratching your head is distracting, then make a conscious effort to eliminate this unwanted behaviour.

Voice

You have to speak loudly without shouting. This takes practice, but it can be learned. You can also vary the volume, speaking up to add emphasis, or dropping to a near whisper to signify the sharing of a secret. Also, you have to vary your speed of delivery and the pitch of your voice. There are a number of books which deal well with these aspects and if you are frequently told that your voice is a problem, invest in one of them and persevere with the exercises that they contain. These include:

- breathing exercises – to strengthen your ribcage muscles and to increase the volume of air that you inhale and exhale and thus improve your audibility

- articulation exercises – to make indistinct speakers clearer

- pitch exercises – to lessen a monotonous delivery

- quality exercises – to correct breathy, hoarse, strident or nasal voices.

Obviously, some speech problems are innate and not easily corrected, if at all. But the most common problems I have encountered are to do with people who speak too softly or who mumble their words. It is usually possible for these faults to be corrected, but it requires sustained practice and a commitment to improve.

Using the equipment

Thoroughly familiarise yourself with how the equipment works. There may be only a few controls, but be sure you know where they are and what they do. Make sure that you know what to do if, for example, a projector lamp blows.

There are various keyboard shortcuts that may be useful during a presentation using PowerPoint slides: see Table 19.

Table 19 *Keyboard shortcuts for PowerPoint slide presentations*

Action required	Keyboard shortcut
Get out of slideshow	Esc *or* minus sign (–)
Make screen go white (toggle)	W *or* ,
Make screen go black (toggle)	B *or* .
Go back	Backspace arrow, Up arrow, Page Up, *or* P
Go forward	Return, Enter, Page Down, Forward arrow, Down arrow, *or* N
Go to slide <number>	<number> + Enter
Stop or start automatic show	S
Return to first slide	*Both mouse buttons for 2 seconds*
Display button	A
Change the pointer to a pen	CTRL+P
Hide the pointer and button temporarily	CTRL+H
Hide the pointer and button always	CTRL+L
Display shortcut menu	Shift+F10 *or* right-click
See list of controls	F1

Remember,

- The projector should be switched off when not in use.

- Never leave a slide up after you have moved on in the session.

- Never leave the projector beaming out white light. It draws the eye and is a distraction.

If you are using a flipchart or whiteboard as a 'live' aid for you to note down key words or sketch diagrams, use big lettering that can be seen from the back of the room. Capital letters are more legible than script (handwriting) for most people. Always have enough flipchart paper to last, and ensure that you have an adequate supply of the right kind of pen.

ENLIVENING YOUR PRESENTATION

When presenting factual information, it is important that the information is clear and accurate. However, it is also important that the information is not given in relentlessly dull, dry, language. Take any opportunity to introduce colourful, vivid, emotional language to liven up a presentation.

Use words that are evocative:

crazy   fabulous   awesome   scary   sexy   fantastic ......

Whether you like his style or not, watch a video showing Tom Peters giving a presentation. His delivery is absolutely full of these vivid words – and most people find him spellbinding.

Paint pictures with your words that cause the audience to envisage scenes in their own minds. You can actually ask them directly to do this:

- 'Imagine being invited out for a meal with some friends, and having to decline because you are diabetic and must eat your meals at set times. Imagine ... '

- 'Suppose that everyone in your office had a smile on his or her face whenever a visitor walked through the door. A prospective customer walks in ...'

- 'Picture the scene when the social worker turns up in her brand new car at the home of a single mother with two pre-school toddlers and a babe in arms. Visualise a building that is in such a state of neglect ...'

Remember that a presentation is not a report. You can use adjectives, exaggeration, repetition and colloquial language to make it come to life:

- 'This serum is a gorgeous pink syrup ...'

- 'Millions and millions of beautiful little babies will be bathed with our new ...'

- 'Two exhausted and sweaty trainers had finally completed the induction manual ...'

Whenever you are transposing a written report or text into a presentation, look for opportunities to make it livelier, more dramatic or easier on the ear.

EXAMPLE 1 (MEDICAL)

'This is a serious condition that reduces life expectancy in otherwise healthy 35-year-old males by around 20 years.'

could become:

'A 35-year-old man diagnosed with this terrible condition could expect to die some 20 years earlier than his friends of the same age.'

EXAMPLE 2 (RETAIL)

'As a company, we try to focus on providing distinctive clothes for young people. Accordingly, we must strive to follow the evolution of consumer tastes, trends and spending in the apparel market.'

could become:

'As a company, we offer exceptional, daring and youthful clothing. We must know what the kids want before they do.'

> ## EXAMPLE 3 (INDUSTRIAL)
>
> 'After attempting to synthesise the compound by the method published in the journal nine times, but without success, alternative approaches in earlier papers were considered.'
>
> *could become:*
>
> 'We tried to make this compound following the published method not once, not twice, but nine times. We hate failure – so we trawled the archives in search of any magic spell or incantation that we might have been missing.'

Look at Example 3 again. Which words or phrases would you *stress* to make the message have more impact? It could become:

> '**We tried** to make this compound following the published method not once, not twice, but **nine times**. We hate failure – so we trawled the archives in search of **any** magic spell or incantation that we might have been missing.'

Another way you can enliven your presentation is to vary the pace. Observe how successful politicians, comedians or television personalities do this. Rather than deliver their information at a steady pace, most use a range of speeds to deliver information. Speed up to convey excitement or when the information is easy to take in; slow down to stress importance or to put across complex ideas. This is what most of us do in everyday conversation.

USING ANALOGIES, METAPHORS AND HUMOUR

A simple and effective way of making a complex training presentation easier for your audience to understand is to use analogies and metaphors.

An analogy is when you liken one thing to another. It is best used when you can liken something strange or new to something familiar. But as well as aiding understanding, it can also add colour or humour:

- 'This process is like making a three-layered cake.'

- 'This is the Genghis Khan of viruses.'

- 'If you were building a house, you would start with sound foundations. So too when constructing a training programme. First, get your shovel!'

A metaphor is the application of a name or descriptive term to an object which is imaginatively but not literally applicable. Thus a phrase such as 'a glowing example' is metaphorical, because examples do not literally glow. But we instantly know that the example in question has some of the positive properties of something that glows. Other examples are:

- a cowardly Act of parliament

- a burning issue

- an aloof fabric

- an enthusiastic piece of software.

Humour should be used appropriately, not too frequently, and in your own natural style. Try to avoid offending anyone, and do not make anyone (except yourself) the butt of your jokes unless you know them extremely well and know that they will be happy about it:

- 'We looked at the distribution chain for free-range chickens – *poultry in motion* as it were – and ...'

- 'These hardware failures are as rare as parking spaces outside this building!'

- 'No amount of safety equipment can protect against idiotic behaviour. So, having injured myself, ...'

Inappropriate or ill-judged humour can result in awkward and embarrassing silence. Your audience may well be very busy people who will have to catch up on their work when they return to their normal duties. They will resent excessive time spent on entertainment, no matter how amusing.

SUMMARY

This chapter has dealt with presentation skills. Aspects of delivery that have been discussed include:

- preparing and planning presentations
- verbal and non-verbal delivery
- varying the pace and vocal delivery
- the appropriate use of language in a presentation.

Presentation skills cannot, however, be learned by reading. They can only be learned through practice.

FURTHER READING

Berry, C. (2000) *Your Voice and How to Use It*, 2nd edition, London, Virgin Publishing

Jay, A. and Jay. R. (1996) *Effective Presentation*, London, Pitman

McCallion, M. (1988) *The Voice Book*, London, Faber & Faber

Morrison, M. (2001) *Clear Speech*, 4th edition, London, A & C Black

Pease, A. (1981) *Body Language*, Sydney, Sheldon Press

Rae, L. (1995) *Techniques of Training*, 3rd edition, Aldershot, Gower

Useful websites

www.presentersonline.com Very useful resource for presenting   www

www.saidwhat.co.uk Quotations

www.metaphor.org.uk About metaphors and their use

www.presentationhelper.co.uk More help with presentations and PowerPoint

ACTIVITIES – CHAPTER 8

1 Stress and presenting

In small groups, produce a list of the symptoms of stress when presenting – including the effect on the voice.

Then produce some ideas about how to overcome these effects.

Prepare a brief presentation to feed back your ideas to the other groups.

Timing

Allow about half hour for preparation, five minutes per team for presentation, and around 15 minutes for discussion. With larger groups, select one or two ideas from each team to avoid duplication.

2 Presenting a case to gain commitment

Introduction

Apart from the basic skills of presentation, trainers must learn to be effective as persuaders. This is an activity which requires the presenters to structure a case so as to convince others to support it.

Aims

To provoke thought and discussion about how a case should be structured in a training context, and to provide an opportunity to present and defend a training proposal.

Method

Divide the group into teams of three or four. Each team is asked to prepare a presentation about one of the following:

- purchasing some new training equipment
- refurbishing training facilities
- recruiting an additional trainer
- recruiting an additional/new training administrator
- spending a large sum of money on a management development programme
- increasing the length of an existing training programme.

Each team then takes its turn to make its presentation to the rest of the group. When being presented to, the group role-plays senior managers and asks probing questions which the presenters must respond to. Each presentation is then assessed by the group. Discussion is focused on the factors which made one presentation more persuasive than another. The assessment sheet shown as Table 20 may be useful for this activity.

Table 20 *Presentation assessment form*

Introduction	Comments
Introduced self/team Introduced subject Stated the range of the presentation	
Making a case	
Explained the need for the change/ the problem to be solved Demonstrated that alternative solutions had been considered Put forward persuasive arguments	
Presentation	
Structure Pace Clarity Answering questions Use of visual aids Effectiveness Timing Overall comments:	

Timing

Allow an hour for preparation, ten minutes per team for presentation, and around 20 minutes for discussion.

Participative
delivery techniques

CHAPTER 9

I was gratified to be able to answer promptly, and I did. I said I didn't know.

Mark Twain

CHAPTER OBJECTIVES

When you have finished this chapter you should be able to:

- **describe a variety of participative training methods and the skills needed to employ those methods**

- **select an appropriate room layout and take account of health and safety issues when conducting a participative training session**

- **manage group dynamics and behaviour in groups, and deal better with problems that may arise.**

THE LESSON

Many of the points about presentation techniques apply to the lesson as well. By 'lesson', I mean an interactive, participative, training session. This will typically mean that the trainer is giving some input and is using visual aids, but is also interacting with the group. The group is no longer a passive audience but takes part in the session by making comments, questioning, and giving its opinions. This is generally more enjoyable for them and, importantly, produces better understanding and learning. Preparation for a lesson is similar to preparation for a presentation, but will include planning for interactive sections within the lesson.

For example, an overhead projection slide about manpower planning might be followed by a question to the group: 'Who is responsible for manpower planning in your company?'

The time to deal with the response must be estimated and allowed for. This can be quite difficult because, of course, you do not know what they are going to say. However, with experience you will be able to estimate more accurately. Also, you can adapt as you go along. If the session is behind schedule, you may make up time by simply telling them something rather than asking them to arrive at the answer for themselves.

The main techniques used in a lesson, along with presentation techniques, are:

- questioning and discussing

- questioning and charting

- asking for definitions

- asking for examples from their experience

- asking for reactions.

Questioning and discussing

Trainer: 'Why do you think that people involved in car crashes often cannot remember the moment of impact?'

Learner 1:   'Because it's too frightening, and so they blank it out.'

Trainer: 'Possibly, in some cases. But there's another reason relating to the model of memory we looked at yesterday.'

Learner 2:   'Is it to do with the information not having got from the short-term memory store into the long-term memory store before they've lost consciousness?'

Trainer: 'Yes. Well done. Let me expand on that ...'

This approach stimulates people to think. It is very effective – but it has some pitfalls. You should never 'rubbish' or 'put down' a contribution. All contributions should be welcomed and rewarded. Try not to be patronising when you do this, though:

Trainer: 'Can anyone remember who developed the MUD taxonomy?'

Learner: 'Was it Sylvia Downs?'

Trainer: 'Oh well done, Clive! You are clever. Isn't Clive clever, everyone?'

Also remember that people need to be told when they are wrong. Do it clearly, but in a way that makes them feel appreciated for having made an effort rather than told off for guessing wrongly.

Finally, know when to give up. If you keep asking and no one knows the answer, or cannot understand the question, just tell them.

Questioning and charting

This is very useful when you know that the knowledge is present in the group. You can have a visual aid listing 'Uses for job descriptions', or you can instead ask:

Trainer: 'What uses are job descriptions put to in an organisation? Call out and I'll write them on the whiteboard.'

Learner 1:   'Job evaluation.'

Trainer: 'Good.' (Writes 'Job evaluation' on board.)

Learner 2:   'Recruitment.'

Trainer: 'Yes. Excellent.' (Writes 'Recruitment' on board.)

Learner 3:   'Job grading,'

Trainer: 'Wouldn't that come under "job evaluation"?'

and so on.

Key points are:

- Write down exactly what they say unless they agree to your wording.

- Don't reject points just because you didn't think of them.

- Discuss points as they arise, or after they are all on the board, as you judge appropriate.

- Make sure everyone gets a fair chance to join in.

Asking for definitions

This is often useful to stimulate thought: 'What do we mean by "motivation"? What is it?'

Key point:

- Have a clear definition ready!

Asking for examples from their experience

'Has anyone here ever had to sack someone? You have, Jane. Would you be prepared to tell us about how you felt?'

It is often better to get anecdotes from within the group rather than to tell your own stories. It can be stimulating for you, and you learn from them while they learn from you.

Key points:

- Have a fall-back story in case nothing comes out.

- Be prepared to interrupt if someone starts a rambling and/or irrelevant story.

Asking for reactions

'What do people feel about this model of learning? Is it useful?'

This is a very good way to find out there and then what people's reactions are. It is valuable feedback for you. Do not become too defensive if they have opposite views to yours. It would be a strange world if we all agreed about everything.

Key points:

- Listen carefully.

- Be prepared to agree to differ.

ROOM LAYOUT

Training rooms can be arranged in a variety of ways. For a presentation there are many possibilities that will work. For an interactive session, rather fewer. In a presentation, the main thing is that the presenter and his or her visual aids can be seen. For a group discussion, it is important that the learners can see each other. In some training situations, the trainer may wish to enter the middle of the group, or walk around the edge of it. Options will be limited by the type of furniture available, by the number of participants, and the size and shape of the room. Some of the options available are discussed below.

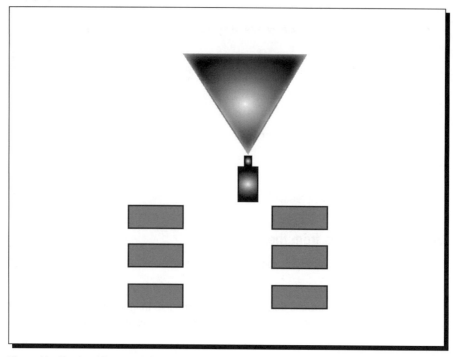

Figure 11 *Theatre-style presentation seating-plan arrangement*

In the theatre-style arrangement (see Figure 11) the audience is seated in rows ... as in a theatre. This enables the maximum number of people to be seated in a given area. Often hotels or other training venues give a room capacity figure based on this layout, and this can be very misleading if you are not aware of what it means. Theatre-style layouts are fine for formal presentations, but prevent members of the audience from interacting well with each other. Even making eye contact is difficult, except for the people sitting next to each other.

The horseshoe, or U-shape, arrangement (see Figure 12) is much more conducive to group interaction. The trainer can also move into the middle of the group if desired. The main problem with this arrangement is that it limits the number of people that can be trained in a particular room.

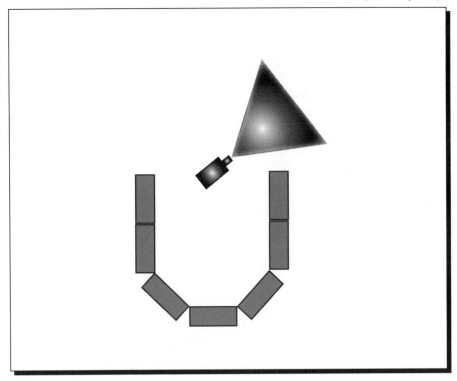

Figure 12 *Horseshoe arrangement*

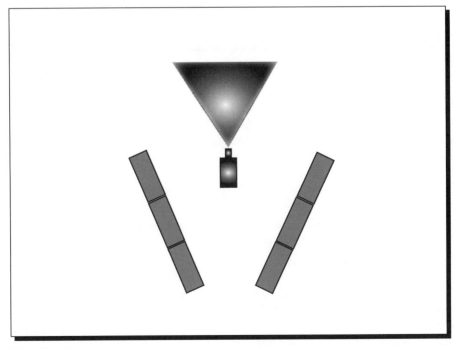

Figure 13 *The vee*

The vee (see Figure 13) is a variation on the horseshoe. Some trainers feel that it facilitates eye contact better than the horseshoe. Personally, I use it if the tables are too big to arrange into a neat horseshoe.

Boardrooms often double as training rooms. They tend to be dominated by huge tables, and the learners sit around the circumference (see Figure 14). This is not ideal because the trainer cannot enter into the middle of the group. Also, it limits options for the placing of visual aids such that everyone can see them. It is, however, an efficient use of space. It is also good when the group discusses issues amongst itself.

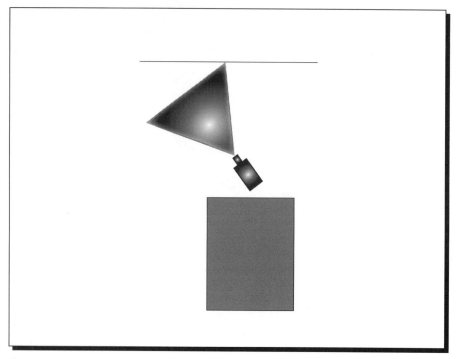

Figure 14 *Boardroom arrangement*

GROUP DISCUSSIONS

A group discussion is a method that may be used by a trainer to create a learning situation where attitudes and opinions are sought and examined. There are three key features about the process:

- The participative environment encourages the sharing of experiences and the introduction and development of ideas.

- The fact that all the participants are actively involved in thinking, listening and speaking leads to better learning and fuller understanding.

- Adults like to learn in this way.

These effects do not, however, occur automatically. If the group knows little or nothing about a topic, then you are unlikely to get much of a discussion. Even if a topic is chosen that everyone knows about, it may be difficult for the participants to get started if they are not given some help. Accordingly, before initiating a group discussion, the trainer has to prepare.

Preparation

Not all topics are best taught by group discussion. Indeed, the process itself may introduce no new facts to the group. What does happen, however, is the sharing of information held by the various group members (which may include the trainer). The process is valuable in the exchange of views and ideas, in problem-solving and in the clarification of attitudes and understanding. You may, for example, choose to examine the ways in which a disciplinary situation might be handled by means of a group discussion. Because people will bring a range of different experiences with them, an interesting and lively discussion is likely from which group members will learn and attitudes may be altered.

Purposes

The group discussion process may have various purposes, such as:

- to disseminate knowledge about a subject
- to solve problems and make decisions
- to develop interpersonal skills
- to influence attitudes
- to enliven a training event
- to develop relationships within the group.

Sometimes it is appropriate to have clearly defined learning objectives; sometimes it is not.

Environment

People should be sitting down fairly close to each other, ideally in a circle. If the group is too big, some will not participate, so splitting into smaller groups may be appropriate. It may also be useful to provide flipcharts or other aids to assist the group. For some topics, privacy and confidentiality will be essential.

Getting started

There are various ways in which the initial discussion may be stimulated. With some groups and some topics it may work simply to say 'Now have a group discussion about topic X.' However, group discussions are normally more successful if they follow some other sort of input, such as:

- an introductory talk or presentation
- a film or video
- a case study or written handout
- an exercise or game.

For example, if you wanted to explore the topic of self-development you might try one of these approaches:

- a talk about the psychology of self-development
- a video about self-development
- a short case study highlighting self-development
- asking if there are those present who feel they have contributed to their own career progression through self-development.

How to achieve the objectives

Once you have got the discussion started, how will you make sure that your objectives will be achieved? What will you do if the participants are unable to see the points you had in mind? What if there is an adverse reaction to the topic, or someone gets upset?

The first time you try to create a group discussion of a topic, you will have little idea how long it will last and what degree of interest it will stimulate. It may also generate friction between the participants, or lead to some participants being frozen out. You must, as far as possible, prepare for all these eventualities. This may involve having back-up case study or presentation material, and you should think through how to handle any difficult situations that may arise.

Control

The degree of control will vary according to the objectives of the trainer and the nature of the group. The skill of a trainer is in selecting the appropriate style of control as much as it is in exercising that control. The style may vary during the course of a discussion, the trainer judging when it is right to intervene and when it is right to withdraw. The following three styles may therefore be considered as a range of options that merge into each other rather than as discrete entities.

Close control

The discussion leader controls the discussion by asking questions that are replied to by group members directing the response to the leader. The leader may even decide who will contribute at which point by naming who will respond, and may suppress uninvited contributions. Watch TV 'audience discussion' shows for examples of how this is done. The leader will evaluate all contributions, and may pass judgement in terms of 'That's right', or 'That's wrong'. The success of the discussion will be judged by the leader on whether or not the group has reflected the leader's attitudes back to him or her.

This style is often employed where there is a specific problem to be discussed in a limited time. The degree of control, while high, is often not perceived as unwelcome by the group. Indeed, group participants may be impressed by the authority that is displayed. They feel they have participated, but are aware of the high proportion of the leader's contribution, and may value this, particularly if they know they require such high control to be efficient.

The success of this style will depend to a large extent on the willingness to accept it, and the level of expertise of the leader compared to the group. The style will lead to conflict or non-participation if the group resents the leader's approach. In particular, a group that has been used to less control may react very negatively if this approach is adopted by a new course tutor.

Medium control

Here the trainer initiates the discussion, but permits and encourages the group to talk to each other directly, rather than through the chair. Some of the control mechanisms are suppressed, and the trainer leaves it to the group to evaluate contributions. He or she intervenes from time to time to expand on points that have arisen, and to point the discussion in the required direction. This may be by encouraging certain individuals to expand their contributions, by stating 'Perhaps we are moving too far ahead,' or by making some other such comment to restrict digression.

To encourage the group further to participate without going through him or her, the leader may sit among the group to reduce the emphasis on the leader role, and may keep silent for quite long periods. If the discussion goes well, the leader does not interfere. This may sound easy, but not joining in a lively and interesting group discussion requires great restraint.

Low control

The leader may withdraw from the discussion completely, or may sit at the back of the room and observe – participating only when invited, or when things are obviously going wrong. A group that is not used to this style often finds it uncomfortable to begin with. It tends to work better when the full group has been divided into smaller groups to discuss something. They then do not expect to be led.

The leader is invited to contribute facts or to give procedural advice. If the group asks for his or her opinion of the matter under discussion, he or she will avoid giving it. Instead, the leader will turn the question back to the group, or may state a number of different opinions to give the group something to work on.

The facilitator role

The text above uses the term 'leader'. However, it will be seen that in the medium-control or low-control situation the trainer is actively avoiding leading the group for much of the time. The trainer may then be viewed as a facilitator who is there to help the group reach its objectives – and these may have been determined by the group, not the trainer.

In order to function in a facilitating role, the trainer must be perceived as a trustworthy person who understands what is happening, and can be relied upon to prevent conflict or personal antagonism getting out of hand. In particular, the facilitator may perform the following functions:

- encourage contributions, particularly from the less self-confident
- ensure that the more verbose do not completely take over
- control conflict by stepping in if necessary to divert the discussion to a less contentious issue, by pointing out areas of agreement, or by analysing what has caused the conflict so that the participants can take a more objective, less emotional, view
- summarise from time to time, and perhaps pose a question or make a suggestion to take the discussion forward
- assist 'weaker' participants by rephrasing their arguments for them so that these do not get lost just because they are not forcefully put across – this may also be done by testing understanding of their contribution by questioning
- ensure that individuals receive positive feedback from the group, perhaps by acknowledging contributions that the group ignores, or by seeking positive contributions from others if a negative evaluation is given
- provide the group as a whole with feedback on its performance
- provide the information and resources for the group to function effectively
- stay quiet when all is well; permit silences, and allow time for people to think
- ensure that the discussion is brought to a close when the topic is exhausted
- ensure that the whole group attains common goals, and derives its greatest satisfaction from having done this together.

RUNNING EXERCISES

Apart from devising your own exercises, it is nowadays possible to purchase collections of exercises or activities at very reasonable prices. These often include instructions on how to use the material provided. However, you should always bear in mind that the people who wrote these instructions have probably been using the exercise in question for a few years. It is very easy for them to inadvertently leave out a key part of what they say or do, or for them to give you the impression that the exercise 'runs itself' with no need for further input from you.

Preparation

The first thing you must do with any exercise that you are using for the first time is to read it thoroughly. You should be clear in your own mind what is likely to happen, and be satisfied that it will bring out the learning points you require. Carefully study the list of resources needed and satisfy yourself that you have, or can get, everything necessary. If the instructions specify '30 metres of rope' how will you obtain it? I have certainly had bosses who would have taken a lot of persuasion to sanction such a purchase, whereas 'four rubber bands' seems perfectly manageable. Also read carefully what will be required in terms of the number of participants. Some exercises written for college classes require 20 or 30 people; others are designed for no more than 12. Some activities require an exact number of people, or require participants to work in threes (triads) or fours. Think what you would do with a group size of 11. Would it still work?

Assuming that you decide to proceed, clarify for yourself what preparation you will need to make. You may need a large space to work in, or syndicate rooms, as well as the materials specified. Remember to warn participants in advance if the exercise is likely to involve any physical exertion, or the possibility of getting wet or dirty. Advise them so that they can dress appropriately. Otherwise, you may well find people reluctant to take part once they think that their clothes will be spoilt.

Safety

Be very careful with any activity that has a possibility of hurting people. For example, some activities ask the group to climb onto tables, or to carry someone across a room. Unless you have a good reason for choosing such an exercise, try to find a safer substitute. Many years ago, when I was being trained as a trainer, our tutors organised a series of 'trust' exercises for us to experience. These included allowing oneself to fall backwards only to be saved by other members of the group. This worked well.

Another activity was explained as follows: 'Everyone except George go and stand over by the wall. In a minute, we are going to ask George to close his eyes and run headlong at the wall. The rest of you will close around George with your bodies, cushioning him and preventing him from hitting the wall.'

Unfortunately, 'George' (I can't remember his real name) did not wait for the group to get ready, or for a signal from the trainers. Instead, he said 'Right,' lowered his head, and charged! The group scattered leaving only me between George and the brick wall of the gym. I braced myself and thrust an elbow forward. George hit this at full pelt with the centre of his chest, and then collapsed on the floor where he remained for several minutes looking very distressed. Eventually, he recovered. The exercise was abandoned, and I made a decision never to take part in, let alone run, such an exercise again. Presumably George did too.

Most exercises do not have such dangers, and their use can greatly enliven a training course as well as facilitating experiential learning. There are some other potential pitfalls, though.

Face validity

Sometimes the purpose of the activity may not seem obvious, and participants may demand an explanation of it before commencing. 'We work in insurance. How does this exercise about a car factory relate to us?' Face validity is a term used in psychometric testing to describe whether a test looks relevant – 'on the face of it' – to the characteristic it purports to measure. Tests with poor face validity are often not liked, even if very accurate. I think it is a useful term to use to assess the similar property in training activities. Be prepared to explain if asked, but also try to head off such objections by explaining before you are asked what the relevance of the exercise is. This is not always easy without giving too much away.

Non-participation

Some people may refuse to take part in some activities. This may be because they have a moral objection to the activity. For example, one popular exercise requires participants to pretend that they have to choose the order in which people will be rescued from a flooding cave. I have known people refuse to do this activity for ethical reasons, and this then leaves the trainer with a problem. Other people will not take part in any exercise that has military overtones.

Another reason people refuse to participate is that they decide the activity is just too silly. There are exercises which ask people to communicate only by grunting, or to pretend to be farmyard animals. Know the group well before attempting such activities! Some people attend training events against their will and are looking for an excuse to refuse to participate in order to make a point. If you suspect this might happen and would prefer to avoid it, choose exercises with great care.

Many people will not take part happily in activities that require bodily contact with one another. An icebreaking exercise I have in a book includes blindfolding people and asking them to 'mill around', getting to know each other 'by any means you choose, such as talking and touching'. This may be a perfectly valid activity, but it is one I would be very reluctant to try because I have met a lot of people who would refuse to do it.

However, this does not mean such activities should never be used. If you know the people concerned and believe that there is sufficient value in the activity to take the risk of objections or refusal, then go ahead. You can, of course, ask them whether or not they are prepared to try it. It is not normally a good idea to pressurise people to take part in an activity they have reservations about. Perhaps you can ask them to observe.

The later section on dealing with difficulties considers other reasons for non-cooperation.

Review

The purpose of an exercise is, of course, to stimulate learning. It is the trainer's job to ensure that the learning possibilities that lie within an exercise are fully exploited. This is done in the review process at the end of the activity. There are several ways to structure a review:

- informal discussion
- structured discussion
- reports by observers
- video playback
- completion of a worksheet.

Informal discussion

This is often the most popular way of reviewing an activity. Simply lead a discussion of what happened, making sure that the key learning points are explored adequately.

Structured discussion

A discussion can be structured in that you can nominate who will speak, and in what order. You can pose specific questions, perhaps writing them up, to direct the discussion.

Reports by observers

You may have asked one or more people to observe an activity. Their observations are fed back to the group before a discussion of what happened.

Video playback

The participants can watch themselves on video, and learning points can be drawn from the playback.

Completion of a worksheet

Participants may be asked to complete a worksheet, or 'review' sheet, which asks such questions as: 'How well did your group work together?' This can either precede or follow a discussion.

READING GROUP DYNAMICS

Before considering how to read group dynamics we must first define what we mean by the term 'group dynamics'. To do that, we must first define the term 'group'. Many definitions exist, but that by Brown (1988) is a suitable one for trainers:

> **'A group exists when two or more people define themselves as members of it and when its existence is recognised by at least one other.'**

The 'other' in this context may be other learners, managers, or the trainer or trainers. If this definition is accepted, it follows that in one classroom of a dozen people it may be possible to find one group, or six groups, or any other number in between. It is also possible to belong to more than one group at the same time, and therefore the potential number of groups can be much larger. For the sake of clarity, these 'groups within groups' are often termed 'sub-groups'.

In practice, a group of 12 will often contain only two or three sub-groups that are identifiable to the trainer. Depending on the nature of the training you are conducting, it may or may not be important to make these identifications and to be aware of what is happening within each sub-group as well as the whole. In some kinds of training, such as team-building, this awareness is absolutely central to the learning process.

The term 'group dynamics' describes the interactions and processes that occur within and between groups. These interactions include how relationships between individuals are formed and developed, the degree of group cohesion, how power is distributed and used, and how group norms are evolved and enforced. The processes include how the group is formed, how it resolves or tolerates conflicts, how it makes decisions, and how it copes with change.

It can be seen, therefore, that the study of group dynamics can be a highly involved and complex science. There are some very heavy academic texts on the subject. However, some of the basic principles of how groups function can be readily understood. The reading of group dynamics is as much art as science, but a knowledge of the jargon used can made the description of group processes considerably easier. This can be of great assistance when trying to describe aspects of a group's functioning to others, or indeed to the group itself.

Group formation

A descriptive system developed by Tuckman in 1965 has entered the trainer's vocabulary largely because it is so easy to remember. This is the 'Forming, Storming, Norming and Performing' model which you may be familiar with already.

The *forming* stage is when the group members do not yet know each other. There is some anxiety, testing out of the rules, and trying to find out what behaviour is acceptable. A trainer can reduce the anxiety felt by group members in various ways – for example, by organising 'icebreaking' activities, or by discussing rules openly: 'It's okay to disagree,' 'There will be no report back to your managers.' Some people feel anxious about what clothes to wear, and this anxiety can be reduced in the joining instructions so that everyone knows to wear either formal or casual clothes.

The *storming* stage may or may not happen. It is when conflict may surface between sub-groups and there may be a rebellion against the leader. The leader in a training context may be the trainer, and this stage can be quite uncomfortable! On a very short course, there may not be enough time for the storming stage to evolve, and the individuals may consciously choose not to tackle issues that would otherwise concern them because they are aware that the group is a very temporary one.

The *norming* stage emerges after the storming stage has been resolved: the group can continue its development by establishing 'norms'. Norms are the tacitly agreed and understood ways of behaving which the group has evolved. They can include modes of dress, language, time-keeping, participation, and so forth. There is an open and healthy exchange of views and feelings.

The *performing* stage may never appear in some kinds of learning group. It is the stage when a team has emerged from the group and tasks are accomplished efficiently and effectively. Obviously, this may be required in a group of people who are going to be working together, but is not relevant to people who will never see each other again. Nonetheless, this stage can be reached in such circumstances, and some groups can feel a real sense of loss when a highly integrated group is disbanded at the end of a programme.

Analysing behaviours in groups

It can often be interesting to observe a group performing a task or discussing something. It may be possible to assess what stage of development the group is at, the degree of cohesiveness it exhibits, and so on. It may also be useful to analyse communication patterns. This can be done for your own information, or can be fed back to the group for further discussion or analysis. The easiest kind of behaviour to analyse is verbal behaviour, and several techniques are available to us to facilitate this.

Simple contribution analysis

Record how many times someone speaks by simply making a tick or a mark against his or her name. As a rule of thumb, you may wish to define a contribution as any meaningful utterance of five words or more addressed to the group. You will then end up with a record of the contributions of the group members something like this:

Name	Marks	Total
Andy	✓ ✓ ✓ ✓ ✓ ✓ ✓ ✓ ✓ ✓ ✓ ✓ ✓ ✓ ✓ ✓	16
Clare	✓ ✓ ✓ ✓ ✓	5
Grahame	✓ ✓ ✓ ✓ ✓ ✓ ✓ ✓ ✓ ✓ ✓ ✓ ✓	13
Jill	✓ ✓	23
Ming	✓ ✓ ✓ ✓ ✓ ✓ ✓ ✓ ✓ ✓	10
Louis	✓ ✓ ✓ ✓	4

How do we interpret this pattern? Perhaps it indicates that Clare and Louise are not participating fully. Perhaps it indicates that Jill does not know when to shut up. You will, of course, have heard the discussion as well as simply scoring it, and so you will be in a better position to give feedback than simply from the numerical data.

Sequenced contribution analysis

An alternative method is to record the person's contribution, perhaps by use of an initial letter, to show the pattern of the discussion. Using the names given above, we could end up with a pattern such as:

A J A J M A J L A J L A J A J A M C A J A J A C A J A C A J M L M A J A C A C A J A ...

If we want to, we can still total up the number of contributions from each person. However, the pattern can tell us much more. If Andy has initiated the discussion, he is unwilling to let go of it. Also, often after Andy has spoken, the next contribution has come from Jill. Are they aware of this? Does it indicate favouritism or animosity? In fact, Jill has only ever spoken after Andy. Why is this?

Obviously, you will have much more information because you observed the discussion. This kind of 'evidence', though, can be much more powerful when given as feedback to someone than your subjective impressions can be.

Directional contribution analysis

Another way to make a record of the contributions people make is to represent them as circles on a piece of paper. If someone speaks, mark an arrow from the letter representing that person towards the person he or she spoke to. Should the contribution be directed towards the group as a whole, then the arrow points outside the circle. An interruption can be marked with, for example, a short stroke across the line. See Figure 15.

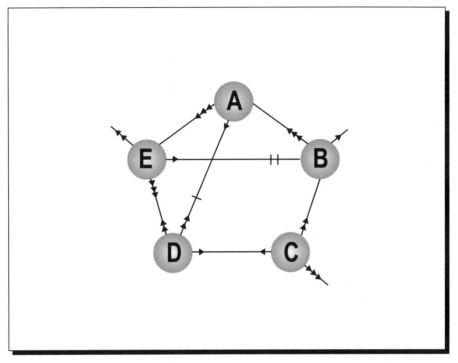

Figure 15 *Directional contribution analysis of a group discussion*

An alternative method is to construct a matrix and use this to record the way contributions are made: see, for example, Table 21.

Table 21 *Directional contribution analysis using a matrix*

To: From:	Ahmed	Betty	Charles	Debbie	Total
Ahmed	–	8	6	14	28
Betty	7	–	3	11	21
Charles	14	2	–	1	17
Debbie	9	7	1	–	17
Total	30	17	10	26	83

Interaction process analysis

R. F. Bales in 1950 invented a system for categorising the contributions of group members in terms such as 'shows solidarity' or 'asks for opinion'. In all, Bales provided 12 categories for contributions to be assigned to. Since then, there have been a number of similar systems produced. The problem with Bales's system, and its derivatives, is that it is difficult for someone to assess where a contribution should go and record it before the next contribution has been made. In my opinion, these more sophisticated systems have limited use for trainers. Perhaps they are manageable with the use of video recording, and the interested reader can find a fuller description of such systems in the book *Techniques of Training* by Leslie Rae.

It is, however, possible to create your own more limited system to suit your specific needs. For example, see Table 22.

Table 22 *Contribution analysis*

	Asks question	Offers answer	Positive contribution	Negative contribution
Alex				
Femi				
Mark				
Steve				
Ursula				

If you are feeding such information back to a group, it is obviously going to be necessary to give examples of what you mean by 'positive' or 'negative' in this context. For example:

'We recorded "I really don't like this kind of exercise" as a negative contribution, and "I think we should go with Alex's idea" as a positive contribution.'

Observation sheets

Apart from the detailed systematic approaches described above, it is also common to record what happened in more general terms. It is certainly not essential to have a prepared observation sheet, but many people find it helpful to have headings from which to work. As an alternative, it is possible to use a timed recording sheet. This gives some discipline to the recording process, which can be tedious, and ensures that observations are made at regular intervals. A sample of each type is given below, but it is often better to design your own to bring out the particular learning points that you want.

OBSERVATION SHEET

Use this sheet to record your observations. On the left hand side of the sheet the time is given in minutes from commencement of the activity. On the right hand side, write down what is happening in the group every 2 minutes. Make notes about who is leading the activity, who is being left out or ignored, who is providing ideas, and so on. Do not take part at all, or voice any suggestions to the group. Your observations will be important in the discussion of how the group operated which will follow the activity.

Time started:

Minutes   **Observations**

0

2

4

6

8

10

12

14

16	
18	
20	
22	
24	
26	
28	
30	

OBSERVATION SHEET

Use this sheet to record your observations. Make notes under the headings given. Do not take part at all, or voice any suggestions to the group. Your observations will be important in the discussion of how the group operated which will follow the activity.

Time started:

The leader: How did the leader organise the team? What did he or she do which was effective or ineffective?

Teamwork: How did the group function together? Make notes about any particular behaviours which contributed to, or inhibited, success.

Decision-making: How were decisions made? Did the leader decide, or the group as a whole?

Record anything else of relevance or interest. Do not forget to note effective behaviours examples as well as ineffective behaviours.

DEALING WITH DIFFICULTIES

First, it is not always possible to 'deal with' difficulties. Some difficulties will mean that the training event will fail to meet its objectives or must even be abandoned altogether. Second, one person's difficulty may be another person's attempt to get things put right. After all, if a learner believes that the training he or she is undertaking is inappropriate, we really should welcome the fact that he or she is going to say something about it even though this may be uncomfortable for us. However, we have to try to overcome difficulties that arise in order to achieve our objectives. When thinking about how the difficulty arose in the first place, always be prepared to examine your own conduct and be ready to learn from any mistakes you have made.

Unresponsive group

Some groups are more responsive than others. Sometimes the presence or absence of just one person makes a tremendous difference to the whole group. The reason the group is not responding must be ascertained before taking any action. Is the group always unresponsive? Or is it just with you? Is it this particular topic? Are they tired? The most unresponsive groups I have encountered were unresponsive because of poor identification of training needs or poor briefing by the line management. However, we normally have to make do with the group we have, so select one or more of the following approaches to try to rectify the situation:

- Change the delivery style. Move from a lesson approach to small-group work, with them reporting back. If the group is unresponsive because of laziness, make them work harder by requiring them to prepare a presentation.

- Give extra breaks.

- If the group has other things on its mind, allow time for these things to be got out of the way. I was once running a course for an organisation whose staff union had just voted for industrial action. The group was preoccupied with this and was being unresponsive. One of them asked if they could have half an hour to discuss the implications of the vote. After that session, the group was back to its normal, responsive, self.

- Break them up into small groups and ask them to come up with answers to the question: 'How do we make this course livelier and more participative?' Be prepared for them to criticise you. Listen to any criticisms or suggestions and respond to them.

- Open the windows.

- Keep a score sheet to record who has contributed and who has not. Speak privately to those who have not participated and ask them why. If it is appropriate, tell learners that success on the programme is partly dependent on participation in the lessons and that their contribution rate is below the standard expected.

- If one or two people are deliberately not participating to make a protest, allow them to discuss it, but tell them that if they are not prepared to join in, they must leave. Be prepared to account for your actions afterwards. If 'throwing people out' becomes a regular event, it may be you that is the problem.

Hostility

If the group is hostile, it is probably because its members do not recognise any value for them in the learning process that they are undertaking. This may be because of poor briefing, or it may be due to factors unconnected with the training itself. The group may be hostile to the concepts you are trying to purvey. For example, if you are trying to conduct a course on a new performance management system and the group believes the system will be used in a punitive fashion, then they will respond negatively to the training. On one occasion I started to deliver a course on appraisal to a group and was trying to sell the idea of appraisal as an indication of the management's concern for the long-term development of its employees. The group informed me that redundancies had been announced the day before and they were waiting to hear who was affected. Again, you have to try to assess the underlying reason for the problem as well as the likely outcome before selecting any of the following:

- Spend longer than you had planned explaining the reasons for the training and how it might benefit them.
- Ask them to tell you why they are angry. Listen carefully. Do not try to defend the indefensible, but acknowledge their feelings. Never say anything critical about the senior management that could be quoted to others out of context. After some of the heat has dissipated, ask them for agreement to carry on.
- Seek common ground. There is nearly always something you can agree with. If there are criticisms directed at you personally, you can always agree that 'I'm sure I could do better.'
- If appropriate, agree with whoever is concerned to pass on complaints in return for their agreement to participate more fully in the course.
- Don't go on the attack. Stand your ground, but avoid criticising them. Remember, you are outnumbered!

Conflict

If there is conflict within the group, again you must try to understand why. Avoid exercises that promote conflict very early in a training course. Assess whether the conflict is a symptom of the group going through its storming stage. Is the conflict merely a resurfacing of old grievances?

- Control outright attacks by intervening. If someone is openly aggressive, tell him or her that this is unacceptable behaviour. If necessary, remove the person concerned from the course.
- Allow other group members to contribute to the reconciliation process when appropriate.
- If two people have fallen out, keep them apart for a while when selecting syndicate groups. Put them together, perhaps a day or two later, to give them the opportunity to mend fences.
- Talk to the protagonists individually. Try not to take sides, but listen to both so that you can achieve an understanding of the reason for the conflict. Sometimes, other group members will be able to explain to you what is going on.
- The conflict may be a symptom of a struggle for leadership or influence in the group. There may be little you can do other than to contain it.

Learners who are upset

Sometimes the learning process can be painful. Feedback, even if intended to be constructive and supportive, may in fact lead to people feeling attacked or hurt. Some of the people you may have on a training course can be extremely blunt and insensitive to one another. The fact that someone is upset may be indicated by a dramatic change in behaviour, such as crying, or by more subtle changes, such as withdrawing from the group. It is not always necessary or advisable to do anything. Many people get upset by a careless word, but are perfectly all right ten minutes later. However, sometimes action is needed. If someone has an emotional outburst and then runs out of the room, the trainer must take action. It is always a good idea to have at least two trainers involved in any training perceived as having a high risk of causing distress, such as training in bereavement counselling. One trainer can stay with the group while the other attempts to help the upset person.

- Allow someone who is upset some time and space to recover his or her composure. Protect him or her from any teasing or insensitive banter.

- Try to have a word with the person in private if you realise that something is wrong but do not know what. Adopt a counselling approach – that is, listening and empathising – but recognise the person's right not to confide in you.

- Remember that someone can be upset because of domestic issues, or because of things happening in the workplace unconnected with training.

- It may be that one person's behaviour is upsetting someone else. Consider whether to have a quiet word with the person causing the distress.

- Someone who is upset because he or she is having trouble keeping up with the learning may need reassurance.

- Someone who is really upset is not going to learn anything. Let him or her leave the course to try to resolve the relevant issues.

Diversity issues

One problem that may be encountered stems from the fact that some people express views that other people find offensive. Although there are many issues that can be involved, sexism and racism are two which are fairly frequently encountered. The trainer must ensure that no person is picked on or teased because of his or her gender, race, nationality, age, sexual orientation, disability, or any other difference. Apart from ethical considerations, failure to ensure equal opportunities within a course could lead to a complaint being made under the relevant legislation.

- Set a good example. Never tell racist, sexist, or potentially offensive jokes.

- If someone else tells such jokes, or makes other offensive remarks, you have a duty to stop him or her.

- Ensure that your handouts and visual aids are not racist or sexist. Training films should be selected with equal opportunities in mind, although sometimes you may have to use what is available.

- Coarse language or vulgar behaviour by some course members may constitute sexual harassment towards others. If *everyone* thinks that the behaviour is acceptable and amusing – and if it is not disrupting the learning process – then it may be all right. But if just one person looks uncomfortable, embarrassed, or distressed, that behaviour must be stopped or moderated.

Time-keeping

Your carefully planned training can be ruined by poor time-keeping. Sometimes this is due to circumstances beyond the individual's control, but more often it is an attitudinal issue.

- Set a good example; always ensure that you are in the room early.

- Start promptly, even if some people have yet to arrive.

- If that is not appropriate, consider asking the group that is there to discuss: 'How should we handle the problem of people arriving late?' Latecomers are asked to join the group and contribute.

- Arrange for coffee to be available up to the proper starting time. Have it removed then so that latecomers have to wait until the first break.

- Is the starting time reasonable? Discuss it with the group and agree a definite time that they all commit to arrive by.

- Ask people who arrive late to stay behind so that you can tell them what they have missed.

Domestic problems

Many courses are ruined by problems associated with the domestic arrangements. Although these are problems that really should not affect the learning process, the fact is that they do. It is not possible to foresee every contingency, but some problems can be avoided by careful planning.

- Always ensure that tea and coffee are available. Check if anyone requires decaffeinated products.

- Always check if anyone has special dietary needs. Offer a vegetarian alternative if lunch is provided.

- Cater for smokers.

- Inform people of car parking arrangements, where the nearest station is, and so forth.

- Know where the nearest telephone, toilet, first-aid point and fire exits are.

- You may need to ban mobile telephones, bleepers, or other interruptions.

- Check accessibility for any learners with mobility problems.

SUMMARY

This section has dealt with a number of different delivery methods, and has also looked at some of the things that go on within groups in the training context. Aspects of delivery that have been discussed include:

- lessons
- group discussions
- running exercises
- group dynamics
- dealing with difficulties.

Trainers must experiment with techniques, and evolve their own style and range of methodologies. Training delivery is, of course, an interactive process. What works well with one group may fall flat the next time. It is not possible to get it right every time, but trainers who are consistently well received have five things in common:

- They prepare thoroughly.

- They respect and care about the learners.
- They are flexible and responsive.
- They let their own personalities come out through the training.
- They enjoy training.

FURTHER READING

Brown, R. (1988) *Group Processes: Dynamics within and between groups*, Oxford, Basil Blackwell

Bales, R. F. (1950) *Interaction Process Analysis: A method for the study of small groups*, Chicago, University of Chicago Press

Havergal, M. and Edmonstone, J. (2003) *The Facilitator's Toolkit*, 2nd edition, Aldershot, Gower

Kolb, D. A., Rubin, I. M. and Osland, J. S. (1995) *Organizational Behavior: An experiential approach*, 6th edition, Englewood Cliffs, NJ, Prentice-Hall

Rae, L. (1995) *Techniques of Training*, 3rd edition, Aldershot, Gower

Rae, L. (1996) *Using Activities in Training and Development*, London, Kogan Page

Schindler-Rainman, E. (1988) *Taking Your Meetings Out of the Doldrums*, Revised edition, San Diego, University Associates

Tuckman B. W. (1965) Development sequences in small groups, in *Psychological Bulletin*, 63, pp384–99

Useful websites

www

http://www.cipd.co.uk/onlineinfodocuments/toolacts/trainact.htm
Training activities from the CIPD

http://www.learningpages.org/ Includes some free material and exercises

http://www.managementhelp.org/grp_skll/theory/theory.htm Many links to material about group development and functioning

ACTIVITIES – CHAPTER 9

1 Leading a group discussion

Introduction

Rather than simply practising discussion-leading with an irrelevant topic, this activity produces both skill practice for the person leading the discussion as well as learning through discussion for the rest of the group.

Aims

To provide skill practice in group discussion-leading and learning about training-related subjects.

Method

Following input and discussion about group discussion-leading, each learner selects one of the following topics. Each must choose a different topic. They then prepare to introduce the topic and conduct a group discussion on it. For large groups, people may work in pairs.

Suggested topics:

- Outdoor training and development
- Training venues
- Distance learning/ E-learning
- Role-play
- Interesting ways to start training courses
- Equal opportunities in training
- New technologies in training
- Should training and personnel be separate functions?

Feedback is then given, together with discussion about points of technique. The assessment sheet shown as Table 23 may be useful for this activity.

Table 23 *Assessment form for leading a group discussion*

Introduction	Comments
Introduced self	
Introduced subject	
Stated the objective of the session	
Control	
Involvement of all participants	
Keeping to subject	
Dealing with aggression and/or disruption	
Answering questions	
Summarising	
Effectiveness of discussion	
Timing	
Overall comments:	

Timing

Although extensive preparation is not necessary, most people like to think about the topic for some time before the activity. So perhaps allow people to prepare overnight. The discussions may be limited to, say, 20 or 30 minutes as required. Feedback and discussion of the process takes a further ten minutes per discussion.

2 Group dynamics exercise

Introduction

A short exercise that is quite memorable.

Aims

To clarify understanding about the effect of goal clarity on group functioning.

Method

One or two people are asked to observe the rest of the group undertake two short group exercises. Any method of recording or observation may be used.

Part 1:

Tell the group that you will give them a question to discuss about group dynamics, and that they will not be allowed to ask any questions. Then show the group the following question, prepared on the flipchart or overhead slide in advance:

> 'What are the most significant considerations regarding group dynamics to be borne in mind when facilitating inter-group interactions using analogous communication as opposed to multilateral logical syntax?'

Part 2:

Show the group the following question, prepared on the flipchart or overhead slide in advance:

> 'What examples can you give of team activities which a teenager might take part in?'

The exercise is concluded by feedback from the observers and discussion about the effect of goal clarity on group dynamics, relating this to training situations.

Timing
Allow five minutes for each question, followed by about 15 minutes' discussion.

3 Dealing with difficulties

Introduction
Most people who have been involved with training will have experienced difficult situations which may or may not have been handled well. These will provide the material for discussion.

Aim
This activity is intended to explore a variety of strategies and discuss their effectiveness.

Method
Ask each member of the group to think of a difficult situation which has arisen in a training context. This can be to do with operational problems – such as a room being double-booked, equipment failure, or fire alarms sounding – emotional, learning or interpersonal problems. It may be that they were central to the problem, or they may have been a witness to the problem. Ask them to make notes about how it was handled and the consequences of the actions taken.

In small groups (three to six people), individuals describe the problems, actions taken and the eventual outcomes. Each problem is to be considered and alternative strategies discussed. At the end of the discussion, the most interesting problem is selected and presented back to the whole group with the syndicate group giving its ideas about how well the problem was handled and any alternative strategies which they think might have worked better.

Timing
Allow five minutes for each syndicate member, followed by about 15 minutes' plenary discussion.

Evaluate

Assessment

CHAPTER 10

*There is nothing so useless as doing efficiently that which should
not be done at all.*

Peter F. Drucker

CHAPTER OBJECTIVES

When you have finished this chapter you should be able to:

- describe the scope, purpose and principles of assessment

- describe a number of methods of assessment

- describe how to give constructive feedback on performance

- list the key points to consider when establishing a record system to comply
  with the Data Protection Act.

OVERVIEW

There has probably never been as much emphasis on the assessment of performance and the
evaluation of training as there is now. Assessment impacts on training in various ways:

- There is assessment to identify learning needs.

- There is assessment in order to certify competence, often linked to qualifications, but
  also linked to performance management.

- There is assessment as part of the selection process in recruitment and also in
  development.

- There is assessment in order to prove the effectiveness or otherwise of the training
  process. This is the area where assessment forms part of the evaluation process and
  is considered further in Chapter 11.

Assessment in training has also been emphasised through government initiatives in the United
Kingdom. The National Vocational Qualification (NVQ) system has assessment at its very
heart. Similarly, the Investors in People award requires organisations to perform assessments
in various areas. In particular, for an organisation to become an Investor in People, it must
evaluate its investment in training and development to assess achievement and improve future
effectiveness. Organisations seeking the award are required to evaluate training at individual,
team and organisational levels. The NVQ system helps organisations to do this, although it is
not the only way to do so.

Unfortunately, the undoubted benefits to be gained from rigorous assessment and evaluation
are offset, to some degree at least, by some of the downsides. Really thorough assessment

and evaluation processes are time-consuming, bureaucratic, and expensive. The line manager likes the idea that the training function must prove its worth. What he or she does not always like is the involvement he or she must give to this process. In many instances, assessments must be carried out by the line management in the workplace. Some assessment systems are perceived as being complex and bureaucratic, and this can result in alienation.

Similarly, any meaningful assessment system has to include assessing some people as falling *below* the standard required. This can bring a schoolroom atmosphere to training which can have a negative impact on the learning process. At the time of writing, the NVQ system in the United Kingdom has attracted strong support in some organisations, but little or none in many others. In 2005, the QCA website stated:

> **'It is estimated that around 12% of the national workforce have attained an NVQ. However, the level of penetration is not uniform across industrial sectors: approximately 75% of certificates were awarded to those in engineering, providing business services and providing goods and services.'**

If an organisation embraces NVQs wholeheartedly, the system produces a framework for assessment which provides both a process for the identification of training needs and for the evaluation of learning. It also provides a comprehensive record system. All this costs money, and unless it is funded adequately, the introduction of NVQs can result in less training activity rather than more.

Initial, formative and summative assessment

One way in which assessments can be classified is to categorise them into one of three types, which are really distinguished by when and why the assessments are performed:

- *Initial assessment* – This is when the level of a learner's existing skill and knowledge is assessed before or at the start of a training programme. Its purpose may be to identify the most suitable programme for the learner, to ensure that particular needs are addressed, and to minimise time spent on aspects in which the learner has already achieved competence. It can also form the basis for evaluation of learning.

- *Formative assessment* is a term used to describe assessment carried out during the learning process. Its main purpose is to gain information about how the learner is progressing in relation to his or her goals. This gives feedback to both the learner and the trainer so that amendments to the learning programme, if required, can be made in good time and so that the learner knows whether he or she is working on the right lines.

- *Summative assessment* is a term used to describe assessment performed to determine whether or not a learner has achieved a standard (passed or failed). It can be used for grading, for evaluation and/or for determining future learning needs.

Some aspects of assessment are dealt with in Chapter 2, which deals with the identification of training needs.

There are a range of methods available to trainers for assessment. Which one to use will depend upon a number of factors, in particular the type of learning involved – memorising, understanding or doing – and the situation in which it is to be applied. It is best to be as direct as possible in assessment, but there are times when indirect methods are needed.

Norm-referenced assessment

When the performance of one person is compared to that of other people, and a judgement is formed on the basis of that comparison, then a norm-referenced evaluation is being made. So if we have trained ten young people as welders, and then put them into a rank order of 'best to worst', we have made a norm-referenced assessment. Suppose that we give the best two welders a grade A, the next best two a grade B, and so on. The worst two get an E. What someone knows about the young welders is simply that some are better than others. Of course, they might all be very poor – some less poor than others. Or they might all be very good – some even better than others, but all capable of holding down a professional welding job. Unless we know what a 'grade A' person can do, and what a 'grade E' person cannot, we cannot tell.

In some instances, norm-referenced assessment is appropriate – especially in situations where no clear criteria of performance exist – but wherever possible in training, criterion-referenced assessment is preferred because it is more meaningful and useful.

Criterion-referenced assessment

This is a term used to describe an assessment against a clear objective standard. In performance terms, it relates directly to behavioural objectives. Can the person do something under specified circumstances to a specified standard or not? In Chapter 4 we looked at the way behavioural objectives were written, and gave the example shown in Table 24.

Table 24 *The components of an objective*

Performance	Conditions	Standards
Mow the lawn	An electric mower in good condition Square or rectangular flat lawn Initial grass length 3cm to 5cm Dry grass	No areas missed No cuttings left Clear straight line pattern No scalping At the rate of 600 square metres per hour

It should now be blindingly obvious how to assess whether learning has been achieved which meets these objectives. We need to get the learner to demonstrate his or her performance, under these conditions, and we need to have an assessor who will be rigorous and consistent in determining whether the criteria for the performance – the standards – have been met.

Even in the straightforward example given, there is the potential for variation. Would one blade of grass left on the lawn disqualify the person? Do we need to measure straightness with a theodolite, or will doing so by eye be good enough? The problem gets worse with objectives, however well defined, which contain inherently subjective elements, or which are hard to observe or quantify. This can lead to an emphasis on the assessment of what is easy to assess rather than what is important. For example, someone delivering a presentation is easy to assess in terms of time management and use of visual aids. He or she is much harder to assess in terms of effectiveness. This does not mean that we should not try to make such assessments, but that we must strive to make such assessments as consistent and meaningful as possible.

For the assessment of observable performance skills – such as lawn-mowing, shirt-making, typing, and bricklaying – criterion-referenced assessments should always be used. For performance concerned with conceptual or interpersonal skills, criterion-referenced assessment is less meaningful, and other methods have to be employed in order to make a judgement about competence. In the NVQ system, the forms of evidence considered can include written documentation, written reports probed by questioning and witness testimony. One of the dangers of assessments of this nature is that they can be influenced by the skill and effort applied to presenting evidence as well as by true competence.

ASSESSMENT METHODS FOR KNOWLEDGE AND UNDERSTANDING

Essays

In the context of assessment, an essay is an answer to a question in the form of continuous writing in which the writer has considerable discretion in terms of how to express himself or herself. Essays can be of indeterminate length, or may be subject to some sort of limit (eg between two and four pages or between 600 and 800 words). Essays can be set as part of a continuous assessment programme, or as part of an examination. There are three purposes for the use of an essay as an assessment device:

- to assess the command of language and the ability to express oneself in writing
- to assess the level of knowledge and understanding of a particular subject
- to assess the ability to interpret facts and to analyse the relationship between them.

The first of these purposes is probably of more concern in educational contexts than in training, although it can be useful in selecting people for employment or promotion if such abilities are required. The second purpose is often seen as part of the learning process as well as assessment. If the learner is required to read up certain information in order to write the essay, it can improve both memorisation of the facts and understanding of them. Lack of understanding is often readily apparent in an essay. The third purpose is frequently of great relevance in a training situation. It is a way of assessing if the information given in the classroom (or wherever) can be used to understand a particular situation.

In an examination, the examiner may set a question as 'open book', which means that the learners can bring books and/or notes in with them. This has the advantage of reducing the pressure to memorise information prior to the examination, and allows the learner to concentrate more on interpretation and analysis. Obviously, an open book examination is not an appropriate means of assessing the retention of factual information but can be useful to check if someone can find relevant information quickly. One problem with open book examinations, and also in essays set as course work, is that some people simply copy out a section of a book or handout material to answer a question. Care must be taken in the setting of the question, and in the instructions to the learners, to ensure that the abilities under study are going to be displayed.

Marking of essays is always subjective to some degree. In order to allow the writer discretion with regard to essay content, it does not make sense to have a very rigid marking scheme.

However, if the essay is primarily designed to test retained knowledge, it is possible to put in a structure which gives points for the inclusion of specific facts (eg the names of key competitors). In most situations where essays are appropriate, marking will have to be a mixture of looking at the *content* and the *interpretation*. It is good practice to let people know the marking balance in advance so that they can apportion their efforts appropriately. For example:

Outline a model of team roles that you are familiar with (40% of marks), and describe how such a model can be used in the selection and training of personnel for a project team (60% of marks).

If you are marking a number of essays, it is helpful to read rapidly through all of them to gain a general idea of the standard. Then read through more carefully, perhaps sorting the essays out into piles of 'good', 'average', and 'poor'. Marking essays is essentially a comparative process. When you start, you have little idea of what you would regard as 'good' or 'poor', but a picture will gradually emerge. The number of piles you end up with may depend on the number of grades or marks you will give. A three-point scheme of 'fail', 'pass' and 'merit' might be adequate. At the other extreme there are percentages – with a theoretical range of zero to 100.

Sometimes learners will ask 'I only got 60 per cent. Where did I lose the other 40 per cent?' To reduce misunderstandings, try to give guidance beforehand about how you mark. For example, say: 'The top mark I have ever given for this topic was 95 per cent. This was a quite exceptional essay which brought in ideas which we hadn't covered in the course, and involved a lot of library research. A mark of around 80 per cent would be very high, and on average only about one in ten people scores at that level. A good mark would be around 60 to 70 per cent. The pass mark is 50 per cent. If you score below this level, I will talk to you about how to improve your marks and let you try again.'

Even then, you will have to explain, and if necessary defend, the marks you have given. Usually, the essay will have a learning purpose as well as an assessment purpose, and the process should, as far as possible, remain a motivating one for the learners.

Projects

Many of the points about essays also apply to the marking of projects. A substantial project may be marked against a number of criteria, and it is even more important than for an essay that people know what these criteria are before they start. For example (as percentages):

Presentation	15
Information-gathering	20
Technical content	30
Analysis	20
Strength of proposals	15

If possible, let people see examples of completed and successful projects before they start. Completing a project can be a powerful learning exercise for someone. A project not only allows you to assess the learner's competence, but also enables the learner to put much of what he or she has learned into practice. The project can help people outside the training function see and appreciate the effects of the learning on performance.

Free response tests

Although essays and projects are very good for looking at some types of learning, they are never a complete examination of somebody's knowledge. When it is important to assess whether someone has achieved a thorough knowledge and understanding of technical subjects, tests can be more useful.

A 'free response' question is one which does not suggest an answer in any way:

What is the capital of Denmark?
A variation on such a straightforward style of question is the 'structured question'. A 'structured question' is one which has an initial, descriptive, introductory statement followed by successive sub-questions which are designed to check comprehension or knowledge. For example:

An engineering company placed an advertisement for an electrician in a local newspaper. They received ten applications – nine from men and one from a woman. The company interviewed four of the men and appointed one of them. The woman decided to complain that she had been subject to discrimination.

a)   What is the most relevant piece of legislation covering this situation?

b)   How long would she have to register a complaint?

c)   Does the burden of proof lie with the company or with the woman?

d)   What would be the maximum amount of compensation she might receive if successful?

e)   Give three arguments that the company might use in its defence against the allegation.

One of the important things to ensure when setting such a question is that you have a clear idea of what would constitute an acceptable or unacceptable answer. For example, would you require a date for part a)? If so, would it not be fairer to amend the question to indicate this? Part e) has some scope for the individual to select from a range of a possible arguments. Think through whether such a question would actually discriminate between people who understood the topic fully and those who were just good at guessing.

Multiple-choice questions

A multiple-choice item consists of a question or incomplete statement followed by a choice of answers. Usually only one of the answers is correct.

What is the capital of France?

a)   Lyons

b)   Marseilles

c)   Paris

d)   Poole

e)   Rennes.

Variations on this format have been developed, such as asking respondents to choose from a selection of combinations. For example:

The following are all locations in Europe:

Barcelona

Cognac

Rome

Oporto

Which of them does our company have offices in?

a)   all of them

b)   Barcelona, Cognac, and Rome

c)   Barcelona, Cognac, and Oporto

d)   Cognac, Rome and Oporto

e)   Barcelona and Oporto only

f)   Barcelona and Cognac only

g)   Barcelona and Rome only

h)   Cognac and Oporto only

i)   Cognac and Rome only

j)   Rome and Oporto only.

The first advantage of structuring the question in this way – rather than asking 'Which of the following does the company have an office in?' – is that only one response is necessary, which simplifies marking. The second advantage is that the respondent is not confused into thinking that he or she only has to choose one of the options.

ASSESSMENT FOR SKILLS

As previously discussed, wherever possible skills should be assessed against clear criteria. Often the technique used will be observation against a written down set of criteria:

- Did the learner check the handbrake before setting off?
- Did the learner smile when greeting the customer?

Such assessments may be made in the workplace or in the learning situation. Certain practical skills can be assessed without observation of the process – simply by checking the end result – but more usually the process will be observed (at least from time to time) so that any errors in the process can be addressed. In many instances, training methods can be adapted as assessment methods. For example, role-plays or case studies can be used for assessment against a checklist or rating scheme:

- Did the learner offer to help the customer with her luggage?
- Did the learner thank the customer for choosing our hotel?
- Did the learner ask if the customer wanted to reserve a table for dinner?

or

How effective was the learner at asking questions that provoked further thought?

Very effective   5   4   3   2   1   *Not effective*

How effective was the learner at establishing rapport with the client?

Very effective   5   4   3   2   1   *Not effective*

In some situations it is useful to get a range of assessments which can include the assessments of:

- the trainer

- the learner

- other learners.

A learner's own assessment (self-assessment) may be compared with that of the trainer, and reasons for differences discussed. When other learners are included in the process (peer assessment), a number of views are being brought into play and the learner may be much more ready to accept the assessments than he or she would the opinion of the trainer. When peer assessment is used, it can be useful to involve everybody in setting the criteria on which the assessments are made and the groundrules for how the assessments will be given. The following section about feedback will be particularly relevant.

GIVING FEEDBACK

There are some situations when assessments are made without feedback, or with limited feedback. For example, if you take an educational qualification examination, you will probably be told only the grade that your efforts were assessed as being worth. In most training situations, you have to do more than this. You have to explain the reasons for giving the assessment that you did and what the learner must do to correct any deficiencies. This process requires tact and sensitivity. There are two outcomes to be particularly avoided:

- telling people that what they are doing is fine when in fact it is not

- crushing them so that they do not wish to continue with the learning.

Personally, I enjoy giving people praise and dislike criticising them (to their faces, at least). I therefore have to discipline myself when giving feedback to include 'points for improvement'. Incidentally, it does not matter what you call such feedback – some people will regard it as criticism. It is important to spend time diminishing this feeling by explaining the purpose of the feedback before the assessment event, and ensuring that certain rules are followed.

In technical training, feedback is often easily given in that there may be a definite right or wrong answer. In 'softer' subjects a degree of subjectivity is present which can lead to differences of opinion and interpretation. Often more than one person can be involved in giving the feedback, and other learners' perceptions may be as good as or better than the trainer's.

Certain rules may apply to the giving of feedback:

- It should always be remembered that giving feedback in front of others is a very special situation. People have a right to their individuality and integrity, and the opportunity to give feedback is not a licence to 'have a go' at someone.

- Offer feedback on what has been observed and try not to read motives into someone's behaviour which might not really be there:
  Say: 'I noticed that you avoided eye contact with the interviewee,'
  rather than 'You seemed to be scared of the interviewee.'

- Try to avoid being judgmental. Terms such as 'poor' or 'bad', or phrases like 'You shouldn't have …' will make you sound like an old-fashioned schoolteacher. Instead, point out what was effective or ineffective. You can, however, say how you *felt*: 'I felt I was being put on the spot when you chose me.'

- Focus on behaviour that can be changed. Telling someone that he tends to turn his back to the audience a lot may be useful; telling him that he would be more imposing if he were taller is not. Some feedback, even if valuable, needs to be given in private rather than in front of a group (eg comments about clothing or grooming).

- Do not overload people with things to work on or change. Concentrate on two or three key aspects for improvement. If someone is given a long list of areas that need improvement, he or she will feel demoralised and will not know where to start.

- Asking people what they thought of their own performance can be useful. It allows them a chance to acknowledge shortcomings for themselves, which may be more comfortable. You can also ask them why they did certain things and not others. Perhaps a learner will say that she chose to experiment, to do things differently from how she normally does. This can then lead on to a useful discussion of the two approaches.

- In many feedback situations mistakes are all right. The whole point of the exercise is to learn from making mistakes. People also learn from observing others' mistakes. For this reason, those who go first are at a disadvantage, and later participants will have had the chance to avoid certain pitfalls. Bear this in mind if assessing performance.

- Comment on the things that were done well. Sometimes people are not aware of their own competence and need to be told. This helps to build confidence and sustain motivation.

One problem with verbal feedback is that it can be quickly forgotten. A useful idea when a video-camera has been used to make a recording, perhaps of a presentation or an interview, is to leave the tape running to record the feedback as well. The learner can then play this back to himself or herself as required. Another option is to give written feedback. If you are making systematic assessments of a skilled performance, it makes sense to use the same format for feedback to the learner. It is also good practice to let people know what they will be assessed on and given feedback on before they perform rather than afterwards. An example of a potential assessment sheet is given as Table 25.

Table 25 *Assessment sheet format*

Introduction		Comments
Introduced self	~	
Introduced subject	~	
Explained the need	~	
Stated the range of the session	~	
Stated the objective of the session	~	
Put the learner at ease	~	
Instruction		
Structure	~	
Interaction with learner	~	
Clarity of instructions	~	
Answering questions	~	
Checking understanding	~	
Effectiveness	~	
Time usage	~	
Comments:		
Pass/Refer/Fail		

RECORDS

Having completed any form of training, you will need to enter the details in some form of recording system. There are many reasons why training records should be kept:

- to monitor the overall level of training activity
- to form the basis for assessing the effectiveness of the training function
- to meet statutory requirements
- to meet the requirements of a quality system
- to build up a record of an individual's learning and achievements
- to provide evidence for CPD submissions
- to provide, or point to, evidence of prior learning for NVQ assessments
- to form a database of what individual trainers or external companies have done
- to link back to the training needs analysis.

All record-keeping is tedious for most of us. But it is absolutely essential so that we can answer legitimate questions such as:

- Has anyone from here ever attended a course at the XYZ centre?

- What training has Sarah Smith been given since she started?

- Has everyone been on the Diversity Awareness programme now?

- Can I have a list of everyone who went on that outdoor development programme last year?

- How do we monitor our training to ensure that it is conducted in accordance with the Equal Opportunities Commission guidelines?

- What was the average overall rating of these three programmes?

- On average, how many days training do managers get here each year?

- Did that chap who had the accident with the grinding wheel attend the regulation training?

- Who ran that brilliant leadership programme four years ago?

- I'm applying for that job at Head Office. Can you give me a list of all the training I've attended since I came here?

Nowadays, there is a lot of readily available software to assist with this. You may already have a system in place, or you might need to set one up from scratch. Some of the providers of training administration software will supply demonstration disks to help you assess their suitability for your needs. You may need special features such as fancy graphics and compatibility with other software – or a simple home-grown spreadsheet might suffice. Otherwise, ask other trainers what they use – and whether they are happy with it. Most training departments would be pleased to help, and would probably let you have a look at their systems.

You may be able to manage without a computerised system, especially in a small organisation. Even if you do use a computerised system, you will also (probably) need a file for each individual where paper records, copies of certificates, handwritten assessments, etc, will be kept. If you decide to become paperless, absolutely everything will need to be entered.

You will also (probably) want to keep a file on each training event. This will contain a copy of the programme, participants, joining instructions, maybe a leaflet from the hotel used, evaluation forms and other information. Although computers are great, for some purposes it is often faster to pull out a folder and look through it rather than search through a complex computer database.

Data protection

Employers are data processors for the purposes of the Data Protection Act (1998) and accordingly must ensure that personal data about employees is obtained and retained only for specific and lawful purposes. In most instances, training records would be regarded as legitimate records for an employer to keep while the person was still in employment. There is no period laid down for how long the records should be kept once someone has left the organisation. In my view, it is sensible to keep the records for a long time because:

- The former employee may return to the organisation in the future.

- There may be instances where a record of training is relevant to a claim for compensation that may arise years after the employee has left – for example, in order to prove that someone had received training in the use of hearing protection, in the safe handling of hazardous chemicals, or to comply with the law regarding the sale of financial services.

- The former employee, or possibly a prospective employer, may contact you to ask for information about his or her training. This is not prohibited by the Data Protection Act, but must only be done with due diligence. (Is the person asking really the person the information is about? Is the asker a bona fide prospective employer with a legitimate reason to ask?) What is termed 'sensitive data' must not be disclosed. See the website of the Information Commissioner for further guidance.

In any event, any records held must be kept secure and confidential. The Employment Practices Code recommends that manual records be kept under lock and key and that computerised records be password-protected. Only people with a legitimate reason to view records should be able to. Again, refer to the website of the Information Commissioner for further guidance.

If the organisation decides that it wishes to dispose of paper or other physical records, this should be done thoroughly (eg by shredding).

Employees have the right to request copies of data that is held about them, and to receive a copy of their personnel file (excluding confidential references about them given by their previous employer) within 40 days. A charge of up to £10 may be levied by the employer for this. Any inaccuracies in data should be remedied as soon as possible. It is therefore important that no potentially embarrassing records are kept, such as:

- 'David is rather dim and took a long time to grasp this.'
- 'The rest of the group took a strong dislike to Anita because of her clumsy interpersonal skills.'
- 'If he could do something about his scruffy appearance, he could make a decent supervisor.'

Note that records such as video recordings are also covered by the Act. Covert monitoring is not normally permitted. So if you record people on, for example, a presentation skills course, delete or destroy the recordings when you have finished with them – or give them to the learners for them to keep if they want, but do not keep copies. If, for instance, you want to keep a recording for use as a training aid – because it was so good or because something interesting happened – get the signed consent of everyone on the recording.

SUMMARY

This chapter has looked at the area of assessment and giving feedback. These are important aspects of the role of the trainer which have been given increasing prominence in recent years.

A number of approaches to assessment have been considered, from straightforward criterion-referenced approaches through less direct methods such as essay-writing.

The art of giving feedback has also been outlined. Although this topic could with fair reason have been included in the chapter on delivery skills, the feedback process has an inherent element of assessment. In essence feedback is a method of communicating assessments, however informally it is done.

Guidance on the keeping of records, and on the obligations of the Data Protection Act, has been given.

FURTHER READING

Buckley, R. and Caple, J. (2004) *The Theory and Practice of Training*, 5th edition, London, Kogan Page

Harrison, R. (1992) *Employee Development*, London, IPM

Mager, R. F. (1990) *Measuring Instructional Results*, 2nd edition, London, Kogan Page

Reid, M. A., Barrington, H. and Kenney, J. (1992) *Training Interventions*, 3rd edition, London, IPM

Reid, M. A., Barrington, H. and Brown, M. (2004) *Human Resource Development – Beyond training interventions*, 7th edition, London, CIPD

Strudwick, L. (2002) *Training for Assessors*, Aldershot, Gower

Useful websites

www.autoscribe.co.uk/training2.shtml Training management software particularly for the scientific community

www.informationcommissioner.gov.uk/ Government site dealing with, among other things, the Data Protection Act

www.rmsuk.com/ Training management software

http://www.qca.org.uk The Qualifications and Curriculum Authority site

http://www.rit.edu/~609www/ch/faculty/effective8.htm Guidance on effective teaching techniques for distance learning. from the Rochester (US) Institute of Technology

http://www.trainingzone.co.uk A large site full of resources – some for sale

ACTIVITIES – CHAPTER 10

1 Feedback demonstration

Introduction

A short but memorable way to put across the importance of giving informative feedback.

Aims

To stress the importance of giving as much information as possible to improve performance.

Method

Divide the group into pairs, seated at tables equipped with a pencil, paper and ruler. One person from each pair is then blindfolded. The blindfolded person is then asked to draw a line exactly 10 centimetres in length. They are allowed ten attempts. After each attempt, the other person measures the line and announces 'right' or 'wrong' to the blindfolded person. To be 'right', the line must be within 2 millimetres of the required 10 centimetres length.

After ten attempts, the rules for feedback change. The person giving feedback may now tell the blindfolded person exactly how long or short the line is. After ten further attempts the blindfolds are removed and the two sets of lines compared.

Timing

About 20 minutes.

2 Giving feedback exercise

Introduction

This is a simple exercise but it has the potential to cause some distress and so needs to be handled with care.

Aims

To give practice in the giving of feedback.

Method

The class is split into two groups. Group 1 sits in a circle and discusses a topic which may be given to them or chosen by them. This lasts for 20 minutes. Each of the people in Group 2 is assigned the responsibility of observing one particular individual in Group 1's discussion. At the end of the 20 minutes, each participant is paired up with his or her observer who then gives feedback to him or her about how he or she behaved in the group discussion. The observers now form the discussion group, and the previous participants now observe. It may be better not to have the same people paired as previously.

Variations

- The participant may be asked not to respond or comment during the feedback.

- The participant may be asked to give his or her reaction to the observer about the quality of the feedback given.

- The class may be divided into three. The third group's role is to observe the feedback process and then give feedback (in turn) on the quality of the process.

- You may introduce rules about whether or not to have an even number of positive and negative observations, no negative observations, and so on.

Timing

Depending on the way the exercise is structured, about an hour.

Evaluation

CHAPTER 11

When I want your opinion I'll give it to you.

Laurence J. Peter

CHAPTER OBJECTIVES

When you have finished this chapter you should be able to:

- **describe the principles, scope and purposes of evaluation**

- **describe the four-stage model of evaluation developed by Donald Kirkpatrick, the CIRO model, and the concept of return on investment as refined by Jack Phillips**

- **employ a range of techniques to conduct evaluations of training.**

INTRODUCTION

Evaluation of training has a far higher profile now than it did in the past. As a profession, training has long promised: 'Give us the resources and we'll transform the business.' Line management is now replying: 'Prove it!' There is a requirement to prove the connection between an investment in training and an improvement in organisational performance. While this is understandable, it creates some difficulties for trainers. The fact is that the benefits of sustained long-term investment in training are usually impossible to calculate accurately. An organisation that has sanctioned a major increase in training expenditure will also be doing other things differently: there will be new managers, new products, and new markets, and so on. However, it is not acceptable to use this as a rationale to justify lack of accountability, and trainers must be able to make some estimation of the impact of their efforts or lose credibility.

There is, therefore, a strong case for attempting to evaluate training, particularly in view of the very large sums of money that are spent on it. However, there are a number of problems associated with the evaluation process which must be considered.

The first difficulty is that, in an ideal world, it would be necessary to measure the exact knowledge and skill of each trainee *before* the start of the training. Without this information it is impossible to assess what has been learned by the end. What someone is capable of doing at the end of the training may primarily reflect what they could do before the training. To separate out the new learning may necessitate a pre-test, which is practicable in some learning situations but becomes much more difficult in other situations. For example, if we were to introduce the pre-testing of senior managers before a course on leadership, we could anticipate some resentment which could actually inhibit learning. With subjects such as assertiveness, someone's ability to display assertive behaviour could be greatly reduced by the anxiety generated in the assessment process. Pre-testing in many situations may also inhibit the process of establishing rapport with the course members, and can result in the learning experience becoming a 'What do I have to do to get through it?' ordeal. Sensitivity must be applied to any assessment process.

Another difficulty is that an ongoing review tends to result in changes to the detail of the programme before it can be thoroughly evaluated. It is not sensible to say to line managers 'I know it's not working, but I want to prove that systematically before changing it.' Sometimes a rigorous evaluation methodology must be sacrificed for the sake of expediency.

A third difficulty is the sheer workload that thorough evaluation can require. Although evaluation is important, is it more important than delivery or design? What would the senior management rather you spent your time on? Many line managers can be convinced of the importance of evaluation, but most would not want to see it taking up more than a small proportion of the trainer's time. They would rather see you training than evaluating. Before approaching an evaluation project, we must ask ourselves:

Why is the evaluation required?

There are various reasons for evaluating training:

- The evaluation enables the effectiveness of an investment in training to be appraised which can help to justify expenditure on future programmes.

- It allows the effectiveness of differing approaches to be compared.

- It provides feedback for the trainers about their performance and methods.

- It enables improvements to be made, either on the next occasion, or if the evaluation is ongoing, as the training proceeds.

- Recording learning achievements can be motivational for learners.

- The evaluation indicates to what extent the objectives have been met and therefore whether any further training needs remain.

What should be evaluated, and when?

A number of different models have been developed by various writers, some of which are described below to answer this question. Knowledge of at least one of these models or frameworks is necessary to help to get to grips with the evaluation process.

KIRKPATRICK'S LEVELS OF EVALUATION

In four articles published in 1959 and 1960 (later consolidated in books) Donald L. Kirkpatrick proposed a model for training evaluation that remains widely accepted today. Alternative models have emerged since, but most are based upon his original framework.

Kirkpatrick's framework for evaluation is by far the most widely used. Indeed, a survey conducted by ASTD found that 67 per cent of the organisations in the USA which evaluated training used it. It has endured because it is simple, logical and useful. There are four levels in Kirkpatrick's framework:

1. *Reaction* – the participants' opinion of the materials, facilities, methods, content, trainers, duration and relevance of the programme. What did the learners think about the training?

2   *Learning* – the skills, knowledge and attitudes learned during the programme. Have the learning objectives been met?

3   *Behaviour* – the change in on-the-job performance which can be attributed to the programme. Did the learning transfer to the job?

4   *Results* – the effect on the organisation of the changes in behaviour, such as cost savings, quality improvements, increases in output. Has the training helped departmental or organisational performance?

Although to some degree these are sequential stages in the process, it is not always necessary to conduct the lower levels of evaluation before conducting the higher levels. However, if the link between training and *results* is to be established, then the effect of the training on *behaviour* would usually be demonstrated by proving that the *learning* was a result of the training. If the learners do not endorse this relationship in their *reactions*, then the effectiveness of the training may not be believed.

CIRO – WARR, BIRD AND RACKHAM

A somewhat different approach was put forward by Warr, Bird and Rackham (1970). This also has four levels, the first letters of which form the acronym CIRO:

- Context
- Input
- Reaction
- Outcome.

Reaction evaluation has the same meaning for both Kirkpatrick and CIRO. Outcome evaluation is subdivided into *immediate, intermediate* and *ultimate*. These correspond well with Kirkpatrick's last three levels. The more interesting areas are therefore in Context evaluation and Input evaluation.

Context evaluation examines the reasons why the training or development event is required. It enables an effective strategy to be agreed upon and prompts the organisation to identify both the learning and financial goals of the strategy. This permits you to determine the level of investment required against the potential returns. In other words, it is a review of the training needs assessment, the learning objectives and an estimation of the likely outcomes and potential costs and benefits of any proposed action.

Input evaluation is to do with looking at the inputs required to deliver a successful programme. This includes the selection of trainers or facilitators, deciding on the time available, determining the relative methods of different training methods, and deciding on materials and budgets. Determining the appropriateness and accuracy of the inputs is essential to the successful delivery of the training or development initiative. In other words, input evaluation is about careful advance consideration of what will be required to make the training intervention likely to succeed. Failing to determine the inputs will make much of the measurement meaningless. It is a useful step between identifying learning needs and the detailed design of an intervention.

JACK PHILLIPS

Basically, Phillips has taken Kirkpatrick's framework for evaluation, and added a fifth level. His modified version of Kirkpatrick's four-level evaluation model, adapted to include measuring for *return on investment* (ROI), looks like this:

Level

1   reaction and planned action

2   learning

3   on-the-job application

4   business results

5   return on investment.

In many ways, level 5 is simply an extension of level 4. That is, Phillips is looking more deeply at the financial implications of the impact of the training process and by analysing this in cost-benefit terms is producing a cash value for the training. This can actually be negative if the training is ineffective or unduly expensive. Much of the importance of the work of Phillips is due to the methods he has devised to calculate ROI for hard-to-measure situations. Even then, he recognises that not everything is measurable. He has added a 'sixth indicator' which he has termed 'intangible benefits'.

'Intangible benefits' refers to situations where the available data is too difficult to convert to monetary values, or would be too costly to convert to monetary values, or where the line management (or others) are satisfied with intangible data. An example could be where there is a noticeable improvement in employee satisfaction following a training intervention – the management may decide that there would be no real point in spending time and money in quantifying the value of this, even though they believe that a value exists.

MEASUREMENT

Different approaches are appropriate for each level of evaluation. I will use Kirkpatrick's framework for his four levels, and then consider Phillips's ROI level.

Kirkpatrick's framework

Level 1 – reaction
Questionnaires, interviews, group discussion, or asking trainees to write a report can be used. Care must be taken with all of these methods. Very often participants have enjoyed a course, even if they learned very little. Factors such as the quality of the lunch provided, or the comfort of the chairs, may influence the assessment of the training given. The other participants may have spoilt a basically sound course, or conversely saved a basically poor course.

Trainees are not always in a position to know immediately whether what they have learned will be useful and it may be best to wait some considerable time before asking for an opinion. Sometimes a trainee may have felt unfairly criticised during a course, and so may 'rubbish' it in retaliation. I also feel that the more training a person receives, the more critical he or she is likely to become. Standards and expectations rise with experience.

Using more than one technique can be helpful to gain a broader picture. Also look out for cues such as an increase or decrease in demand for the training (where there is a choice), or if the line managers start asking for one particular trainer in preference to another.

Level 2 – learning
Tests, examinations, workplace-based assessments of competence, projects, or attitude questionnaires are the key techniques here. Some learning situations are easy to test for (eg typing ability), whereas others necessarily involve a good deal of subjectivity

(eg counselling skills). Yet other learning is so long-term in its nature that direct methods are frankly not appropriate. For example, if a newly appointed supervisor attends a course, then an end test or examination can only tell us if he or she has learned certain terms, concepts or models. It cannot tell us if he or she will become a good supervisor by applying that learning in the work situation.

The processes used at level 2 are often termed *validation*. This term is considered later on in this chapter.

Level 3 – behaviour

This level requires assessment of improved performance on the job. This is easiest in jobs where before-and-after measures can easily be made (eg the speed at which an insurance proposal form can be processed). It becomes more difficult to evaluate performance in jobs which are less prescribed and where measurement is imprecise (eg training design). There may be a time-lag between training and the appearance of indicators of performance improvement. For instance, upon returning to work after attending a course on leadership, a manager may immediately practise what he or she has learned – but the results of this take two or three months to become apparent.

During that time other factors in the situation may have changed – there may have been some new staff recruited, or some redundancies have affected morale. If we were to instigate a long-term assessment process, we would also find it difficult to separate out the influence of day-to-day experience from the influence of the formal training course. It is often impossible to isolate the precise influence of the training. Often the trainer has to resort to indirect performance assessment measures to gauge the influence of the training.

Level 4 – results

Because departmental and organisational results depend upon many people and it is difficult to attribute improvements to the efforts of specific individuals, evaluation at this level often has to be conducted in a more general way. Does the overall training programme result in greater efficiency, profitability, or whatever? If we were to try to look at the impact of a large training programme on a part of a large organisation, we can take an experimental approach. Ideally, we take two identical units. One is given lots of training, the other is given none. Two years later, the difference in performance is apparent!

Obviously such an approach is not one which can be easily advocated. If we really believe that the training is likely to be of value, it is unfair, perhaps even unethical, to withhold it from one of the units in order to conduct an experiment. However, it is sometimes possible to obtain historical information which shows a correlation between spending (or some other measure) on training and organisational performance. Perhaps two similar units within the same organisation can be compared and the relationship between past training activity and other measures can be assessed (eg accident rate, machine downtime, customer complaints).

Reaction evaluation

There are several reasons why we may want to record the reaction of learners to a training event. This is an easy and quick way to achieve some form of evaluation, and although of limited scope, it often gives useful information. Reaction evaluation forms are used:

- to assess the level of satisfaction with the course
- to enable learners to express their views and feelings about the learning

EXAMPLE TRAINING EVALUATION FORM

Please take a few minutes to complete this form and return it to the tutor on completion of your course. Your feedback is important to us, and will be taken into account when running future courses. If you need more room for your comments, please use the back of the form.

Thank you.

Course title:.............................Tutor(s):..................................

Held at:...................................... From:............... To:...............

Your name:.................................

Job title:...................................Company:...............................

ASSESSMENT		COMMENTS
Did you identify your learning objectives before attending the course?	☐Yes ☐No	
Did you discuss these with your manager?	☐Yes ☐No	
To what extent were your objectives met?	☐Fully ☐Substantially ☐To a small extent ☐Not at all	
Do you think the design of the course or the material in it should be changed?	☐Yes, substantially ☐Yes, slightly ☐Don't know ☐No	
How competent was the trainer at delivering this course?	☐Very good ☐Good ☐Satisfactory ☐Below the standard expected	
What is your overall rating of the course?	☐Very good ☐Good ☐Satisfactory ☐Below the standard expected	
Anything you would like to add?		

More comments on the other side of this form ...

- to give feedback to the trainer so that improvements may be made to the training
- to give a quality control mechanism (at level 1)
- to link the training to the workplace
- to assess domestic and resource provision, and possibly to compile evidence for improvements to facilities.

There are many different ways to construct reaction evaluation forms and many ways to use them. When designing a form, try to think through what information you really want to know. It is possible to design a form in a manipulative way, asking people to praise you rather than say what they really think, but there is little point to this. I once co-tutored a course in a company which used a form that had several levels of satisfaction available. If the learners ticked the highest category, that was all they had to do and could leave. If they ticked any other category, they had to explain why. We got very good marks!

When considering what questions to include in the form, remember that there is often no benefit to the individual who is actually completing the form. For him or her, the training is over. It has come and gone, and whatever changes are made thereafter are of only academic interest. If the form is to be completed at the end of the course, perhaps a few minutes before 'home time', the learners will not want to spend a long time filling in an elaborate form and providing in-depth analysis. In my view, therefore, we should make the form quick and simple to complete while at the same time allowing the learners an opportunity to express their views and give us useful feedback.

Sometimes organisations prefer to allow people time to consider their views before completing a reaction evaluation form. A disadvantage of this is that many people forget to complete the form. If they have to be chased, then they are not likely to give the form much consideration anyway. A sample form is illustrated opposite. For fuller discussion of reaction form design, the book by Leslie Rae (1995) is recommended.

The performance grid

A concept developed by Stewart (1986) which can be useful for the evaluation of training at level 3 (behaviour) is the performance grid. This provides an indirect measurement of performance which can be useful as a training need identification aid, but which becomes a strong assessment tool when used before and after training for people whose jobs are not easily measured by direct means.

The concept is based on the notion that two main components of current performance are *motivation* and *skills*. The individual's innate *ability* level is also important, but because that may be considered to be fixed, it may be disregarded for this purpose. Similarly, the *opportunity* to use skills may usually be ignored when comparing performance in a stable situation.

Managers or supervisors are asked to assess the two elements of performance separately for each person and place them in the performance grid shown as Table 26.

Table 26 *The performance grid*

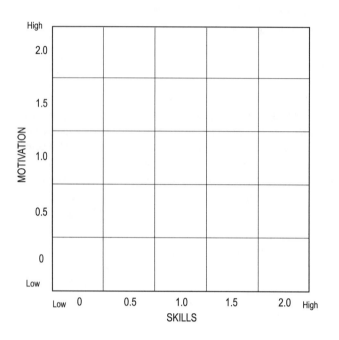

The supervisor or manager is asked to identify the best and worst performer and to place each of them on the grid by reference to their motivation and skills level. A rating of 2 is at the 'Best I've ever known' level, and 0 is at the 'Worst I've ever known' level. This process is repeated – second best/second worst, and so on. Additional guidance may be given by the use of behavioural guidance 'anchors'. An example is given below, but you might prefer to adapt the terms used in an existing system, such as a performance appraisal scheme.

Skills

0	Almost no skills or knowledge required in the job
0.5	Some skills and knowledge, but below the required standard
1	Skills and knowledge match the job requirements
1.5	Skills and knowledge exceed the job requirements
2	Skills and knowledge exceed the job requirements substantially

Motivation

0	No interest in the work whatsoever
0.5	motivation
1	Averagely motivated
1.5	Above-average motivation
2	Very high motivation

A performance rating (PR) can now be calculated:

$$PR = \frac{\text{motivation} + \text{skills}}{2}$$

For convenience, the sum of the scores of the two factors is halved so that staff who are assessed as competent have the score of 1 (they can perform the job to 100 per cent of the requirement for that job).

Once the performance ratings for a group are calculated, they can be plotted on a performance distribution graph. After the training programme, the ratings are made again, and a new graph is drawn. Any changes in the whole group's performance is now demonstrable. This method is particularly useful when a series of inputs is given over a period of time as the cumulative impact of the training is measured.

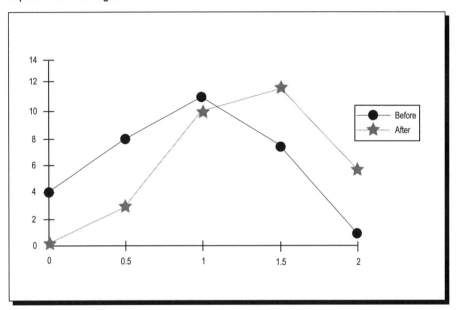

Figure 16 *Performance distribution graph*

Cost-benefit analysis

One of the key ways in which level 4 evaluation can be tackled is to attempt to calculate the benefit of the training in relation to the cost of the training.

Cost-benefit analysis is a way of determining whether a particular solution has produced a greater financial benefit than the cost incurred. As an approach, it can also be used in advance to assess whether a particular training solution is likely to make sense financially. It may be a fundamental requirement of senior managers asked to approve a costly solution.

Steps

1   Determine the time period to which your analysis will apply.

2   Generate a list of cost factors related to the solution.

3   Determine the cost associated with each factor (roughly for an initial analysis; accurately at later stages in a proposal or for evaluation).

4   Total these costs.

5   Determine the financial benefits of the solution.

6   Express the results as a ratio: $\dfrac{\text{Benefits}}{\text{Costs}}$.

Example

Let us consider sending two members of staff on a training course.

Cost of training two existing telesales staff by sending them on a three-day course:

Course fees	£450 x 2	= £900
Travel	£90 x 2	= £180
Hotel	£160 x 2	= £320
Cover by agency temps while away	£300 x 2	= £600
Total		**£2,000**

It is hoped that the training will improve sales performance by 10 per cent.

The estimated value of these increased sales is therefore 10 per cent of the current annual sales of £300,000. That is, £30,000 p.a. *per person.*

The profit margin is 20 per cent, so the value of the benefit is £6,000 (20% x £30,000) per person. For both of them the benefit would be £12,000 p.a.

We might need to know how long this benefit would last. The personnel department tells us that telesales staff stay, on average, 18 months (1½ years).

The benefit is thus £12,000 x 1.5 = **£18,000**.

The cost-benefit calculation is:

$$\frac{\textbf{Benefits}}{\textbf{Costs}} = \frac{£18,000}{£2,000} = £9 \quad \ldots \text{ that is, for every £1 spent, £9 is made}$$

At the proposal stage, this should be amply persuasive. However, the manager of the sales department should also want to ensure that these projected sales actually happen. The calculation must therefore be performed again after a suitable period to check whether the anticipated benefits have actually come through. Suppose that they have. The sales manager, now very enthusiastic about training and evaluation, has six new members of staff. Why not send each of them to a different training provider, and calculate the cost-benefit ratio in each case? The only pitfall here is that the results may reflect the natural talent of the individual concerned rather than the skill of the training provider. However, as an approach it is basically sound and can be used in many types of evaluation to compare different options.

The 'increased sales' scenario is comparatively easy to measure. In other situations, more complex measurements must be attempted. Costing can be a very complicated exercise indeed, but a simple approach is often enough to enable judgements to be made in the training situation. Firstly, let us consider how to cost training in two types of training situation:

- on-the-job training

- off-the-job training.

On-the-job training is the term applied to learning while working within the normal work area and actually doing the job. A trainee gardener who is pruning roses in a public park and who is under guidance from an experienced gardener is thus receiving on-the-job training. Similarly, trainee shop assistants dealing with real customers or trainee machinists making 'real' products are receiving on-the-job training.

Off-the-job training is the term applied to classroom training, or to training outside working hours using machinery that is not 'live'. Instead of real customers, perhaps the trainees are taking it in turns to role-play customers.

The key costs in on-the-job training are:

- the trainees' wages and other employment costs
- the loss of production/sales/etc
- any additional payment made to the instructor
- the value of any excess materials used
- the value of any excess damage or spoilage.

The key costs in off-the-job training are:

- the trainees' wages and other employment costs
- the trainers' wages and other employment costs
- the value of the materials used
- depreciation of equipment
- overheads.

Suppose we look at a fictitious example of how these costings can be used as an evaluation measure. Let us assume that it currently takes 20 weeks for someone to learn how to perform a production job. The trainee costs the company £200 a week to employ. During the 20 weeks the trainee is an additional person to the regular operator, and so all the employment costs must be included. The operator is paid an 'instructor's allowance' of £10 per week for the period. At the beginning, the output is considerably reduced because the operator has to explain everything slowly, and the machine speed is purposely reduced. Also, more of the raw materials are spoiled than would normally be the case. Fortunately (as in real life), we can get the value of these items from the management accountant. The costs look like this:

The trainees' wages and other employment costs	£200 x 20 = £4,000
The loss of production	£4,000
The additional payment made to the instructor	£10 x 20 = £200
The value of any excess materials used	£800
Total	**£9,000**

The training department then restructures the training to make it *off-the-job*. It decides to take in six trainees at a time. Because the training is full-time, the trainees become fully proficient in only 10 weeks. The trainer's salary and employment costs for that ten weeks amount to £5,000. Materials consumed amount to £1,500. The machinery used depreciates by £2,500, and the overheads amount to £7,000 – mainly due to the cost of the room used. The sums now look like this:

The trainees' wages and other employment costs	£200 x 10 x 6 = £12,000
The trainer's wages and other employment costs	£5,000
The value of the materials used	£1,500
Depreciation of equipment	£2,500
Overheads	£7,000
Total	**£27,000**

However, this is the cost of training six people, so the cost per head is only £4,500 compared with the on-the-job system cost of £9,000 per head. Obviously, this is a simplified example. In many instances the various cost elements can be difficult to quantify, but usually a reasonable estimate can be obtained. Also note how many of the costs of off-the-job training continue when no training is being performed. If the training facilities are only used once a year, the sums should really include the depreciation and overheads for the full year when calculating the costs.

This approach can be used in many situations to measure whether changes to the training arrangements are paying off, and therefore, whether to continue with them or seek out more cost-effective solutions. An extended discussion of costing can be found in Harrison's book (1992).

Validation

There are differences of opinion as to what this term actually means. I stated before that the processes at level 2 in Kirkpatrick's system were sometimes termed 'validation'. This usage is supported by many writers. For example, Anderson (1993) states:

> **'the emphasis on evaluation is on value; the emphasis on validation is meeting specific objectives.'**

Evaluation is sometimes defined as being different and separate from validation. In my view, validation is a form of evaluation. It is concerned with answering the question 'Did the training meet its objectives?' (level 2). This is not the same question as 'Was this training worthwhile in business terms?' (level 4), or 'Are people using this learning on the job?' (level 3). To complicate matters further, some trainers use the term to describe reaction evaluation (level 1). For example, Rae (1995) talks at length about 'end-of-course validation questionnaires'. Others use the term to consider whether the objectives of the training were the right ones (therefore valid) in the first place. The term is also used by many people as a synonym for 'accreditation by an external body'.

It is not actually necessary to use the term at all, and if it causes confusion, perhaps it is best avoided.

RETURN ON INVESTMENT

Jack Phillips has published extensively on the process of calculating ROI. We have already looked at cost-benefit (or benefit-cost as Phillips says) calculations. An alternative formula is the one he gives for ROI:

$$\text{ROI} = \frac{\text{Net training benefits}}{\text{Training costs}} \times 100 \text{ (thus as a percentage)}$$

Net training benefits are training benefits minus training costs. Essentially, this is an alternative way of expressing the impact using the same figures as you would for cost-benefit analysis.

Phillips deals with data collection and how to cost data in great depth. He distinguishes between hard data such as

- items produced
- forms processed
- error rates
- tasks completed

and soft data such as

- job satisfaction
- performance appraisal ratings
- number of suggestions implemented
- violation of safety rules.

He gives techniques for converting soft data into hard data, and assigning a monetary value to it. For example, if a restaurant chain monitors the number of complaints it receives before and after training, it may find that the number of complaints is down by 20 per cent. However, there may be other initiatives in place, such as improved raw food quality, which might have also had a positive impact. The line managers are therefore asked to estimate how much of the improvement is due to training. Let us suppose they agree that about 50 per cent is due to training.

We can then ask them how confident they are about that estimate. The line managers feel 75 per cent confident about that estimation. We can then say that the reduction of complaints attributable to training is 20% x 0.50 x 0.75 = 7.5%.

Now, if the line managers or accountants think that each 1 per cent reduction in complaints is worth £5,000 to the company (taking into account refunds, lost repeat business, lost recommendations, etc), then the benefit attributable to training is 7.5 x £5,000 – which is £37,500. ROI can now be calculated.

Note that this process has been deliberately cautious. If the training function tries to take the full credit for all the improvements, it is likely to be subject to attack or even ridicule. Note also that in this approach it is *not* the training function that is making these estimations – it is the line managers (or it can sometimes be the employees). Establishing and maintaining credibility is vital when presenting such data and calculations.

SUMMARY

The topic of training evaluation has been explored with particular emphasis on the structure put forward by Kirkpatrick. It is one of the most widely-used frameworks and is relatively straightforward. An alternative system, CIRO, devised by Warr, Bird and Rackham, has been discussed briefly, and the work of Jack Phillips on return on investment (ROI) has been introduced. Several techniques for evaluation have been described.

There are numerous other writers on evaluation who have not been covered here. For example, the contributions of Whitelaw (1972) and Hamblin (1974), which are discussed in some detail by Reid, Barrington and Kenney (1992). Even more models are described in the book by Tamkin, Yarnall and Kerrin (2002).

FURTHER READING

Anderson, A. H. (1993) *Successful Training Practice: A manager's guide to personnel development*, Oxford, Blackwell

Garbutt, D. (1969) *Training Costs*, London, Gee

Jackson, T. (1989) *Evaluation: Relating training to business performance*, London, Kogan Page

Kirkpatrick, D. L. and Kirkpatrick, J. D. (2005) *Evaluating Training Programs: The four levels*, 3rd edition, San Francisco, Berrett-Koehler

Phillips, J. J. and Stone, R. D. (2002) *How to Measure Training Results*, New York, McGraw Hill

Rae, L. (1995) *Techniques of Training*, 3rd edition, Aldershot, Gower

Reid, M. A., Barrington, H. and Kenney, J. (1992) *Training Interventions*, 3rd edition, London, IPM

Sanderson, G. (1995) Objectives and evaluation, in Truelove, S. (ed.) *The Handbook of Training and Development*, Oxford, Blackwell

Tamkin, P., Yarnall, J. and Kerrin, M. (2002) *Kirkpatrick and Beyond: A review of models of training evaluation*, Brighton, Institute for Employment Studies

Useful websites

www.astd.org American Society for Training and Development – some resources openly available: it has an ROI network

www.businessballs.com Free resources and articles, some on evaluation

www.cipd.co.uk The CIPD website

ACTIVITIES – CHAPTER 11

1 Evaluation exercise A

Introduction

This is an evaluation process design exercise that can be used as a follow-up activity to the programme design exercise given in Chapter 5.

Aims

To allow practice in the application of evaluation principles and discussion of issues arising.

Method

Divide the class into small groups. Ask them to examine an existing training programme for which there is no real evaluation system in existence. Their task is to produce an evaluation plan showing how evaluation would be carried out at each of Kirkpatrick's four levels. This can then be presented to the whole class and discussed. An alternative is to use the programme design produced in accordance with the instructions in Exercise 1 at the end of Chapter 5.

It will be necessary to clarify and agree the degree of detail required in the plan. Decide whether 'a multiple-choice' test is an adequate description, or whether 'a multiple-choice test consisting of 20 questions will be devised covering the following areas ...' is required.

Timing

Depending on the degree of detail required, between 45 minutes and 2 hours.

2 Evaluation exercise B

Introduction

This is a detailed evaluation design exercise that can be used as a follow-up activity to the evaluation design exercise given above.

Aims

To allow practice in the application of detailed evaluation techniques and discussion of issues arising.

Method

Divide the class into small groups. Ask them to produce a finished test as proposed in the previous exercise. This can then be presented to the whole class and discussed. An alternative is to ask for a *customised reaction evaluation form* to be produced.

Timing

Depending on the complexity of the task, between 30 minutes and 1 hour.

Psychometric testing

CHAPTER 12

The difference between one man and another is not mere ability – it is energy.

Thomas Arnold

CHAPTER OBJECTIVES

When you have finished this chapter you should be able to:

- **define the main types of psychometric test**

- **explain the ways in which psychometric tests can be useful in selection and development.**

Psychometric (literally, 'mind measurement') tests have long been used in the field of human resource management. This has been generally to aid the process of selection for employment. They can, however, also be used for identifying candidates for training programmes. This can help to reduce the chances that people will attempt to undertake programmes that are beyond their ability level. More recently, the publishers of tests have started to offer products that have application in the context of feedback about personal qualities at work that in turn can help to identify development needs. The same products can subsequently be used to measure whether developmental changes have taken place.

HISTORY

The need for an objective measure of ability was first noted in the educational/clinical field. In France, at the turn of the twentieth century, Alfred Binet developed tests to clarify which children had learning difficulties – and who would not be able to benefit from conventional schooling. The tests used were later developed into measures for use with adults. The concept of 'mental age' came into being. This was compared with chronological age, and the term Intelligence Quotient (IQ) was coined:

$$IQ = \frac{\textbf{Mental age}}{\textbf{Chronological age}} \times \textbf{100} \quad \text{(thus representing a percentage)}$$

By definition, it was the *average* IQ that therefore was 100 (per cent). This concept was very useful in the clinical field. Over the years more tests were developed to measure IQ, among adults as well as children, and eventually the idea of doing this as an aid to selection for employment was born.

Nowadays, the idea of measuring IQ is considered inappropriate for selection because people differ in their abilities to function in a variety of mental areas, and a general IQ score can be misleading. IQ tests measure general ability, and not the ability to do a specific job. Accordingly, modern tests used in non-clinical situations do not attempt to measure IQ, but instead measure aptitudes in clearly defined mental skills which are considered relevant to a particular job.

APTITUDE TESTS

Aptitude (looking at potential) and ability tests (looking at current capability) measure performance in areas such as numerical reasoning, verbal reasoning, or working with diagrams. They are usually targeted at a particular level of ability such as graduate-level or apprentice-level. They are usually easy to administer, score and interpret. They are used extensively for selection purposes. Because they are designed to measure ability as distinct from acquired knowledge, they are not useful as an evaluation measure in a training context. Some tests have been developed which look at very specific areas – such as aptitude for computer programming.

One of the issues to be considered with the use of aptitude tests is that of administration. The more accurate tests use a lot of questions – or items – but therefore take a long time to administer. Shorter tests are quicker, but may be less accurate. With multiple-choice tests, as most are, some people will get some questions correct by chance – but the longer the test is, the less this chance effect will influence the result. To some extent this problem is reduced by administering a number (or 'battery') of tests.

Another consideration is that some people will have taken a particular test more than once, and therefore improve their results through practice. For this reason, many tests are published in a variety of versions – and some large organisations have their own tests developed to be sure that there is no such influence. Anyone trained to administer proper psychometric tests to the British Psychological Society level A is thoroughly drilled with the importance of keeping test materials utterly secure – otherwise, they quickly become devalued.

Discrimination

One of the major advantages of using an aptitude test in a selection procedure (eg to select entrants for a training scheme) is that it can give a degree of objectivity to the process.

For example, a line manager may have a prejudice against employing females in his department. He has learned not to articulate this prejudice because he (quite rightly) gets a lot of pressure and censure from the HR department. So he may discriminate more subtly by making evaluations of ability following interviews which favour male applicants. Even if you suspect this, it can be difficult to prove without evidence. Aptitude tests can provide this evidence. If a female candidate scores much more highly than all the male candidates, the manager can no longer use his judgement as a reason to prefer a male candidate.

Conversely, an applicant who does poorly on tests, and who is rejected purely on the grounds of having lower ability than required, may still complain if he or she believes that the reason for rejection was discrimination. Keeping the test scores gives the organisation evidence to support its decision and to defend its actions.

One problem area is when candidates using English as a second language take tests – particularly those with a large verbal component. They are obviously disadvantaged, but it is simply not possible to say by how much. What you can say is that the score they get represents an indication of the minimum level of their ability, and that their true ability level would probably be somewhat higher.

Advanced tests

As has already been mentioned, there are many tests which look at verbal and numerical reasoning – for verbal and/or numerical ability can be important in many jobs. Simple verbal ability tests may look at knowledge of vocabulary and the meanings of words. For example:

Rain is to summer as ……….….. is to winter.

or

Which is the odd word out?

Cheerful   Happy   Satisfied   Jolly

Whereas such tests can give a quick and useful indication of ability (of course with many such items in a timed test), they do not really reflect the kind of problem-solving and interpretation which many professional jobs require. Below is part of a sample test which requires the person taking it to read a complex piece of written material and then answer questions designed to find out whether or not true comprehension has been reached.

EXAMPLE COMPREHENSION TEST EXTRACT

The following is an extract (six out of 15 questions) from the Verbal Practice Test which may be completed online at the website of Knight Chapman Psychological Ltd, to whom copyright belongs. This is reproduced here with their kind permission.

Financial Regulations

Compliance with the Financial Regulations is compulsory for all staff employed by the College. A member of staff who fails to comply with the Financial Regulations may be subject to disciplinary action under the College's disciplinary policy as set out in the Staff Handbook. Any such breach will be notified to the Audit Committee and thence to Council.

It is the responsibility of Heads of Departments to ensure that their staff are made aware of the existence and content of the College's Financial Regulations and that they have access to the document via the Finance Office web pages or hard copy.

1 The College Council is not notified directly of any breach of the Financial Regulations.
  ○ *True*   ○ *False*   ○ *Insufficient information*

2 The Financial Regulations are set out in the Staff Handbook.
  ○ *True*   ○ *False*   ○ *Insufficient information*

3 The Audit Committee is responsible for the content of the College's Financial Regulations.
  ○ *True*   ○ *False*   ○ *Insufficient information*

Marketing Policy

We recognise that some parents buy mobile phones to give to their children. For this reason we have written and issued personal security guides to customers and have also signed up to the industry's Code of Practice to ensure that young people who use our mobile phones are protected from adult material.

We have now restricted access to sites that are suitable for over-18s only. If a customer wants to access these sites, they must prove their age first. This must be done in writing with the user providing documentary proof of date of birth.

Restricted access also applies to unmoderated chat rooms where young people may be particularly vulnerable.

> 4 Mobile phone users don't receive a personal security guide.
> ○ True ○ False ○ Insufficient information
> 5 Users must notify the company orally of their date of birth.
> ○ True ○ False ○ Insufficient information
> 6 Under-18s are not given access to chat rooms.
> ○ True ○ False ○ Insufficient information

Similarly, simple numerical ability tests may contain calculations which must be performed, or numerical sequences which must be determined. For example:

Insert the next number in the sequence:

4   5   7   11   19 .....

(The answer is 35 – the sequence increases by 1, 2, 4, 8 ... and the next increase is therefore by 16.)

Again, such tests can give a quick and useful indication of ability but do not really reflect the kind of interpretation of numbers which many professional jobs require. The extract below contains part of a sample test which requires the person taking it to select the right figures to perform calculations on and also to demonstrate that he or she understands terms such as 'ratio' and can interpret graphically presented data. Note that the test is taken using a calculator – reflecting the reality of everyday working life.

EXAMPLE NUMERICAL TEST EXTRACT

The following is an extract (eight out of 16 questions) from the Numerical Practice Test which may be completed online at the website of Knight Chapman Psychological Ltd to whom copyright belongs. This is reproduced here with their kind permission.

An office furniture company supplied a customer called AMR Corporation with desks, cupboards and chairs in the ratio 8 : 6 : 2 . The total value of the sale was £6,700.

1 How much did the cupboards cost?
  ○ £1,116.67   ○ £2,512.50   ○ £3,350   ○ £300   ○£837.50
2 What percentage of the total amount was the price of the chairs?
  ○ 37.5%   ○ 45%   ○ 25.5%   ○ 12.5%   ○ 50.0%
3 Another company spent a total of £3,250 on similar furniture, but the ratios were the same as those of AMR Corporation. What was the difference between the two companies in the amounts paid for cupboards?
  ○ £1,293.75   ○ £3,450   ○ £1,725   ○ £431.25   ○ Insufficient data
4 Richmond Oil purchased desks and chairs in the ratio 2 : 5. If Vacey Ltd's chairs cost half as much as the chairs Richmond Oil bought, how much did the desks at Richmond Oil cost?
  ○ £1,340   ○ £8,040   ○ £6,700   ○ £5,360   ○ Insufficient data

Jennifer and Jonathan sell subscriptions to a lifestyle magazine directly to the public. The magazine pays them each a basic hourly rate plus a commission for 10 or more subscriptions sold in a single day:

	Basic pay	Commission
Jennifer	£10 per hour	£1.10 for each subscription above 9 sold in a day
Jonathan	£8 per hour	90p for each subscription above 9 sold in a day

5 Between 9am and 10am on a particular day Jennifer sells 3 subscriptions and Jonathan sells 5 subscriptions. How much is their combined pay for the hour?

   ○ £74.00   ○ £40.00   ○ £70.20   ○ £18.00   ○ £70.00

6 If the company has paid £162.80 for Jennifer and Jonathan to work for 8 hours, and Jennifer has sold 22 subscriptions, how many subscriptions has Jonathan sold?

   ○ 41   ○ 14   ○ 11   ○ 33   ○ Insufficient data

7 If Jonathan is paid £377.80 for working 38 hours this week, how many subscriptions has he sold?

   ○ 82   ○ 83   ○ 80   ○ 91   ○ Insufficient data

8 If Jennifer sells 12 subscriptions in an hour and Jonathan sells 17 subscriptions during that same hour, how much does the company pay them in total wages per subscription sold that day?

   ○ 91p   ○ £1.61   ○ £1.02   ○ 98p   ○ Insufficient data

PERSONALITY QUESTIONNAIRES

The concept of personality is complex, and actually a quite difficult one to define. Personality is not the same thing as motivation, culture or attitude. Nor is it the same thing as ability – although all these things interact. A search on the Internet will produce many different definitions of the term 'personality', and psychologists do not all use the term in exactly the same way.

However, the following is a typical definition (which I have put together from a few found through the Internet) and will suffice for our purposes here. We can define personality as

> **'The relatively stable and enduring characteristics of an individual which distinguish him or her from other people and which may be used as predictors of behaviour.'**

Note that this definition says 'relatively stable and enduring'. How we behave is influenced by factors such as stress, fatigue, mood and experiences. But when we think of someone that we know well, we can usually use descriptive words such as 'calm', 'excitable', 'aggressive', 'warm' or 'distant' to illustrate that person's usual demeanour and likely behaviour. Indeed, if someone acts in a way which is very unlike his or her normal behaviour, we say something like:

- 'He acted out of character.'
- 'It's not like her to be late.'
- 'He wasn't himself.'
- 'She wasn't the person I know.'

For most of us most of the time, people who have a good knowledge of our personalities would be able to predict our behaviour fairly well (but not precisely) in a variety of situations. They will do this on the basis of their knowledge of how we have behaved in the past. But, of course, they will not always know how we felt about our behaviour, how close we were to behaving differently, or whether we have a different pattern of behaviour in private situations.

Personality questionnaires are an attempt to shortcut the process of getting to know someone very well. They endeavour to analyse personality on the basis of the individual's answers to questions. These questions normally ask them to assess how they usually behave in certain situations, or what they would rather do when they have a choice, or how they consider themselves to be. For example:

I consider myself to worry less than average. **True / False**

The questionnaires available vary considerably in style and in the underlying theoretical concepts about personality that they are based on. For example, one of the best-known models of personality is that developed by Raymond Cattell. In 1949 Cattell published research which asserted that human personality traits could be summarised by 16 personality factors (PF) or main traits. As examples, these include 'Openness to change', 'Perfectionism' and 'Privateness'. Everybody has some degree of every trait, according to Cattell, and the key to assessment is determining where on the continuum an individual falls. The personality questionnaire based on this model is called the 16PF.

Another well known instrument is the MBTI (Myers-Briggs Type Indicator). It was developed by Isabel Briggs Myers and her mother Katharine C. Briggs on the basis of Carl Gustav Jung's research in personality. The MBTI is a four-factor model that looks mainly at how we deal with the world around us. It has the following dimensions:

- *Extraversion–Introversion* – do people prefer to focus their attention and get their energy from outside themselves, or from their inner world of ideas and experiences?
- *Sensing–Intuition* – do people prefer to take in information using their five senses, or to use their 'intuiting' function which shows meanings, relationships and possibilities beyond the information from the five senses?
- *Thinking–Feeling* – do people prefer to make decisions based on logical analysis or guided by concern for their impact on others?
- *Judging–Perceiving* – do people prefer to deal with the outer world in a planned orderly way, or in a flexible spontaneous way (using sensing or intuition)?

Questionnaires such as these are difficult to score and interpret, and require some skill to give feedback to people without upsetting them. Increasingly, test publishers are producing, at a cost, software which produces written reports automatically. Whether these questionnaires are very useful in the training context is a matter of opinion. There are some aspects of personality that can be considered fundamental to us and impossible to change – particularly so for mature adults.

Other aspects do change with time and experience. For example, you may have known someone who was once fairly shy and lacking in confidence but who got a job which, over time, transformed him or her into a more outgoing and confident person. These effects do not happen rapidly, and personality questionnaires may not always be an appropriate way of measuring such changes. Nonetheless, they can give information on the effectiveness or otherwise of long-term development programmes, particularly those concerned with interpersonal skills, assertive behaviour and stress management.

Personality questionnaires may also give information about whether someone is likely to enjoy working with detail or not, will tolerate chaos well, or needs challenge in a job. Does this person seek the limelight? Is he or she more comfortable in a role with clear boundaries, or would a risky, less structured role be more satisfying? Again, such information can be helpful in determining who should undergo training.

Some of the most easily used and interpreted tests, such as Saville and Holdsworth's (SHL's) Occupational Personality Questionnaire (OPQ) and Knight Chapman Psychological's (KCP's) Managerial and Professional Profiler (MAPP) have been developed specifically for the occupational market. Some of the other personality questionnaires have been based on clinical psychology needs and their use within occupational settings is less easy, and is difficult to justify. Below are some questions from part of a personality questionnaire.

EXAMPLE PERSONALITY QUESTIONNAIRE EXTRACT

The following statements are 20 (out of 70) requiring responses taken from the Roberts Practice Personality Questionnaire. They are used with the express permission of Knight Chapman Psychological Ltd, to whom copyright belongs, and may not be reproduced without such authorisation.

Respond to these statements by selecting from the range of responses:
- Strongly agree
- Agree
- Neither agree nor disagree – in between
- Disagree
- Strongly disagree

1   'I like to be actively involved in what the team is doing.'

2   'I prefer work that I can do on my own.'

3   'I like to get the details right.'

4   'Others have described my approach to work as disorganised.'

5   'I always persevere with a job to its completion.'

6   'After a day's work, I like to sit and do nothing.'

7   'I am quite thick-skinned.'

8   'Sometimes I feel that teamwork gets in the way of results.'

9   'I like to surround myself with lots of people.'

10   'As long as I get most of a task right, I don't worry about little mistakes.'

11	'I make sure I have everything I need before I start on a job.'
12	'I find it difficult to keep going with jobs after something has gone wrong.'
13	'I enjoy work that keeps me active.'
14	'I am very sensitive about the way people behave towards me.'
15	'I prefer co-operation to competition within a team.'
16	'I might be described as a loner.'
17	'I enjoy work that has to be done precisely.'
18	'Though I may be disorganised, I get there in the end.'
19	'Once I get started on a task, nothing can distract me.'
20	'Sometimes I feel too tired to do anything.'

OTHER INSTRUMENTS

Interest inventories

These ask about career and lifestyle preferences. They are often used in career counselling, and nowadays in outplacement. They are usually easy to use. One readily available instrument is the Careers Orientation Inventory available in *Career Anchors* by Edgar Schein (1990) and distributed by Pfeiffer and Company (see *Useful websites*).

Feedback instruments

In response to the trend to provide managers with feedback from the people they work with, a number of companies have developed instruments designed to produce information which can be useful when comparing the individual's self-perception with that of colleagues, bosses, or subordinates. This is sometimes referred to as 360-degree feedback. One such instrument is the Personal Feedback Questionnaire (PFQ) produced by Knight Chapman Psychological. This provides measurements of the following dimensions:

Managing relationships

- Leadership
- Team membership
- Influencing
- Interpersonal awareness
- Development of others

Managing self

- Results orientation
- Energy and determination
- Resilience
- Structure
- Flexibility

Managing operations

- Strategic awareness
- Creativity
- Problem-solving
- Decision-making
- Change management.

AVAILABILITY

For many years access to tests has been controlled so that:

- Tests do not circulate freely and thereby lose their validity as people practise and rehearse them.

- Consistent usage is assured, and standards do not vary from one administration to the next.

- Damage that can be caused by misuse is avoided.

- Test developers can be sure of recouping their outlay because photocopying and plagiarism is discouraged.

All test providers have a registration system. In recent years, the British Psychological Society has developed a generic system to standardise the approach to this, but some publishers still insist that you train with them to be able to buy their products. The BPS scheme is:

- Level A

  This is available after a course that assesses the delegate's competence in a number of core areas and which gives access to most ability tests.

- Level B

  This follows on from level A and consists of further training and competence assessment. Level B gives access to a specific substantive personality questionnaire (intermediate level) or to a wide range (full).

See the *Useful websites* list at the end of this chapter to find test publishers.

Online testing

A major development over the past few years has been in the use of online testing. It is still (usually) very necessary to have a trained administrator on hand to ensure that there is no 'cheating', and there has to be an Internet-connected computer for every person at any one time, but the advantage is that the tests or questionnaires can be scored and analysed virtually instantly. The results can then be emailed back to the organisation very quickly.

Unfortunately, this has also led to an explosion of poorly-developed and unsound instruments being made available. Sometimes the producers use such phrases as 'based on Jung-Myers-

Briggs typology' to imply that you are using the well-known and thoroughly researched test when in fact you are using an amateur version. Take great care – especially if the instrument is from an unknown source.

Indeed, there are some long-established publishers whose standards are much lower than required by the BPS. They sell personality tests of doubtful validity and allow people to purchase and use them after attending a one-day course. Their sales personnel usually do not have a grounding in either psychology or human resources. One technique that they employ is to approach a senior person in the organisation with the offer of a free personality profile. The Chief Executive, for instance, agrees to this and is given feedback which flatters his or her ego and is convinced that this is a wonderful instrument.

The use of online testing is still developing. Some interest and personality questionnaires may be completed without close supervision, and remote supervision using cameras may be employed to prevent cheating. Advanced techniques such as identification and authentication using thumbprint or retinal eye-pattern recognition may also extend the use of online testing. At the present time, though, there are still many situations where traditional paper-and-pencil testing is more appropriate.

SUMMARY

This chapter has attempted to give an introduction to the main categories of psychometric tests, and other instruments, and relate these to the uses which members of the training profession may find for them.

Samples of advanced verbal and numerical tests have been given, as has a sample section of a personality questionnaire. An outline of the requirements for training and certification in the use of these instruments has been given, and there has been an introduction to the developing practice of online testing.

FURTHER READING

Rust, J. and Golombok, S. (1999) *Modern Psychometrics: The science of psychological assessment*, 2nd edition, London, Taylor & Francis

Schein, E. H. (1990) *Career Anchors: Discovering your real values*, San Diego, Pfeiffer

Shavick, A. (2005) *Practice Psychometric Tests: How to familiarise yourself with genuine recruitment tests and get the job you want*, Oxford, How To Books

Useful websites (see also Appendix 3)

www

http://allpsych.com/personalitysynopsis A site which gives an overview of personality theories

www.ase-solutions.co.uk The site of ASE, a test publisher

www.bps.org.uk/ The site of the British Psychological Society

www.kcpltd.com The website of Knight Chapman Psychological Ltd, test publishers, with some practice tests

www.morrisby.com/default.asp A company with particular expertise in vocational guidance

www.pfeiffer.com Publishers of Schein's *Career Anchors* materials, and much more

www.psychometrics-uk.com/bapt.html The Berger Aptitude for Programming Test with sample questions

www.shldirect.com The site of SHL, test publishers with samples to practise

www.thepsychometricscentre.co.uk Information from the City University, London

ACTIVITIES – CHAPTER 12

1 What personality do we want?

Introduction

The use of personality questionnaires in the selection of people for particular roles can be very helpful – but only if the decision-makers are clear about what they want.

Aims

To stimulate thought and discussion about the use of personality questionnaires, and to clarify the way in which questionnaires work.

Method

In small groups, consider a fictional or real training job, possibly from one of your organisations, and produce a specification (in everyday language) of the personality that you would regard as ideal for the position.

Then refer to the Example Personality Questionnaire Extract (on page 211) above. Look at each question in turn and consider:

- What aspect of personality is being assessed?
- What would be the ideal response from someone suitable for the job?

Issues arising can be discussed in the full class.

2 Take some free tests

Bearing in mind the lack of rigorous controls and possible doubtful validity, search the Internet and try a few free (but make sure they really are) tests and/or personality questionnaires. Report back about any particularly useful or dodgy ones that you may find.

A site rich in material is: **http://similarminds.com** .

Appendices

Useful contacts

I hope you find the following list useful. I have not listed postal addresses or telephone numbers because they are subject to change. If you need them, they are usually available from the website. This is not, and cannot be, a comprehensive list – but some of these sites give further listings and links.

Government sites

www.dfes.gov.uk/nvq/ The NVQ website
www.investorsinpeople.co.uk The Investors in People website
www.qca.org.uk The Qualifications and Curriculum Authority site
www.sqa.org.uk The Scottish Qualifications Authority
www.ssda.org.uk The Sector Skills Development Agency

Societies and institutes

www.cipd.co.uk The Chartered Institute of Personnel and development
www.astd.org The American Society for Training and Development
www.traininginstitute.co.uk/ The Institute of training and Occupational Learning
www.iitt.org.uk/ The Institute of IT training
www.amed.org.uk The Association for Management Education and Development
www.solonline.org The Society for Organisational Learning

Others

www.trainerslibrary.com Resources for trainers
www.presentersonline.com Very useful site run by Epson, the printer company
www.gowertraining.co.uk/ Training materials for sale
www.flexlearningmedia.com/ Training materials for sale
www.jumpcutuk.com/ Training materials for sale – mainly for jobseekers
www.capita-ld.co.uk/ Training courses plus training books, videos and CD-ROMs
http://video.google.com/ Some training films can be previewed here, with links
www.btp.uk.com/main.html Search engine for management courses – lots of training companies can be found through here
www.trainingzone.co.uk/index.html Lots of information, resources and links to training providers
www.ukhrd.com/index.jsp Useful information and resources. Also provides a daily emailed 'digest' (by subscription) through which trainers can help each other
www.kantola.com/ American training video company that is a lot cheaper than UK companies and which will supply UK customers
www.videoarts.com/ Long-established UK training film company
www.e-learningcentre.co.uk/ A large collection of reviewed links to e-learning resources
www.pfeiffer.com/WileyCDA/ Specialist publisher of training and development materials, some downloadable

Extract from the report of a 360-degree feedback instrument

Reproduced by kind permission of Knight Chapman Psychological Ltd.

The Personal Feedback Questionnaire

The following double list compares your hierarchy (the elements of your work in the order of their significance to you) with other people's notion of what your hierarchy is.

The second list is based on the *average* score given to you by your colleagues.

Your hierarchy	Their hierarchy
Flexibility	Resilience
Customer focus	Customer focus
Strategic thinking	Flexibility
Decision-making	Self-awareness
Teamwork	Developing others
Developing others	Influence
Structure	Awareness of change
Resilience	Analytical thinking
Awareness of change	Strategic thinking
Analytical thinking	Teamwork
Self-awareness	Decision-making
Business planning	Creativity
Creativity	Business planning
Leadership	Leadership
Influence	Structure

Key points

There are some close relationships between perceived areas of strength and areas for improvement in these hierarchies.

Flexibility and Customer focus feature quite highly. Business planning, Leadership and Creativity equally figure as areas for improvement.

The greatest areas of mismatch are Influence, where others rate you much more highly than you rate yourself; Resilience, where again others give you a higher rating than you do; Decision-making, where your self-perception is stronger than that of others; and to a lesser extent, Strategic thinking, where your view is generally somewhat higher than that of your colleagues.

Psychometric test distributors

I have not listed postal addresses or telephone numbers because they are subject to change. If you need them, they are usually available from the website. This is not a comprehensive list.

www.ase-solutions.co.uk/ Long-established test publishers with a wide range of tests
www.harcourt-uk.com Tests include the Watson-Glaser Critical Thinking Appraisal, and the DAT range
www.kcpltd.com Knight Chapman Psychological Ltd, ability tests plus UK developed personality tests and assessment centre material
www.morrisby.com/default.asp A company with particular expertise in vocational guidance
www.opp.co.uk/ Publishers of the 16PF and MBTI
www.psychometrics-uk.com Specialise in tests for the IT industry
www.psytech.co.uk Publishes arrange of tests
www.shldirect.com The site of SHL, publishers of the OPQ and other tests
www.testagency.com Publishes a range of tests

Index

Membership has its rewards

Join us online today as an Affiliate member and get immediate access to our member services. As a member you'll also be entitled to special discounts on our range of courses, conferences, books and training resources.

To find out more, visit www.cipd.co.uk/affiliate
or call us on 020 8612 6208.

Also from CIPD Publishing . . .

Equality, Diversity and Discrimination

Kathy Daniels and Lynda Macdonald

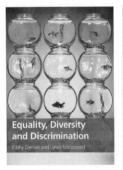

Equality, Diversity and Discrimination
Kathy Daniels and Lynda Macdonald

This text is designed specifically for the increasing number of students taking a module in Equality and Diversity, including those students taking the CIPD specialist elective, Managing Diversity and Equal Opportunities. It will also be relevant on many equality, diversity and equal opportunities modules that are part of general business or HR degrees.

The text contains a range of features, including:
* learning objectives – at the beginning of each chapter summarising the content
* interactive tasks to encourage students to research around the subject
* case studies
* legal cases
* key points and summary at the end of each chapter
* examples to work through at the end of each chapter.

Order your copy now online at www.cipd.co.uk/bookstore or call us on 0870 800 3366

Kathy Daniels teaches at Aston Business School and is a tutor for ICS Ltd in Employment Law and related topics. She is also a tutor on the Advanced Certificate in Employment Law for the Chartered Institute of Personnel and Development. A Fellow of the CIPD, she is a lay member of the Employment Tribunals sitting in Birmingham. Prior to these appointments she was a senior personnel manager in the manufacturing sector.

Lynda Macdonald is a freelance employment law trainer, adviser and writer. For fifteen years prior to setting up her own business, she gained substantial practical experience of employee relations, recruitment and selection, dismissal procedures, employment law and other aspects of human resource management through working in industry. With this solid background in human resource management, she successfully established, and currently runs, her own business in employment law and management training/consultancy.

Published 2005	1 84398 112 2	Paperback	272 pages

The Chartered Institute of Personnel and Development is the leading publisher of books and reports for personnel and training professionals, students and all those concerned with the effective management and development of people at work.

Also from CIPD Publishing . . .

Organisational Theory

David Crowther and Miriam Green

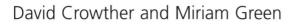

This new text is designed to provide a theoretical framework for students, so that they can place organisational practice in a theoretical context. This text provides a solid knowledge base in organisational theory and its application for both undergraduate students and those on postgraduate and MBA programmes studying organisational theory or organisational behaviour.

Organisational Theory explains the development of theory in the social, cultural, political and ideological contexts in which organisations develop in different societies. It evaluates the theories critically using different theoretical approaches; analysing the interpretation and application of these theories to organisations, their reception and implementation by people in different types of organisation and at different levels; and their influence.

Order your copy now online at www.cipd.co.uk/bookstore or call us on 0870 800 3366

David Crowther is Professor of Corporate Social Responsibility and Director of Research at The Business School, London Metropolitan University. Prior to his time at London Metropolitan University he worked at Aston University for six years. He also has over 20 years experience in industry, commerce and the public sector as an accountant, consultant and general manager.

Miriam Green is a Senior Lecturer in Organisation Studies and Programme Leader for the Higher National Certificate in Business Management at the Business School of London Metropolitan University. She has been a college/university lecturer for over 30 years.

Published 2004	0 85292 999 4	Paperback	224 pages

The Chartered Institute of Personnel and Development is the leading publisher of books and reports for personnel and training professionals, students and all those concerned with the effective management and development of people at work.

Also from CIPD Publishing . . .

People Resourcing

3rd Edition

Stephen Taylor

People Resourcing (formerly *Employee Resourcing*) addresses fundamental management issues such as attracting the best candidates, reducing staff turnover and improving employee performance. It provides a comprehensive overview of and a theoretical underpinning to the subject, while giving practical guidance to students and practitioners alike.

Key areas covered include human resource planning, recruitment, selection, absenteeism, dismissal, grounds for dismissal and best practice, the law and its implications, flexibility, and vital current issues such as emotional intelligence and knowledge management.

The text is also referenced with the latest legislation and research findings. It contains detailed sources of further information, and frequent questions and case studies to enable readers to place theories firmly in a practical context. Each chapter has a clear overview and concise summary, providing ideal points for revision and reference.

Order your copy now online at www.cipd.co.uk/bookstore or call us on 0870 800 3366

Stephen Taylor is a senior lecturer at Manchester Metropolitan University Business School and the CIPD's examiner for the Managing in a Strategic Business Context paper. He teaches and researches in HRM, employee resourcing, reward management and employment law. He has written and co-written several books about HR and regulatory issues.

Published 2005	1 84398 077 0	Paperback	528 pages

The Chartered Institute of Personnel and Development is the leading publisher of books and reports for personnel and training professionals, students and all those concerned with the effective management and development of people at work.

Also from CIPD Publishing . . .

Personal Effectiveness

Diana Winstanley

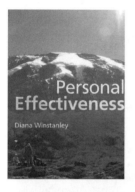

Written by a leading author in this field, this new text on Personal Effectiveness is designed to give students a basic understanding of study skills and management skills, and to give context to other studies.

Suitable for use on a range of undergraduate and postgraduate modules, including those relating to self development, personal skills, learning and development, management skills, study skills and coaching modules, and as part of general business or HR degrees, this text seeks to be both comprehensive and accessible through the use of learning aids.

Each chapter includes:
- learning objectives and a synopsis of content;
- vignette examples to illustrate key points;
- exercises with feedback;
- a self-check exercise and synopsis at the end of the chapter; and
- references and further sources of information.

Order your copy now online at www.cipd.co.uk/bookstore or call us on 0870 800 3366

Diana Winstanley has over 15 years experience of training staff, students and managers in personal effectiveness, as well as in human resource management, and is already a well respected author of a number of books and articles. She has also led, designed and supported a number of PhD and postgraduate programmes in transferable skills and personal effectiveness, and is currently Professor of Management and Director of Postgraduate Programmes at Kingston Business School. Previously she has been Senior Lecturer in Management and Personal Development, Deputy Director of the full-time MBA programme and Senior Tutor at Tanaka Business School, Imperial College London. She also has professional qualifications as a humanistic counsellor.

| Published 2005 | 1 84398 002 9 | Paperback | 256 pages |

The Chartered Institute of Personnel and Development is the leading publisher of books and reports for personnel and training professionals, students and all those concerned with the effective management and development of people at work.

Students

Save 20% when buying direct from the CIPD using the Student Discount Scheme

The Chartered Institute of Personnel and Development (CIPD) is the leading publisher of books and reports for personnel and training professionals, students, and for all those concerned with the effective management and development of people at work.

The CIPD offers ALL students a 20% discount on textbooks and selected practitioner titles.

To claim your discount, and to see a full list of titles available, call 0870 800 3366 quoting 'Student Discount Scheme 1964' – alternatively, visit us online at www.cipd.co.uk/bookstore.

Order online at www.cipd.co.uk/bookstore or call us on 0870 800 3366

NB This offer is exclusive of any other offers from the CIPD and applies to CIPD Publishing textbooks only.

The Chartered Institute of Personnel and Development is the leading publisher of books and reports for personnel and training professionals, students and all those concerned with the effective management and development of people at work.